School Corruption:

Betrayal

of Children

and

the

Public Trust

School Corruption: Betrayal of Children and the Public Trust

ARMAND A. FUSCO, Ed.D.

iUniverse, Inc.
New York Lincoln Shanghai

School Corruption: Betrayal of Children and the Public Trust

Copyright © 2005 by Armand A. Fusco

All rights reserved. No part of this book may be used or reproduced by any means, graphic, electronic, or mechanical, including photocopying, recording, taping or by any information storage retrieval system without the written permission of the publisher except in the case of brief quotations embodied in critical articles and reviews.

iUniverse books may be ordered through booksellers or by contacting:

iUniverse
2021 Pine Lake Road, Suite 100
Lincoln, NE 68512
www.iuniverse.com
1-800-Authors (1-800-288-4677)

ISBN-13: 978-0-595-36557-9 (pbk)
ISBN-13: 978-0-595-80988-2 (ebk)
ISBN-10: 0-595-36557-4 (pbk)
ISBN-10: 0-595-80988-X (ebk)

Printed in the United States of America

Dedication

This book is dedicated to my lovely and loving wife of over 50 years, Constance M. Fusco, Ed.D., who is my confidant, my inspiration, my loving critic, and my reason for living. She is the most trusting and honest person I know.

She spent over 30 years in public education retiring as an Assistant Superintendent of Schools.

If all educators had her passion for the profession and her moral and ethical integrity, there would be no corruption in our schools.

Her critical comments and assistance in reviewing the original manuscript were invaluable.

Contents

Preface	The Corruption Process	xiii
Introduction	Corruption Overview	xvii
Chapter One	The Robin Hood Hogs	1
Chapter Two	Cheating And Deceit—CheDe	6
Chapter Three	CheDe Examples	15
Chapter Four	Waste And Mismanagement—WaMi	40
Chapter Five	WaMi Examples	51
Chapter Six	Fraud and Stealing—FraSte	130
Chapter Seven	FraSte Examples	135
Chapter Eight	Corrupt U.S. Department of Education (DOE)	208
Chapter Nine	School Failures: State And City Takeovers	221
Chapter Ten	Reconstitution: Recycling Failed Schools	256
Chapter Eleven	Inept School Governance	267
Chapter Twelve	The Final Corruption	286
Chapter Thirteen	Conclusion and Remedy	295
Appendix I	Guiding Principles	309
Appendix II	Prevention	311
Endnotes		315

Note: To protect confidentiality, the cases and incidents cited are identified only by location, position and title—if applicable—not by name unless it appears in the title of the reference.

THE CORRUPTOR'S CODE OF CONDUCT

MY CREDO IS GREED
If I can touch it
If it is within my reach
If I can control it
If I can manipulate it
If I feel entitled to it
If I want it
I will take it
and the public trust
and
children
be damned!

Armand A. Fusco, Ed.D.

Acknowledgements

The author wishes to acknowledge the invaluable news resources from Education Week, School Reform News (Heartland Institute), EducationNews.org (Jimmy Kilpatrick), and the excellent education information published by the Education Commission of the States.

The newspaper sources must also be recognized for reporting the corruption in their districts, and, in some cases, doing real investigative stories. Without the newspaper stories, this book could not have been written.

It should be noted, with some bewilderment, that with over 850 references practically none came from education journals. For whatever reason, they do not publicize corrupt activities found in education, and this is why the education community itself is unaware of its extent.

PREFACE
THE CORRUPTION PROCESS

"The time to guard against corruption and tyranny is before they shall have gotten hold of us." Thomas Jefferson

Although the term "corruption" has been used to describe a variety of fraudulent acts in corporate, institutional, and governmental sectors, "school corruption" is a relatively new concept. Schools are typically not viewed as being corrupt; therefore, it is important to understand that "corruption" is being used in a broad sense, but in keeping with its definition.

<u>Corruption: breach of trust, bribery, crime, crookedness, deceit, deception, dishonesty, exploitation, evil, extortion, fraud, graft, malfeasance, nepotism, payoff, profiteering, tainted, unethical, untrustworthy and unscrupulousness.</u>[1]

School corruption, as used in this book, includes school districts, the U.S. Department of Education, state departments of education, and school boards all of which are sustained by taxpayer dollars. It also refers to any other endeavor and funds that exist because of the schools such as the PTA/PTO groups, student activity funds, scholarship foundations, private grants, educational associations, etc.

It is critically important to keep this definition of corruption in mind in order to thoroughly understand how all-encompassing it is in schools, the devastating effect it has on the education (or lack of it) of children, and how it betrays the public trust.

School corruption takes many forms, but it falls into three main categories: cheating and deceit, waste and mismanagement, and fraud and stealing.

Cheating and Deceit—CheDe (cheaty)

CheDe infects all schools (and organizations) to some degree. It's really the moral and ethical decay of the school or culture. Dishonesty emanates from all human forces found in schools—students, school employees, and board members.

The following stories are good examples of CheDe at work:

> "At a public junior high school which has consistently scored within the top 5% of New York City schools, a teacher was formally reprimanded because she taught punctuation. A letter was placed in her personnel file memorializing her mistake. Her error was not that she didn't go about teaching it correctly, but that she covered the topic at all...another teacher was scolded because she told her class that spelling counts." This was the ironic punch line: "The supervisor was upheld in her ruling because spelling is not in the curriculum, it has no place in the classroom."[2]
>
> "In Orange County's largest school district a high school principal's memo urged teachers to pass 98 failing students so they could graduate and allow the school to meet federal graduation requirements,"[3]

The above examples do not involve money, but illustrate the corruption of academic standards, and how CheDe affects the credibility of academic performance.

Waste and Mismanagement—WaMi (whammy)

Once there is a decay of values and ethics, complacency usually follows and this really "whams" the school resources that are wasted through mismanagement. WaMi is not normally viewed as a form of corruption, but it is. Whether waste and mismanagement is purposeful or due to incompetence makes no difference because either can be controlled and corrected. Since it is preventable and correctable, such failure to get the "best from each buck" is an act of corruption.

WaMi is vividly illustrated in the following example that is almost incredible to believe:

A finance officer, in a one-school district, was paid $375,000 in one year. As a result, he will get a pension of over $200,000 per year.[4]

WaMi does not typically result in personal financial gain, but usually there is personal gain involved such as less work, less effort, empire building, etc. What must be accepted as fact is that there is an <u>implied sacred covenant between the taxpayer and schools</u> to spend dollars efficiently and effectively. WaMi violates the sacred covenant and that is why it is an act of corruption. Unfortunately, all school districts are endowed with the plague of WaMi to some degree, and neglected it develops more aggressively leading to the ultimate corruption.

Fraud and Stealing—FraSte (frosty)

FraSte should "frost" all taxpayers because it's their dollars that are being stolen in some way (embezzlement and theft) or used to enhance personal financial gain (gifts, favors, and opportunities).

FraSte can be found wherever there is money involved. What needs to be understood is that trying to prevent FraSte from growing its tentacles without also treating CheDe and WaMi is never successful.

What must be accepted as fact is that if anything can be stolen, it will be stolen; and if there is any way to benefit from the education treasure chests, so be it! There are no rules, there are no boundaries, there are no exceptions, and certainly no ethical considerations

This is best illustrated by just two shameful acts. The first is that of a school administrator who, among other corrupt acts, stole all of the children's candy money—money raised from candy sales.[5] The second is a secretary at a middle school who regularly stole money from the student accounts that financed field trips and other activities. "By the time district auditors and police caught up with her, she had allegedly embezzled nearly half a million dollars ($483,000 dollars and then skipped town."[6]

Can it get more shameful and obscene?

It can! For example, FraSte can involve a lapse in ethical behavior when personal financial gain is involved that can influence financial decisions.

> "Texas school vendors are paying superintendents handsomely for their 'so-called' expertise. Hint, nobody thinks 'expertise' is what they're really buying…they have received thousands of dollars from vendors hoping to sell to their districts."[7]

Summary

The numerous examples documented in this book will certainly prove distasteful, disgraceful, demoralizing, discouraging, and even insane to anyone with moral and ethical values and who also believes in academic standards. Some examples may even seem unbelievable; yet, it's what has happened, and it continues to occur on a daily basis.

School corruption will continue on its relentless and pervasive path until it is treated as an aggressive plague upon the schools. This requires that school corruption must be exposed and prosecuted with vigor in order for it to be arrested, controlled, and eradicated.

The reality is that this insidious plague does not even register as a twinkle in the universe of educational issues. Therefore, it is hoped that this book will raise the level of school corruption to a hot topic issue. Only then can it be attacked for what it is—a betrayal of the children and the public trust.

INTRODUCTION
CORRUPTION OVERVIEW

"As long as the empire can keep the pretense alive that things are all right, there will be no grieving and no serious criticism." Walter Brueggemann

This book is an exposé of deceit, stealing, cheating, fraud, embezzlement, waste, mismanagement and malfeasance in public schools and related institutions, agencies, and endeavors. Although it's not a particularly pleasant subject to write about, the fact remains that corruption is a very serious problem that demands attention and it should rank as a hot topic among school issues. Interestingly, it cannot even be found as a category in educational indexes.

The reality is that corruption has become a natural part of the educational landscape, but it's hidden from view by walls of complacency, denial and self-protection. Exposing corrupt practices is shunned because it would caste a dark and foreboding shadow on how all education dollars are expended and on those who have been entrusted with the public trust to safeguard the school treasure chests.

Law enforcement officials say it (corruption) "is allowed to happen because the education community is a brotherhood, where reputations are as important—maybe more important—than stopping the problems."[8]

Sparse Research

The fact is that many of the nation's school districts have very serious problems with corruption. Unfortunately, the public learns most of what they know about corruption from the news media and little of it from the professional community of educators. Of the 5,000 scholarly papers delivered at the 1995 annual meeting of the American Education Research Association, only a handful dealt with wrongdoing by school employees. In addition, the thousands of research papers, articles, books, and dissertations pertaining to educational issues that have been disseminated over the past 20 years have paid no attention to this insidious problem.[9]

A prime reason why there is so little research about this problem is that the research communities have a strong financial interest in maintaining positive relations with school districts. The reason for their reluctance has to do with money. Millions of dollars in consulting fees, contracts, and research grants are at stake, and many professors are reluctant to criticize the schools that provide consulting dollars. It's rather remarkable that research universities have had virtually nothing to say about corruption of education dollars and academic standards, even though many of these universities are located within the districts where the problems are most severe.

Federalized Schools

No one can deny that there are many problems and issues facing public schools. The fact is that public education is under siege and rightly so. However, there is one primary problem that overshadows all others because it is the reason why schools are in denial and under siege. Before the advent of federal involvement in public education, schools were considered as solely a state responsibility (provided by the Constitution) whose purpose was to provide schools that had a clear focus and purpose to teach students the basic academic and societal skills required to be assimilated into the general society. Once the federal government became involved, the schools gradually changed from educational institutions to governmental schools and, thereby, societal institutions.

According to Charlotte Isebyt (former U.S. Department of Education adviser) there is no question the entry of the feds moved "our marvelous system of education, which until 1960 was the best in the world, from academics to one devoted to training children to become compliant human resources to be used by government and industry for their own purposes."[10]

The result has been that the mission of public education has changed from its primary mission of providing academic skills to a primary mission designed to address and resolve social agendas and all social ills. Even combating obesity has been added to the list of school responsibilities.[11]

There is an interesting side to this issue articulated by three-dozen school district superintendents who are asking for more education dollars to accomplish a mission they claim "has changed from providing universal access to a quality education to insuring universal success for all students."[12] They are right to say that it is Mission Impossible!

However, it is not just a problem with federal paternalism. "State officials will never accept accountability for academic failure and state officials are not questioning their own policies in the face of stagnant and falling academic performance over the last two decades."[13]

Being politically governed institutions also means that they are bureaucratic and intransigent to reform. Tragically, taxpayer dollars are viewed as personal treasure chests to be pillaged and abused, all in the name of children, by the hogs whose appetite for school dollars are never satisfied. They know only too well that no matter how much is squandered from the treasure chests through theft, fraud, waste and mismanagement, the taxpayers are forced every year to replenish the chests with more and more dollars.

The problem with institutions or agencies run by any government entity is that they become weighted down with waste and mismanagement, and it becomes the breeding ground for fraud, embezzlement and theft. This is exactly what has happened since federal paternalism has turned public schools into "federalized societal schools."

This is an important and vital concept to understand because it was this transformation from academic institutions to federalized schools that accelerated the deterioration of public education.

Although death and taxes have been cited as the only certainties of life there is one more that must be added—betrayal of the public trust. If there is any doubt, the exposé in this book of rampant and disgusting corruption found in too many public schools and in related institutions and agencies should make every taxpayer, every parent, and every honest education official (there must be a few left) feel betrayed beyond belief.

<u>The reality is that corruption to some degree will be found in every school district because wherever there are school dollars greedy hands and minds will flourish. Educational level or position and school location doesn't matter</u>. This is the reality that must be accepted by everyone responsible for guarding the school treasure chest.

What is also important to understand is that what this book exposes is simply the tip of the iceberg because school officials make every attempt to hide corruption. As an example, in the Shelby, Alabama school district, a former administrator was responsible for "fixing problems—clean them up or toss them out." His job was to make the system and superintendent look good, and to "keep bad things quiet." He kept a stack of unsigned letters of resignation in the trunk of his car. At times of trouble, he would appear with resignation letter in hand to make employees an offer they couldn't refuse. "He would say: "If you sign this today, I guarantee you a good recommendation." [14]

Corporate Corruption

Of course, education is not alone in having its treasure chest pillaged and plundered. Fraud and embezzlement cost the business world over $400 billion annually and the average company loses $9 daily per employee.[15]

In fact, the total lost in the business world is equal to what is spent by tax dollars on all K-12 education. The business world simply sees it as the cost of doing business and the cost is passed on to the consumer. This is the only conclusion that any thinking and sober person can arrive at considering the huge amount of money stolen through fraud and embezzlement. It certainly is no secret that prevention is far less costly, but it is more troublesome.

It's almost incomprehensible to believe that with so much money being siphoned from the corporate treasure chests that there is so little effective oversight and vigilance. The recent expose of the Enron accounting scandal, the Tyco splendor of lavish and excess spending, and the other corporate giants that have followed their lead is a shocking reminder that greed prevails over oversight and monitoring responsibilities, and that ethics have also become corrupt.

School Corruption

Education is different because there is no expectation or acceptance that corruption will or should occur. Unfortunately, it does! It's absolutely appalling to think that those who are entrusted with school resources are arrogant enough to steal from the mouths of those the system is designed to serve —the children—and to mismanage the resources so foolishly and greedily. It's even more revolting to know that those who are obligated to provide oversight are much too complacent about protecting the school treasure chests from being plundered, pillaged, gorged and gouged.

The responsibility on the part of public education is quite different from that of the business world because taxpayer dollars fill the treasure chests and, as such, there is a far greater obligation to guard the dollars with much more vigilance and honesty.

The school resources can be viewed as a buffet table where the "greedy gluttons" help themselves by picking and choosing among the various treasure chests that adorn every school buffet table. There is the treasure chest of contracts (transportation, construction, remodeling, food services, maintenance, consulting, architectural, and engineering), the treasure chest of grants (federal, state, foundation), the treasure chest of nepotism (employing relatives), the treasure chest of jobs (teachers, administrators, custodians, office personnel, aides, security officers), the treasure chest of purchasing (furniture, equipment, supplies, maintenance), the treasure chest of power and influence, the treasure chest of school activity funds (fund raising events, ticket sales, dues), the treasure chest of personal benefits (gifts, gratuities, kickbacks), the treasure chest of expenditures (allowing for waste, theft and fraud), the treasure chest of personnel (poor allocation and utilization), the treasure chest of invoices (falsifying), etc. As will be seen from the many examples of the hogs at work at the buffet table, there are no limits to feeding their greedy and voracious appetites.

Although many incidences of such corrupt indulgences are reported many more are hushed up and are unreported. A report by the Education Intelligence Agency in 1998 stated: "Crimes involving money, or a least some promise of material gain, are widespread; yet, at the same time very much hidden from public view." What is reported is generally limited to local events in local newspapers, and rarely do such events reach national headlines or receive national attention from the media. What's worse is that the educational associations and professional publications basically ignore the problem of the hogs that feast on the school treasure chests because it's too embarrassing to admit. The hidden rallying cry is to protect the institution and profession at all costs and the public and children be damned.

As an example, "No school (in Alabama) or law enforcement agency keeps an accurate count of the misdeeds. The State Department of Education keeps few records on such cases. It could find only three times in the past five years in which school employees holding teaching certificates were disciplined."[16] Alabama is certainly not alone in its failure to accurately track and prevent school corruption.

This is similar to the medical profession protecting incompetent doctors because exposure of malpractice reflects on everyone in the profession. It is wrong because such lack of attention and publicity encourages the hogs to continue feasting on the treasure chests. An unfortunate and tragic example, but ever so relevant, is how the Catholic Church ignored the problem of sexual abuse of children by priests. Hiding the problem accomplished nothing because the truth eventually prevailed. It discovered much too late that the costs have proved staggering in dollars, image, parishioner support; and, of course, the emotional suffering of those who were abused.

What is most fascinating is that although budgets are always considered to be "tight" or "bare bones" there is ample opportunity for the school treasure chests to be plundered, legally and illegally. Actual theft occurs daily as does legalized waste and mismanagement. If these dollars can be saved, and if school dollars can be stretched through improved productivity and quality practices (blasphemous words in education), school budgets can produce more "bang for the buck," and, thereby, meet far more needs and wants.

The problem is that school boards and educators do not understand or accept the fact that fraud and waste occur under their watch. It's really sad to realize that school board members at times are feasting on the treasure chests. Of course, the school districts that have experienced theft, fraud and legalized gouging all felt that they were immune from such ravages of greed. How wrong they were! Those who believe it cannot happen or is not happening right now in their school, school district, educational agency, PTA/PTO, etc. are also blind to the reality of festering corruption.

The fault does not rest entirely on school boards and educators because their national and state associations, as well as, the state departments of education do not address corruption in any meaningful way. They are all endowed with the three-monkey syndrome: see no evil, hear no evil and speak no evil. Simply ignore it and maybe the problem will fade away.

In addition, there is another incredibly fascinating problem: "Many superintendents and school finance officials don't understand the ABC's of finance...the financial training of superintendents or other school executives is woefully inadequate."[17]

This means that the certification programs required by state departments of education and provided by the colleges and universities are totally inadequate. The omission of required training certainly contributes to the proliferation of corruption in education.

Part of the problem is that the school empire pretends like a fairytale that things would be all right if only there was more money in the treasure chests that are filled so willingly by the taxpayers. The reality is that things are not "all right" and more money alone will not solve the problems facing the educational empire. The fact is that as more money is deposited in the treasure chests, the hogs simply have more to gorge on.

Added to this milieu of inept players is that the media has not publicized or sensationalized enough the hogs that wrap themselves in education garments and feast on the school treasure chests. Again, the fault is not entirely theirs since many such frauds are hushed-up and covered-up so the media itself is kept in the dark.

There is certainly enough blame to go around, but blame doesn't change the fact or solve the problem that corruption devours a portion of every school budget. Anyone who believes otherwise has his or her head buried in the pigpen! Any school board member or educator that thinks it can't be happening in their district simply hasn't looked for the corrupt activities. If they seek them out, they will surely find that corruption exists. Unfortunately, most school systems prefer not to find the corrupt acts because it's too unpleasant to think about and to deal with.

One interesting example of this can be found whenever a superintendent is interviewed for a position. It's doubtful if any candidate has ever been asked a very simple and direct question: How would you go about ensuring that no corruption is taking place in the district, and what policies and practices would you recommend and/or support to ensure that corruption does not take place under your watch?

No interviewing committee or school board would ever even think of asking such a question because it would infer that perhaps there is corruption or that corruption could happen. It's simply unthinkable! Of course, candidates for school boards should also be asked the same question.

Therefore, it is hoped that this book will enlighten those responsible for safeguarding and enhancing the treasure chests (school boards, school personnel, town boards, state education agencies, parents and the community) that fraud, embezzlement and waste are far more prevalent in public education than anyone realizes

Until and unless there is an apocalypse of significant proportion to enlighten the players involved that such problems are part of every school landscape, no serious effort will be made to develop and implement meaningful prevention and protection policies, strategies, techniques and practices. It took the apocalyptic event of 9/11 to crumble the complacency of domestic security. Now prevention and protection has become the national priority along with a costly price tag. Enron was an apocalyptic event for the corporate world and the clean up of financial statements is the new agenda. The Catholic Church sex scandal is yet another example of an apocalyptic event and it is still scrambling to see how to clean up the mess it created by silence and subterfuge.

A similar apocalypse must occur in the psyche of those who are responsible and interested in guarding the school treasure chests; it's not an issue of more money, but rather of "will." Hopefully, this book will stimulate an apocalyptic awakening from complacency to a compulsion for vigilance to protect the precious school resources contained in the treasure chests.

A partial apocalyptic event may have indeed occurred but it has not received any real attention. The U.S. Supreme Court, in a unanimous decision, ruled that local governments (cities and school districts) might be sued under a federal law adopted during the Civil War. The act was passed at that time to help prevent fraud from military contractors by authorizing private citizens to sue in the name of the federal government. Those who bring such suits can receive 30 percent of the amount recovered. In other words, local governments were considered "persons" under the False Claims Act of 1863. It's somewhat surprising that lawyers have not seen a business opportunity with this decision (but then they don't know how extensive school corruption is).[18]

What must be clearly understood and appreciated is that there is just a single issue involved: <u>The only ones who have a right to profit from the school treasure chests are the children, and every dollar hogged through corruption reduces their profit to learn and develop.</u>

The fact is that preventing corruption is critical to improving schools particularly in urban districts where corruption seems to flourish, and where school problems are the most severe.

Of course, there are those who sincerely believe that more money is needed to improve schools and provide better opportunities for children. However, time and time again, educational reforms of one kind or another and increased funding have failed to achieve the desired results.

In the 1960's there was a collaborative effort between the United Federation of Teachers and the New York schools to implement a More Effective Schools (MES) program. Selected schools received more money for smaller classes, additional specialists, and the like; all the things that reformers claim are needed to improve schools. But in the 1970's it was dropped because "it proved to be neither effective nor affordable."[19]

A superintendent tells the story of how he increased the budget by 35 percent to reduce class size from thirty to about twenty, and increased the numbers of guidance counselors, psychologists, social workers, classroom aides and remedial teachers. After two years the reality set in when the evaluation of the effort found: "In the end, the cherished faith died...all that was done to make a difference had made no difference. The panaceas were, after all, only false promises—vain expectations. All the patented prescriptions had failed."[20] Such frank honesty is rare.

The grandest experiment of all experiments occurred in Kansas City, Missouri where the schools were put into the hands of a federal judge who was promised by school officials that more money would solve the district's horrendous problems. He gave the district all the money it wanted without limits, and it was spent lavishly and stupidly. The disastrous results would make a great Hollywood movie, but no one would believe that it could possibly be based on a true story (details in Chapter 12).

The numerous examples that will be found in this book do not contain the names of individuals involved with corrupt acts because that is not what's important. It's the event and specific acts that must be pondered and analyzed. Locations are given to show how pervasive the problem is and that it is found in urban, suburban, and rural school districts, and in agencies, associations, and foundations. In addition, a time frame is indicated next to each example in chapters five and seven to put the incident in immediate historical perspective. It is hoped that the extensive and shameful examples will provide the trigger for an apocalyptic awakening that no education dollars are immune from the gluttonous hogs that have an insatiable appetite. In fact, the hogs are feasting everywhere right now because the "watchdogs" are, too often, "lap dogs" sleeping ever so soundly.

It must also be emphasized that some states are far more forthright in publicizing investigations of school WaMi and FraSte because they have a system in place to at least try to identify corruption problems. However, others make it very difficult to locate and provide the documentation and reports; in fact, it seems as though some states simply don't care or don't want to recognize the gravity of the problem.

Therefore, some states are either omitted or have few examples but this should not be inferred to mean that they are free of corruption. If information is made difficult to obtain, it is hard to know the extent of the fraud and mismanagement that is festering in every single school district in every state. Any district that thinks it cannot be happening is living a dream; eventually, the dream will become an unimaginable nightmare that will emerge into shocking reality to discover the public trust and children have been betrayed.

CHAPTER ONE

The Robin Hood Hogs

"We're all born brave, trusting and greedy, and most of us remain greedy."
Mignon McLaughlin

The fairytale of Robin Hood tells how he stole from the rich and gave to the poor, but the fairytale has become a "realtale" with a couple of twists. Today's Robin Hoods no longer steal from the rich barons, but rather from the rich education treasure chests, and now they consider themselves poor and hog the loot for themselves.

The Robin Hood Hogs operate with a host of willing bandits, who are readily available, to plunder the schoolhouse treasures. Although this may be hard to believe, what is harder to believe is that much of the plundering goes unrecognized and unreported. Personal experience suggests that for every publicized case of fraud, five are hidden from public view or knowledge and countless others remain undiscovered. Why? Districts are drugged by complacency and a fortress mentality to protect the system at any and all cost.

Why it occurs would seem to have a simple answer—greed! Not so simple! Other reasons include CheDe practices that create a climate for defrauding, and employees who are angry or frustrated because they feel mistreated or unappreciated and justify stealing as a way to get even. But there is another more insidious reason and one that is somewhat harder to fathom considering that education is one of service and giving.

<u>For whatever reason, there are too many people involved with education dollars that feel they, rather than the children, are entitled to feast on and benefit from the education treasure chests.</u>

The system compounds the problem by making it ever so easy to plunder the treasure chests, and the reason why this happens is understandable to some degree. No one wants to believe that educators would steal from the children they are dedicated to serve, and no one wants to believe that those who serve education would be prone to deceitful and corrupt practices. However, the cold hard and harsh reality is that it has happened, it's happening right now, and it will continue to happen. Corrupt acts whether intentional or because of mismanagement will be found to some degree in every school system and in all related agencies.

For example, who would want to believe that the former National Center for Educational Statistics, a seemingly innocuous agency responsible for collecting and disseminating education information and data, would harbor deceitful practices? Yet, the reality is that the last permanent commissioner was not re-nominated in 1999 because he resisted "improperly politicizing test data" designed to support political agendas. No theft, no embezzlement, no fraud, no waste, and no mismanagement of dollars, but such deceit begins the descent into the pit of malfeasance.[21]

The political agenda moves into the U.S. Department of Education. This dispenser and watchdog of federal education dollars lost track of $500 million due to mismanagement, fraud and theft covering just two years (1998 to 2000), and that it never had a financial management system in place to track the 200 billion dollars it has doled out to schools. Such mismanagement is responsible for breeding corrupt acts. Even creative accounting is used to cook the books by showing $7.5 billion as an asset when, in fact, it was money owed to the treasury department (they must have used Enron accounting practices).[22]

All this may sound like a fairytale, but it isn't! What's more mind-boggling is that there is an Inspector General's Office in the U.S. Department of Education to guard against abuse and mismanagement; it is even required to report semi-annually to Congress. Big deal! After reading the reports covering several years, there is a rather astonishing revelation: The same wasteful practices have been cited time and time again, but nothing really changes.

To add insult to injury, during the waning year of the Clinton presidency, 39 executives in the Department of Education got nearly $500,000 in bonuses. It was the highest payout of all the cabinet agencies. This was done despite a General Accounting Office report that said the department provided "no fiscal year 2000 data for many indicators, no discussion of why goals were not met, and no strategies on how the department would reach its goals." Yep, it's legalized gouging of the education treasure chest and a shameful example for all school districts to follow. As long as it's legal, forget ethics and honesty, its okay to feast on the treasure chests intended for the benefit of children.[23]

The deceit, old-fashioned plain lying, finds its way into every use of taxpayer dollars. For example, in San Francisco, $60 million was diverted from a $350 million publicly approved bond issue for school repairs to pay employee salaries. There was no permission necessary to divert the funds.[24]

The Los Angeles school district inflated attendance figures to get more state aid resulting in a windfall from the state amounting to $120 million. Was anyone punished for this deceit? Of course not! Instead, the governor rewarded the district and let it keep the money. Obviously, deceit does pay and it pays well. That's why corrupt acts are accomplished with such diligence and resourcefulness.[25]

In New York City a five-year, $7 billion school capital improvement plan was found to be short by $2 billion. A report revealed: "The system is so badly broken that the board is incapable of righting itself." However, the Chancellor noted: "Not one dollar was lost to fraud, theft or waste." He must have been taking Ecstasy because an audit found "the school board has limited knowledge of where its employees actually work or where its money goes…it has lost track of how $3.4 billion of its budget is actually spent."[26]

The problem of using specifically authorized bond money for other purposes is not confined to large urban districts. Amity Regional, a small school district in Connecticut, misspent $2.8 million of bond money.

In Florida's Miami-Dade school district thirteen administrators were receiving legislative supplements of up to $15,000 a year as compensation for the hardships of extensive travel even though some rarely left the district. This amount was on top of full reimbursement for actual travel expenses. One administrator who received $30,000 only went to one four-day conference (it must have been to Mars). No one was disciplined because apparently the Superintendent had the authority to award such supplements.[27] This is how legalized corruption works in Education America.

The natural outgrowth of deceit and mismanagement eventually turns into embezzlement and theft. In South Carolina's Sumter School District 17, the role of Robin Hood was filled by the Assistant Supt of Schools and his merry band of bandits who stole over $3.5 million. In addition to his conviction, there were 15 others including three assistant coaches, an assistant principal, the district's auditor, a local travel agency and a New Jersey car dealer.[28]

It always gets more disgusting and appalling as revealed in the following story that may be hard to believe, but governmental institutions and agencies do strange things.

> "When a study revealed that mercury in childhood vaccines may have caused autism in thousands of kids, the government rushed to conceal the data—and to prevent parents from suing drug companies for their role in the epidemic. The meeting took place in June 2000 at the isolated Simpsonwood conference center in Norcross, GA. and was convened by the Centers for Disease Control and Prevention. The 52

attendees who had received private invitations were repeatedly reminded that the data under discussion was strictly embargoed, but instead of taking immediate steps to alert the public and rid the vaccine supply of thimerosal (a mercury based preservative in the vaccines), the officials and executives spent most of the next two days discussing how to cover up the damaging data."[29]

The damaging effect of autism on children and its impact on schools has been awesome (ask any special education director) and the schools must pay for educating the children and the parents are burdened with the related costs. Handling damage control is far more important to governmental bureaucracies than doing what is right; and, in this case, protecting the children.

<u>Clearly, there are no rules, no boundaries, and no real remorse when corruption (CheDe, WaMi and FraSte) proves more profitable than protecting and educating the children.</u>

According to the executive director of the Association of School Business Officials (ASBO), "Embezzlement happens far more frequently than we are willing to admit." However, in spite of the fact that embezzlement is a known quantity in Education America, ASBO does not track cases alleging theft of district funds. How then are school business officials and others to understand the pervasiveness of corruption, and to realize how it is accomplished so systematically and easily? Silence is obviously preferred rather than ruffling the feathers of the establishment.

It is important to keep in mind that the greedy gluttons are not unique to Education America. They also reside in higher education, town, city, and state governments, and certainly the federal government and all its agencies and departments.

There are also hogs found in unions and they even steal from their own members. As organizations they too are at the feeding trough of greed. Negotiated contracts, agreed to by boards of education, actually mangle school management and waste resources by limiting what school administration can and cannot do. Some of the limitations are, of course, legitimate working conditions, but there are others that stranglehold school administration. Many such union incidents and details are found in a newly published book by Professor Lydia G. Segal.[30]

"She has illuminated protracted systemic corruption rooted deep in the structure, organization, and operation of the nation's largest school systems (New York, Chicago, Los Angeles). Even worse, she shows how this systemic corruption distorts the school systems' priorities, putting children's education last. The situation is exacerbated by certain centrally mandated anticorruption controls that do not prevent—and perhaps generate—corruption which block initiative, creativity, and effective decision making."

However, this can be said about thousands of other school districts. School size makes no difference nor does urban and suburban/rural school districts. The reason is rather simple. The obvious clue to finding festering corruption is easy because it occurs wherever there is money involved.

She states: "In every district I studied, when the investigative unit was dependent on management, it would never investigate anything involving the central office and would often sweep important matters under the carpet to avoid embarrassing its superiors."[31]

Even the church is not hog free of the sin of corruption because both clergy and lay have no reluctance to commit fraud and, in most cases, it is the individual you least expect. This issue was illuminated in a Guideline for Pastors: "It has become painfully obvious that both for profit businesses and not-for-profit organizations, such as the Church, are finding fraud to be a significant problem. Over the past several years the Church has been plagued by embezzlement charges. In our Diocese alone we have had a number of instances, both clergy and lay, employees and volunteers, which has allegedly involved fraudulent financial activities."[32]

Frank Abagnale has presented an interesting concept in his book, The Art of the Steal, in which he states: "Fraud is terrorism, and getting worse."[33] Certainly, there can be no doubt that corruption is getting worse. Until corruption is recognized for its insidious impact on education, in the same way terrorism has had on domestic tranquility, a cure for the ills of education will remain elusive.

Summary

It is extremely important to understand the affect corruption has because it goes well beyond the incidents themselves. When viewed more broadly, it begins to explain when there is so much turmoil in public education. Schools that are corrupt by CheDe, WaMi and FraSte become the lighting rod for criticism and that's a major reason why schools are under fire and under siege.

CHAPTER TWO

Cheating And Deceit—CheDe

"It takes two to speak the truth—one to speak, and another to hear."
Henry Thoreau

Corruption is almost guaranteed to occur in a culture permeated with CheDe and it lays the foundation for WaMi and FraSte to develop. It's very uncomfortable for those who believe in the public education system to realize that adults who should be more responsible and accountable allow CheDe to flourish and become part of the system culture.

Some rather common deceitful practices include lying about finances and budgets, attendance figures, and dropout rates. Deceit is also found in various claims that are made about what a particular program or activity is achieving or what it will achieve. The deceit continues when needs are really wants, when programs or services are overstaffed, and when programs or services have outlived their usefulness but are deemed as essential.

CheDe is magnified even more when budgets are fictionalized by not really reporting all critical facts, and when whistleblowers are disciplined for revealing corrupt acts. It's no secret that school officials come down hard on people who come forward with information about corrupt acts.

The issue of class size is a classic CheDe example. The facts are that the number of teachers increased 48 percent from 1971 to 2000; and during that time, the number of students for every teacher decreased from 22.3 to 15.1. Doesn't this mean that class sizes went down? No, because these figures have nothing to do with class size where there was very little change. The average class size of students was 27 in 1971, and by 1996 class size dropped to 24 in the elementary grades, but rose to 31 in secondary grades. So where did all the teachers go?

To put it bluntly, WaMi worked its magic of corruption, and it all started with CheDe. A lot more teachers do a lot less work due to union contracts and administrative malfeasance. The number of students taught per day dropped from 134 in 1971 to 97 in 1996 because fewer classes per teacher are being taught.[34]

Of course, the whopper of CheDe is when the public is told that more money is needed to solve school problems and it never does.

Make no mistake about it, CheDe is part of the definition of what constitutes corruption. Therefore, it must not be viewed as inconsequential or trivial because it is a very serious problem particularly in the context of teaching and learning. What needs to be understood is that there is always some type of profit or gain involved with CheDe otherwise it would not be taking place. Someone or a group benefits in some way, or the system itself benefits at least initially.

The consequences are costly not only in terms of dollars, but in student development and achievement. CheDe causes money to be spent foolishly, and it gives parents and the public a false impression of what students know and what moral and ethical life is all about.

The New York Times, National Public Radio and 60 Minutes have all reported on the culture of cheating that prevails in our nation's colleges, but the fact is that it is found in all school grades and it is much worse than even a decade ago. Because it is so pervasive, students do not see a problem with cheating. It is also obvious that too many teachers and administrators really don't care enough or close their eyes to the problem.

The Josephson Institute of Ethics in California studied the ethical behavior of 12,000 high school students and found a sharp increase in most categories, including cheating, compared with 20 years ago. Of the respondents, 74% said they had cheated on a test compared with 61% in 1992. More discouraging was that cheating in private religious schools was even higher at 78%.[35]

In a book, <u>The Cheating Culture</u>, the author asserts: "Students are cheating more often, more seriously, and are prodded along the path of academic dishonesty by society, parents, and even teachers."[36]

When cheating is so easily practiced in schools by students, it becomes part of their psyche and continues on into adulthood. It is stated very clearly by Jon M. Huntsman Sr:

> "Corporate malfeasance and dishonest acts are thriving, a result of forgotten values and rationalizations…I think we have little by little ground ourselves down to not know the difference between right and wrong…it is an evolutionary process that has gone on over the last 30 to 50 years."[37]

This is the reason why adults, regardless of their profession, educational level, or position, practice it so blatantly.

Tampering with standardized tests is now one of the more common areas for cheating by adults and it's happening with schools border-to-border and ocean-to-ocean. In this culture of blame, the pressure of high stakes testing is touted by many as the reason why adults tamper with tests. Interestingly, The National Center for Fair and Open Testing claims that cheating isn't the problem. "What is massive is teaching to the test...and it is encouraged by states and presidential candidates."[38] Alfie Kohn who supports this belief states: "The real villain is an overemphasis on test scores at the expense of real learning."[39]

However, the Center for Education Reform puts the issue quite differently and probably more correctly: "The cause of cheating is not the test, not the standards movement, but some character flaw. These tests reflect what should be taught in various grades, and if educators are cheating, it means they don't have the ability to get these kids to learn, which means they shouldn't be teaching in the first place."[40]

Another common source of CheDe is the standards movement. More and more often the effort by schools and even states is to move from higher to lower standards so that too many schools and students will not be classified as failing under the No Child Left Behind Act.

Rod Paige, the previous Secretary of Education, found it necessary to send a letter to state officials expressing concern that some states are lowering expectations to evade the law:

> "Unfortunately, some states have lowered the bar of expectations to hide the low performance of their schools. And a few others are discussing how they can ratchet down their standards in order to remove schools from their list of low performers. Sadly, a small number have suggested reducing standards for proficiency in order to artificially present the facts...it is nothing less than shameful that some defenders of the status quo are trying to hide the performance of underachieving schools in order to shield parents from reality...and they will not succeed."[41]

Sadly to say, they will and they are. Some states and local school districts have already taken action allowing students to graduate from high school even if they fail required state tests and even though, in some cases, it is against local policies or state law. Some districts have already stopped students from transferring out of failing schools by simply putting obstacles in the way and limiting the spaces available in other schools. These are just some of the creative ways that will be and are being used to circumvent the law and even more creative ways will be found as the pressure mounts.

There is another reality that must be faced, and it was stated realistically by the Council of the Great City Schools: "My guess is that when parents are faced with the choice of staying in school and getting services or being transported to another part of town, they will opt to stay."[42]

What seems to have been forgotten in the discussions and arguments about standards, testing and accountability was that previously there were no established criteria that made meaningful comparisons between school districts or states. As a result, there was no pressure to improve school outcomes. In fact the result of schooling after 12 years can only be described as rather disastrous and ugly.

A 2002 report, <u>How Well Are American Students Learning</u>, provides disturbing data:

> "In arithmetic, a troubling body of evidence suggests that students' computation skills have stagnated or even declined in recent years. In grades 4, 6, 8 and 10, fewer states reported gains in 2001 than in 2000. Eighth graders experienced the biggest decline with 74 percent performing below the proficiency level and 35 percent performing below the basic level. In 1999, 80% of the states reported math gains in grades 4 and 5; but the gains disappeared in 2001. The trends in grades 4 through 8 warrant national attention and concern."[43]

The fact is that a smaller proportion of 12th graders mastered basic arithmetic than a decade earlier and scores fell significantly from 1990-1999. It's important to know that solid gains were made through the 1980's, but the decline started in 1990 when standards were changed.

In international comparisons, eighth graders ranked 18th out of 38 countries on the most recent comparison, even falling behind Malaysia and Bulgaria. On the 1995 study that tested 12th graders, U.S. students were ranked 18th out of 21 countries in math.

Clearly, the warning signs have been up about this festering problem for years but, although there has been plenty of rhetoric about the problems, reforms have been illusive.

Unfortunately, reading performance has not improved either. The percentage of students making gains in reading over the past three years also declined in grades 4, 5, and 10 with grade 8 showing a modest gain although the overall score was lower than in 1999. The scores extended the decline taking place in previous years so that the overall trend in reading is down. In other words, in the two basic skills of reading and arithmetic a combination of stagnation and decline has been occurring for years.

The 2004 Report was no better and concluded: "Once again the data mirrors that of past editions despite substantial increases in resources being spent on primary and secondary education over the past two decades. Per pupil expenditures have increased by 53.5 percent (after adjusting for inflation) but student performance has improved only slightly. Seventy-three percent of American eighth graders are still performing below proficiency in math, according to the 2003 National Assessment of Education Progress test."[44]

The report goes on to say: "Let's not keep making the same mistakes that have brought our schools to their present condition. We need to challenge the status quo and pursue serious fundamental reform to improve our educational system. Only then can real progress be made in student performance. Our children deserve nothing less."

These words seem to have fallen on deaf ears because the same mistakes are repeated over and over again.

Another study, The Report Card on American Education, makes a state-by-state analysis covering two generations of students (1976-2001). It grades each state using over a hundred measures of educational resources and achievement.[45] The report makes a sobering statement:

> "There is no evident correlation between pupil-to-teacher ratios, spending per pupil, and teacher salaries on the one hand, and educational achievement as measured by various standardized test scores, on the other hand. We cannot simply spend our way to better grades, but must make sure that we are making the right kinds of investments in our schools to promote high student achievement."

To support its position, it compares the dollars expended with achievement results. The ten states that increased per pupil expenditures the most over the past two decades were: West Virginia (+109 percent), Kentucky (+92%), Connecticut (+65 percent), South Carolina (+63 percent), Maine (+60 percent), Hawaii (+56 percent), Tennessee (+55 percent), Vermont (+54%), Indiana (52 percent), and Georgia (+51 percent). None of the states ranked in the top ten in academic achievement."

Interestingly, a report by a British think tank, Standards and Spending: Dispelling the Spending Orthodoxy, also concludes: "Not only is there no positive correlation between spending and results, but there are quite a few negative correlations. It's true that pupils from England and America score high on self-esteem, but the two countries can't compete with other developed nations when it comes to standardized tests."[46]

In yet another report, Education at a Glance: OECD Indicators 2002, by the Organization for Economic Cooperation and Development (OECD), similar conclusions are made: "The U.S. spends more per pupil than most other industrialized countries, but it isn't faring as well as many of those countries in getting students to graduate from high school. In the U.S. only 74 percent graduate, whereas 97 percent graduate in Hungary, and 94 percent in Japan. Finland, France, Germany, Italy, Poland, the Slovak Republic, and Sweden all graduated higher proportions of their high-school-age students."[47]

It also points out that "U.S. high school teachers spend 73 percent more time teaching than their international counterparts, but performance is no better than the rest."

Some answers are found in a survey, conducted by The Brown Center on Educational Policy, of foreign students who attended U.S. high schools, and U.S. high school students who had studied abroad to compare high school experiences in curriculum, homework, motivation, and sports. The survey revealed some rather interesting insights.

U.S. students confirm the key impression of students from abroad that U.S. high schools are not very demanding. Fully 85 percent of students from abroad found classes in American high schools easier than classes at home, and 56 percent of U.S. students agreed that American high school classes are easier than the classes they attended in foreign schools. Thirty percent of U.S. students said classes were hard in American schools, but that was three times the percentage of foreign students that felt that way.

Fifty four percent of American students agreed that they spend less time on schoolwork than students in other countries.

Both American and foreign students shared the perception that American high schools are seen as less focused on academic learning than high schools in other countries. Perhaps this may help to explain why U.S. students are not performing as well as they should.

To put it bluntly, the nation and its policymakers are afraid to adhere to standards and maintain accountability because too many schools would become identified as failing. Instead, the educational spin-masters weave their skills into the fabric of educational gibberish declaring success when there is none, declaring that more money is needed when more has not produced better results, declaring that teacher salaries need to be increased and, when they are, school outcomes are the same or worse, and declaring that standards have been set too high when, in fact, they are lower than foreign comparisons.

The so-called accountability movement will see CheDe explored and bastardized to new depths. "While federal and state legislators congratulate themselves for their newfound focus on school accountability, scant attention is being paid to the quality of the data they are using. Whether the topic is violence, test scores or dropout rates, school officials have found myriad methods to paint a prettier picture of their performance. These distortions hide the extent of school failures, deceive taxpayer about what our ever-increasing budgets are buying, and keep kids locked in failing institutions...and Washington has been complicit in letting states avoid sanctions by fiddling with their definitions of proficiency."[48]

What is really unfortunate and rather disillusioning is not so much that the educational landscape is being polluted with CheDe and other corrupt acts, but that there is no cadre of education environmentalists shedding light on the pollution problem that litters the landscape, and advocating forcefully for stronger laws and policies to protect children from corrupt acts.

<u>The fact is that the environmental dangers facing certain species of worms and bugs get far more attention than the danger of corruption polluting the development and education of children.</u>

The pollution probably begins with professors of education. A 1998 poll by Public Agenda showed that they hold positions totally opposed to what parents and voters want, oppose a rigorous core curriculum, tough homework, and any systematic instruction in reading, writing and mathematics.

> "Only 12 percent believe that it is important for students to end up with the right answer, valuing the process of learning over content. Less than 20 percent hold that teachers should stress correct grammar, spelling and punctuation. Only 37 percent said that maintaining order and discipline in the classroom is important, and 92 percent concluded that teachers should be facilitators of learning, not conveyors of knowledge. Lastly, 80 percent think that the traditional approach to education is outmoded and instead favor those techniques which boost self esteem over systematic instruction."[49]

If this is the philosophy being inculcated into the preparation of tomorrow's teachers, no one should be surprised why there are so many problems in Education America.

"The truth is that the education establishment resents accountability...special interests, from teachers' unions and civil liberty lawyers, to education schools and state bureaucrats, form an imposing bloc against reform. As pressure mounts, expect more unethical behavior and what children learn matters little...what does matter is turf and money."[50]

Another example of the CheDe hype is a cliché that has been used over and over again: "We know what works." If true, then why are so many schools failing? If it's true that we know what works, why isn't the knowledge being put to use in every district, school and classroom? If we know what works why is there still so much groping for solutions?

The fact is we don't know what really works and the utter failure of the urban schools is a particularly stark reminder that solutions are illusive. Geoffrey D. Borman, a professor of education at the University of Wisconsin, analyzed studies of various so-called successful programs and practices. He found 150 studies rigorous enough to be included in his study and concluded that only 3 of 29 model programs were shown to work. In other words, the evidence could not substantiate many model programs that had been touted as highly promising and successful.[51]

The examples in the next chapter represent just the tip of the iceberg because much more CheDe occurs than is ever publicized. It may at times be uncovered in the school or district, but it just doesn't get exposed publicly. One thing is certain, CheDe can be found in every school and school district, as well as, other agencies, departments, and organizations that support public education.

However, there is another issue to address about CheDe. Sometimes it is not intentional because at times, particularly with educational philosophies, there are those who sincerely believe that theirs is a better way. All well and good, except for one small but absolutely critical detail. Why should taxpayers be deluded into paying for an untried scheme? Unless a new practice, whether in school governance, grade alignment, or curriculum, has substantial research to back up its claim, it should not be implemented. It leads policymakers, parents, and the public to believe that some change or reform will make a difference when, in fact, there is no real proof that it will.

In an analysis of public education, Richard Mitchell minces no words to describe how educators manipulate the truth.

> "Mouthing empty slogans about 'quality education' can dull even a good mind into a stupor out of which it will never arise to overthrow the slogan-makers. The apparatus is not intended to distinguish what is worthy from what is not, but what is approved from what is not...Educationists respond to public discontent not by trying to improve what they do, but by trying to 'educate' the public into some other 'perception' of what they do. When the public finally noticed that fewer and fewer children were leaning to read, the educationists quickly discovered that 'learning disabilities' were far more common than anyone had ever suspected.
>
> Far from failing in its intended task, our educational system is in fact succeeding magnificently, because its aim is to keep the American

people thoughtless enough to go on supporting the system...Our educational problems and disorders provide endless and growing employment for the people who made them."[52]

There is another very interesting matter that must be mentioned because it's flagging another dimension to CheDe. School officials that participate in CheDe may become targets of lawsuits for deceiving students into believing that they have basic academic skills, or deceiving parents into believing that there is something wrong with their child when, in fact, the school has literally disabled their child because of incompetent teachers, outdated textbooks, curriculum deficiencies, etc. Although there haven't been any successful outcomes of lawsuits alleging educational malpractice, the culture of victimology, the culture of blame, and the success of suits in professional malpractice, are clear signs that the educational establishment with big financial pockets will not be immune from the malpractice mania of lawsuits.

Summary

What needs to be understood is that CheDe can never be erased from human endeavors, but it is not too idealistic to think that its occurrence should not be so pervasive and blatant in a learning environment. Is anything being done in schools to help stem the tide? Very little! This is not to say that absolutely nothing has been done. For example, an excellent resource containing over 50 measures to prevent, detect, and respond to unethical student conduct should be required reading and training for all teachers, administrators, and parents. It is available on-line and it's free. The teachers.net Gazette: "Dealing with Dishonesty."

The examples in the next chapter will illustrate how the foundation is poured so that the corrupt acts can be honed to perfection, and the other chapters that follow will illustrate how CheDe is the basic ingredient in every illustration of WaMi and FraSte.

CHAPTER THREE

CheDe Examples

"Lies are the refuge of fools and cowards." Philip Dormer Stanehope

It's important to keep in mind that what follows are representative examples and certainly do not indicate all of the CheDe taking place in school districts day in and day out. Therefore, any missing states or school districts should not be interpreted as meaning that CheDe doesn't exist in some form or to some degree.

Furthermore, the causes of CheDe are many, but there is one critical factor that is indicative of where some of the CheDe culture comes from. In a Zogby Poll of college seniors, 73 percent said that when professors taught about ethical issues, "the usual message was that uniform standards of right and wrong don't exist—it depends on differences in individual values and cultural diversity."[53]

In other words, if CheDe is the culture of a school system, it's okay to indulge in deceptive acts and activities. Is it any wonder why there is so much confusion about what is "right" and what is "wrong?" There certainly are standards that the vast majority of people can and do agree with; otherwise, society would be in complete and utter chaos.

Nationwide

No Child Left Behind Act (NCLB)

Federal, state and local officials are taking steps that could and probably will weaken the No Child Left Behind Act. Among its many provisions, NCLB requires schools to have a highly qualified teacher in every classroom by 2006 and requires school aides (paraprofessionals) to have an associate degree or pass a test. Furthermore, disparities in achievement among white, black, and

Hispanic students must be eliminated by 2014, and all students must meet higher standards.

These are fine goals and so too were many other reform efforts and acts, but none have succeeded. The reality is that the NCLB requirements are impossible to meet. In fact, there are estimates indicating that 80 to 90 percent of schools in some states could be labeled as failing. Yes, it has the best of intentions, but it is deceitful in one sense because the fact is that thousands of children will be left behind. The reason is very basic and simple. Motivation or effort on the part of students, teachers, administrators, parents and communities cannot be legislated and effort cannot be equalized.

Even more disturbing is what's happening: "Less than a year after passage state and local officials are taking steps that threaten to weaken crucial elements of the law…states and localities barely waited for the ink to dry when they began to lower their already low standards. Lowering the bar is among the oldest ploys in recorded history."[54]

Districts are also failing to abide by a provision of the law requiring the identification of highly qualified teachers, as well as, providing extra help to students who are failing. In 74 percent of the schools surveyed by the Association of Community Organizations for Reform Now found that districts have not secured the extra academic help they are required to offer to students who attend schools that have failed. In addition, only 25 percent of the districts have met the requirement to notify parents whose children have been taught for four weeks in a row by a teacher who is not "highly qualified."

SAT Sleight of Hand

The College Board announced that math scores are at their highest level in 30 years. Is this a little CheDe at work? The fact is that scores were artificially inflated beginning in 1995 when the College Board began adding points to each students results to bring the averages up to roughly 75 points on the average for verbal and 20 points on math.

They claim that scores were re-centered back to 1967 in order to make historical comparisons. But they used one statistical method to re-center scores from 1987-1995, another for the period 1972-1986 and still another for the years before 1972.

Even after adjusting the test, the SAT results indicate that students are scoring below the levels of the 1960's.[55]

Teacher Test Scam

At least 52 teachers from five states cheated on their competency tests by paying bribes to exam supervisors for extra time and help with the answers. Educational Testing Service asked the FBI to investigate after noticing questionable tests that may have involved fraud or cheating.

A former school employee who worked for the Philander Smith College in Little Rock, Arkansas ran the scam.

The teachers all had their test scores canceled and ETS said: "More teachers are expected to have their scores challenged during the on-going investigation." [56]

Politically Correct Censorship

A parent of a high school senior discovered that the literary texts on the New York Regents examinations had been expurgated. Excerpts from the writings of many prominent authors were doctored, without their knowledge or permission, to delete references to religion, profanity, sex, alcohol or other potentially troublesome topics. This is an example of a federalized "politically correct" curriculum.

This revelation proved so embarrassing to the State Education Department that it ordered the practice stopped.

The reality is that censorship of tests and textbooks has been going on for decades across America and it is now "institutionalized." For example, in California, no textbook can win adoption unless it meets the state's strict demands for gender balance, multicultural representation and avoids mention of unhealthy foods, drugs or alcohol.

Tests are also censored for "bias and sensitivity review." This process was instituted in the 1960's and early 1970's to scrutinize questions for any hint of racial or gender bias so as not to upset students and preventing them from showing their true abilities on a test.

Every major publisher uses bias guidelines listing hundreds of words and images that are banned or avoided. Words like "brotherhood" and "mankind" have been banished. Older people may not be portrayed walking with canes or sitting in rocking chairs. Even a story about mountain climbing may be excluded because it favors test-takers who live near mountains over those who don't.

The National Assessment Governing Board, which is directly responsible for reviewing all test questions on the National Assessment of Educational Progress, considered eliminating a reading passage about Mount Rushmore because the monument offends Lakota Indians who consider the Black Hills of South Dakota a sacred site.[57]

Diane Ravitch, a noted professor of education at New York University, sums up the problem clearly: "The bias and sensitivity review process, as it has recently evolved, is an embarrassment to the educational publishing industry. It may satisfy the demands of the religious right and the politically correct left, but it robs our children of their cultural heritage and their right to read—free of censorship.[58]

It is very doubtful that the public is aware of this senseless but obviously pervasive and idiotic censorship. Freedom from censorship is one of the most basic and fundamental freedoms, at least it was.

Student Cheating

A Princeton University study in 2001 found that 74 percent of high school students had cheated or plagiarized during the prior year. In another poll, 80 percent of top high school students admitted to cheating during their academic careers, and 95 percent of cheaters said they had never been caught.[59]

Middle School Merry-Go-Round

Why do middle schools, usually grades 7-9 or 6-8, dominate the educational landscape? They were touted as the solution to address the needs of the particular age group, so over 9,700 were built or converted costing billions of dollars because policymakers said it was the thing to do. Well the drive is now on to go back to K-8 schools.

Twenty-three Cleveland middle schools have been converted to K-8 schools or are in the process of doing so. This was done after a K-8 pilot program at four schools resulted in better attendance, better test scores, and fewer discipline problems.

In Fayetteville, TN all students will attend either a K-8 school or high school. This resulted from the realization that when kids moved from the sixth grade to the seventh grade there was a huge drop in test scores.

Philadelphia announced a five-year plan to transform most of the city's 42 middle schools into K-8 schools. Their reason was based on the fact that it's notoriously difficult to attract and keep middle school teachers. However, a 1999 study found that students who attended K-8 schools outperformed their middle school counterparts.

In Colorado, the Education Commissioner has been pushing lawmakers to create more K-8 schools.

Many educators now complain that middle schools have grown overly concerned with the emotional development of teens at the expense of academics. Reports have also pointed to middle schools as a weak link in U.S. schooling.

One of the key problems is that there are little rigorous curricula in such important subjects as math, science and English and too few teachers are qualified to teach these subjects.[60]

No doubt in a decade or so there will be a return to the middle school concept. It's a common pattern in education to recycle the same practices over and over again, however, the results are always the same—none.

Private Management Claims

Edison Schools, Mosaic Education, and Chancellor Beacon Academies, private management companies, each make claims of great success in reversing academic declines. But according to a report issued by the General Accounting Office, such claims cannot be substantiated. The report, representing 11 months of research, stated that neither the work of the supporters or the detractors of the movement to privatize public education satisfied minimum standards of scientific rigor.

It faulted studies by the private companies for not testing students both before and after the takeover of a school or district, and for not controlling for demographic variations among groups of students.[61]

The Drug Disaster

The nation's drug czar, John Walters admitted that a $929 million campaign to keep kids off drugs "has been a flop and may have backfired." Anti-drug ads have proven to be ineffective. A joint study of such ads by Westat, a private research firm, and the Univ. of Pennsylvania, revealed a rather astonishing result: an increase in drug use among some teens that saw anti-drug TV ads.[62] Changes are promised, as they always are, and one of them is to test the ads before they appear. Failure to field test the ads was a deceitful act because it was assumed that the ads would work. Is it any wonder why federal programs don't work?

Hibernating Head Start

Head Start, a federally funded preschool program, has been in existence for over 40 years and it is one of the most entrenched programs in existence.

Many studies have shown that by third grade any early benefit a Head Start preschool program provided (schooling, health care, family counseling, and home visits) is gone. The participants score about the same on tests as poor children who never attended preschool. They are just as far behind their middle-class peers. However, whether or not it does much to enhance the educational performance of poor preschool kids, it serves as an informal social service agency, providing a haven for kids and jobs for their parents

Audits by the Governmental Accountability Office found all manner of programmatic and financial sins. "Almost every serious investigation and critical analysis of Head Start has come from the feds or independent researchers…the locals don't care whether Head Start helps the kids as long as the payroll checks don't bounce."[63] The problem is that the program spreads around too much money to be challenged. Efforts to move the program from the Department of Health and Human Services to the Department of Education have failed.

Interestingly, the Maryland Montgomery County school system is phasing out its Head Start program. According to school officials, it leaves out too many students, it is too expensive, and it doesn't work. The district will be substituting a new program called "Fast Start." It's purpose is to give poor children a boost to close the achievement gap, and to give poor children an equal opportunity at the American Dream. Yet, these are virtually the identical goals of the Head Start program. Another reason for phasing out Head Start is that federal mandates are seen as too burdensome. The newest mandate is that by January 2004, Head Start buses must be equipped with child safety restraints. School officials have estimated that this newest mandate will cost over $2 million.[64]

In essence, what school officials are saying is that a program that has been on going for over 40 years is really a failure, but it continues because it has become embedded into just about every school district.

Alabama

Ethics Violations

The State Ethics Commission found the following ethical violations:[65]

The Bullock County superintendent withheld information that allowed his wife to be hired as a supervisor of curriculum and instruction.

The DeKalb County superintendent was investigated for operating a private business out of school headquarters using school resources.

In 1998, a Pike County principal and teacher at Goshen High School were issued administrative resolutions or reprimands because the teacher borrowed money under a phony purchase order and the principal approved it.

Arizona

State

The Arizona Legislature was sued over public school finances. The suit claimed that the lawmakers broke the law by taking $90 million from state school-repair fund to help balance the budget. This procedure had been used in the past four fiscal years. A superior court judgment ruled the practice unconstitutional.[66]

Deer Valley

The superintendent "misused his position in an effort to manipulate the school board election to block his nemesis from vindication on charges of unbalanced budgets and fiscal disarray."[67]

The chief financial officer shocked the board when he revealed that the superintendent ordered him to withhold information about a $1.6 million deficit a month before the election. As a result, the superintendent did resign.[68]

This is a good example of why school finance officers should report directly to the entire board at every board meeting.

Glendale

A student at Sunrise Mountain High School flunked a required English class that she needed in order to graduate. The parents did not protest to the school; instead, they hired a lawyer who demanded that the teacher "take whatever action is necessary to correct this situation so that it can be settled amicably. Failing that, you will force us to institute litigation."

The school administration allowed the student to retake the test, over the teacher's objection. The student passed the test and graduated.[69]

Arkansas

Although over 8,500 U.S. public schools have been identified as "failing," Arkansas has not reported any failing schools. Yet in the Altheimer school district, 90 percent of the students scored below "proficient" last year on the state eighth grade English test. Because of the deplorable conditions and abysmal performance of its students, the district was declared "academically distressed" and placed under the direction of a state-appointed school board and chief academic officer. The district had been under scrutiny and receiving very intense technical assistance for several years with no results.

Staff claims the problem is poorly motivated students because 95 percent of them qualify for free or lower priced lunches. It also seems that the staff is poorly motivated as well. When a group of 20 teachers who were receiving training was asked how many had read the school improvement plan detailing the changes state officials hope to make, only 5 hands went up.

Yet, it is not a failing school. If a state says "we have no failing schools" there is not much that the federal government can do about it because the states have the authority and responsibility to define what failure is under the NCLB legislation, and are allowed to set their own academic standards.[70]

What is rather interesting is that the state has a process for identifying schools in academic distress and a number of schools are on the list, but they apparently are not considered failing schools. CheDe at work!

California

Statewide

Shortcomings uncovered by an Inspector General's audit concern how school districts have carried out the NCLB Act's policy on educational choice for students in unsafe schools. The problems include failures to report all violent incidents.

Interestingly, the state has not identified any schools as "persistently dangerous." The audit concluded that the federal policy was not adequately implemented in the four districts reviewed.[71]

East Palo Alto[72]

Teachers at Costano School, recognized nationally for its success in educating poor and minority students, helped students cheat on standardized tests. Former teachers acknowledged the practice and said the principal ordered them to inflate grades.

In 1999-2000, eighth grade students scored at the 80th percentile on language tests after ranking in the 38th percentile the previous year, a rather remarkable and unprecedented increase in just one year. Tests given in 2000-2001 had an abnormally high number of erasures that changed answers from wrong to right.

In spite of the evidence, the superintendent denied cheating had occurred. The state deputy superintendent of accountability accepted her conclusion "despite the very strong statistical evidence to the contrary." This is a typical example demonstrating the culture of protection that exists in school systems.

Los Angeles School District

Thirteen teachers at Banning High School were disciplined for allegedly test tampering. This is petty test tampering compared to Manual Arts High School. On the surface its performance was like an oasis in the desert of urban educational wastelands. Fully 100 percent of the school's 1999 and 2000 graduates completed every course required for admission to the University of California with a grade of "C" or better, four of five grads enrolled in post-secondary education, and nearly every ninth-grader stayed for four years and graduated. Considering that it is an all minority urban campus, where 87 percent of students come from poor families, its purported accomplishments seemed like magic at work.

The magic was more "slight of hand." Last fall, it was one of 14 schools singled out for possible intervention because of poor academic performance. The principal departed under a cloud as district investigators probed whether ineligible students were allowed to graduate. An Assistant Principal also left after being investigated for allegedly raising the grades of her son, and lowering the grades of her son's rival for quarterback. Isn't it fascinating how CheDe weaves its magic?

The District Attorney declined to file charges characterizing the issue as one of academic integrity. An interesting statement considering the fact that county prosecutors reviewing the report concluded: "A credible case has been made that officials at Manual altered student cumulative records beginning in the 1998-99 school year and continuing into the 2000-01 school year. Moreover, school officials covered up their efforts to graduate ineligible students by forging the initials of those persons whose responsibility it was to maintain the integrity of the files…Several school administrators were involved in raising, and sometimes lowering, student grades without the knowledge or consent of the appropriate teachers."[73]

Obviously laws in Los Angeles differ from the rest of the country where changing and/or falsifying official records are criminal acts and not simply academic mischief.

In spite of the fact that the report has been kept confidential, The Los Angeles Weekly learned of school fund-raisers for which there was neither documentation nor approval. The fund-raisers included having students and coaches collect money from drivers who parked on school grounds during football games. No records show how much money came in or how it was spent.

However, in response, the principal stated: "Principals rarely, if ever, touch moneys made from student fund-raisers."

The fact is that student funds are a prime source of embezzlement by school administrators and teachers, and numerous examples will be found in the FraSte chapter examples.

It also found that grants were not fully accounted for, that some funds were spent for purposes other than originally specified in the grant, and materials for auditing the grants were not readily available even though their availability was a condition of funding.

This is a classic example of how CheDe piles up higher and higher as the digging goes deeper and deeper.

Oakland

A $27 million accounting error and an $8 million shortfall was largely due to the process of changing the fiscal and information system.[74] This kind of an excuse is usually given when financial problems are uncovered.

Villa Park School District

A teacher at Cerro Villa Middle School was placed on paid leave for allegedly giving students study sheets with questions taken from the actual state test.[75]

Woodland Joint Unified School District

Seven Woodland High School science teachers were suspended for photocopying a version of the state's test and teaching the content that appeared in it. They returned to work after five days of administrative leave amid allegations that they shared test questions with their students.[76]

Connecticut

Fairfield

Stratfield Elementary School, in a town of 9 elementary schools, scored 40 percent higher than the other schools and tested highest in the state as well. The school was also rated as one of the nation's best. In fact, it was the envy of other schools and even captivated educators from India and Japan who visited the school seeking the secret for its success. The community and parents revered the principal.

The secret was simple—test tampering. An analysis of its standardized test scores revealed five times the number of erasures than other schools and 89 percent of the answers were changed from wrong to right.

The test company confirmed that test tampering had occurred and a statistical analysis, prepared by a Michigan State University professor, also concluded that tampering had occurred.

An investigation by the Connecticut Department of Education found that the state tests had been tampered with in 1993, 1994, and 1995. The report concluded: "While there is no direct evidence of the principal's tampering with the test documents, his access to the test materials and his responses to inquires leave us unable to exclude him."

When the students were retested under strict security, the scores dropped below those of other schools.

Throughout the long ordeal and investigations costing over $200,000, many parents still refused to believe that any tampering had occurred. The principal denied any wrongdoing even passing a lie detector test. However, he made a secret deal with the board to retire.[77]

District Of Columbia

Testing Shambles[78]

A history teacher at Wilson Senior High School gave an "F" to a student who took his Advanced Placement U.S. history class. It was enough to prevent her from graduating or so he thought. However, at the school commencement, he saw the student graduate.

When the teacher checked, the student's grade had been changed to a "D." A quick investigation by the teacher found at least 11 cases in which grades were raised without the knowledge of the teachers. Altering a grade without a teacher's involvement violates the union contract.

A "D" grade given to a student was protested by her father because she needed a higher grade-point average to go to college. The teacher gave the student another chance to retake the final exam but her score was even lower, so the grade remained, or so the teacher thought. It was changed to a "P" (passing), and the teacher was quoted to have said: "I am absolutely alarmed. It is uncalled for. It is intolerable. It's like cheating. It's like lying. It's like fraud."

The assistant high school principal who was responsible for changing some of the grades was promoted to a principal at another elementary school. The former principal, who also changed grades because "they were unfair," is now an assistant superintendent supervising the city's high schools. CheDe does get rewarded.

The teacher wrote an article detailing his investigation involving reviews of multiple database and paper files, transcripts from previous schools, and teacher interviews.

"My documentation for 2001 and 2002 graduates who did not meet graduation requirements came to 105 pages...when a sample representing roughly half of a graduating class (2001) in one of the nation's top urban public high schools yields a violation rate in the neighborhood of 40%, one can imagine similar violations in many other schools. If these rates are even remotely representative of urban high schools, 'social graduation' may be a major means by which school systems, especially those serving large numbers of African-American and Hispanic students, hide their failure to achieve their education mission...in addition, one-third dropped out."[79]

A district investigation, still not complete, did indicate that "we do have some things to fix...we have serious concerns about the internal rules and record-keeping."[80]

Whatever the final outcome, it is still quite an indictment of urban school non-education and duplicity. This is but one of the numerous examples of such CheDe, and it doesn't just happen in urban schools either.

Florida

Statewide[81]

Social Promotion Promoted

School districts are refusing to end social promotion and hold back fourth-graders who cannot read in spite of the retention law that was part of the A-Plus Plan for Education approved by the Legislature in 1999.

The argument by school officials can best be summed up as "retaining students damages their fragile self-esteem." There seems to be no concern about what happens to their self-esteem when they cannot read in the upper grades or possess the reading skills needed for success on the job. In the double talk found in educational and political jargonese, a governor hopeful said: "He opposes social promotion, but considers it wrong to hold back large numbers of children." This is known as political pandering, a common CheDe.

At least he identified the real problem that too many children would be held back. Holding back large numbers of students would not be politically feasible, or politically correct.

Added to this is the newest wrinkle of fudging the facts. Those schools that fail under the NCLB standard will have a new label—Provisional Adequate Progress. Very creative to say the least! "The constantly changing grading formulas are so arcane that results often don't make sense.[82]

Duvall County[83]

The board unanimously approved a list of 1,136 public school teachers not certified to teach the subject area they are currently instructing. All of the teachers are licensed to teach but lack state certification in certain subjects, and state law requires all school boards to approve any out-of-field teaching.

Of course, now they will be able to qualify as "highly qualified" teachers under the NCLB Act. CheDe just seems to go on and on.

Miami-Dade School District

Under pressure by parents and principals, the district rescinded a policy that would have prohibited high school seniors who did not pass the state test (FCAT) from participating in graduation ceremonies.

Students who met all the other graduation requirements for course work, community service and maintaining a C grade average will now participate in graduation ceremonies and receive a "certificate of completion." This practice is becoming more common.

Illinois

Statewide

Schools suspected of cheating on standardized tests are referred to an investigative team that conducts interviews at the school. Over the past two years, the team has sought evidence of cheating at about 15 schools and substantiated allegations at several of them.[84]

Chicago

Test Cheating Probe

On the same day officials gave out $10,000 cash awards to 60 schools for improving test scores, school officials revealed that a test cheating probe has been expanded to 16 people. In one case, the percent of eighth graders reading at national norms at Armour School was 80 percent whereas the year before only 30 percent made the grade. Investigators found a high level of erasures from wrong to right answers.[85]

Test Security Breached

To safeguard against cheating, the board has long required schools to follow a list of security procedures among which is that teachers in grades 4 through 8 may not administer the test to their own students.

However, teachers themselves report that the security procedures can be sidestepped. Teacher aides who proctor the test joke about the cheating but don't report it. In another school, a teacher said she believes her colleagues team up to cheat: "I'll cheat for you, if you cheat for me."[86]

The principal and guidance counselor at Carpenter Elementary School where a test-tampering scandal was uncovered, were being considered for suspension. Officials discovered widespread cheating for the eighth graders. All 49 of the students had passed the test the first time around, but all scored far lower on the mandatory retests.

There has been no admission by anyone of test tampering, and the two educators are simply being punished for failing to secure the tests.[87]

Hegewisch

The principal and curriculum coordinator at Clay Elementary were suspended for failing to keep standardized tests secure. An investigation found that copies of the state and standardized tests had been distributed to teachers.[88]

Kansas

Piper[89]

A biology teacher at Piper High School flunked 30 students for plagiarizing by stealing sections of their botany project off the Internet. She resigned when the school board, under pressure from angry parents, refused to support her action and ordered her to raise grades.

Two other teachers who tried to give "F's" were "humiliated, intimidated and face litigation."[90]

Such actions send an unequivocal and devastating message to all teachers, e.g. don't maintain standards of any kind. This is how the school culture becomes permeated with CheDe.

Several parents did begin a petition drive to recall three of the board members. The board president, one of the recall targets, said the complaints from the parents whose children were involved had no effect on the decision.

The superintendent resigned because he was criticized for not supporting the teacher, and the principal did not seek renewal of his contract hinting that the plagiarism incident was the cause.

Kentucky

Bourbon

The superintendent was being taken to court by some parents for refusing to provide receipts and other documents from a summer trip he took at school expense. His refused because it would put an unreasonable burden on staff to produce the records.[91] This is a district of only 3,000 students. Apparently, he must have taken an interplanetary flight, otherwise, why should it be so complicated and time consuming to put the data together?

Frankfort

A report by the Program Review and Investigations Committee pointed to errors in the way student attendance is counted and how transportation costs are estimated in individual school districts. The Department of Education was cited for providing little verification of the data. As a result, the state's formula for funding local schools is frequently based on faulty data causing schools to get extra money.

Overstating average daily attendance by just 1 percent would translate to an overpayment of $19.5 million; certainly, no small change.

Louisiana

Tioga

Thirty-four students in 6 classrooms at Tioga High School had to re-take their assessment tests because of apparent cheating. The test analysis company reported that the number of wrong answers changed to right were too far above the norm, meaning someone apparently tampered with the tests. A state department official indicated that "probably" someone changed the answers.[92]

Maryland

Statewide[93]

The State Superintendent hedged the truth about the results of the state performance exams when she said: "We can clearly see that our school reform efforts are working, instruction is improving and students are achieving at higher levels than in 1993."

However, the Baltimore Sun reported at length on the test results and found generally stagnant scores, and "no real gain in reading despite statewide efforts."

Previously she had reported that the problems in Baltimore were underfunding. Yet, over $254 million extra was literally poured into the system, but test gains showed a meager 1.13 percent average gain over the past three years.

More money itself will not and cannot solve the myriad of school problems without honest accountability. Parents, policymakers and taxpayers simply must come to realize this or positive change will not be forthcoming.

Baltimore

Standards Don't Count

For years the school system had an unwritten policy of "social promotion" in which children were promoted no matter how they were performing academically. A promotion policy adopted by the board was designed to stop such promotions.

However, most eighth graders who failed to meet tougher passing standards last academic year were promoted to high school in violation of the promotion policy. In addition, the majority of students who were placed in transitional classes designed to help them catch up were sent to ninth grade midway through the year even though they still did not meet all the requirements.[94]

The Deficit Goes On

The school system exceeded its budget by close to $10 million last year and ended up adding to an existing multimillion-dollar deficit totaling over $18 million despite assurances by district officials two years ago that the deficit would be eliminated.

The explanation for the deficit were centered on four major items: contracting for special education instructors, summer school, repairing aging facilities, and replacing district vehicles. Is it logical to think that none of these items were or could not be anticipated? Poor planning was admitted when the

Chief Executive Officer said: "Better planning is necessary to prevent further worsening of the system's financial situation."[95]

Montgomery County

State test scores at the Potomac Elementary school, the third highest achieving school in the state, were voided after the principal and a teacher were found to have helped students to cheat on the test. The principal resigned shortly after the investigation began.

Interestingly, it was the 5th grade students who reported that they were prompted to change essay responses and were given extra time to finish.

As a result, the school will not be able to participate for several years in the state program providing extra funding for schools that show two consecutive years of improvement.

Seven employees at a middle school were suspended when an advance copy of a state math exam was handed out to several teachers to help them prepare students for the test. Two teachers actually gave students the test questions as homework. Two students identified questions on the test as being the exact same questions that had just completed the night before on their homework.[96]

Massachusetts

Statewide

Members of the Massachusetts Association of School Committees asserted their right to grant diplomas to students who fail the state MCAS exam. Interestingly, high performing schools such as Arlington and Newton supported the resolution. Three districts (Cambridge, Falmouth, and Hampshire Regional) passed their own resolutions saying they will give diplomas to students who don't pass the test even though it is illegal to do so.[97]

When school boards not only defy the law, but also break it, CheDe is at work. No doubt, the courts will have the final say—maybe.

But the effort to circumvent standards doesn't stop with just defying the law. The State Education Commissioner is asking the federal government to participate in the CheDe by giving access to financial aid for college to students who fail the state test.

Michigan

Statewide

Testing Irregularities

Responses to allegations of test cheating on the state test continued flowing into Lansing as superintendents wrapped up investigations and tried to prove their students and teachers did nothing wrong. A list of 71 schools with similar written responses was made public.

An independent panel of superintendents, teachers and principals came in to look at these tests and they came to the same conclusion—"testing irregularities". [98]

Sink Standards

The state has over 1,500 schools (representing one-half of the 3,000 elementary and middle schools) that are targeted under the provisions of the NCLB Act as a "failing schools."

Educators, who had set the original state standards, are now "crying foul saying the earlier standards were set at a high level." The answer to the problem is very simple: lower the standards to meet the lower national standards. Such an action would cut the number of failing schools in half.[99]

Muskegon Heights

Administrators at this urban and mostly black middle school admit to skewing the results of a statewide test by asking the parents of low-achieving students to sign test waiver forms. Forty percent of the 7th graders did not take the test the prior year and, as a result, the percentage of students who scored "satisfactory" on the state test improved significantly.

The practice was defended by school administrators because "failure-prone students could risk further rejection by taking a test they simply have no hope of passing…I would challenge anyone to give a student with a second grade reading level the 7th-grade test…It just contributes to the child's already poor self-esteem."[100]

This is exactly why standards, testing, and accountability have been implemented. Too many schools, particularly those in urban areas, were satisfied with having students promoted to higher grades with no real academic skills.

New York

New York City [101]

Phantom Kids

Enrollment figures, which determine how much state aid is received, were inflated by at least 5 percent. This amounted to $500 million more in state aid.

Fast Service?

One day after the Board of Education voted to increase the number of police officers in the schools, the Chancellor reported a 15 percent decline in serious criminal offenses. It was further revealed that the 1,966 serious crimes reported might not have been committed at all. Perhaps some CheDe was at work.

Test Tampering

Fifty-two educators in 32 schools allegedly started helping their students with statewide tests. Edward Stancik, the city's special investigator, claims that for the past five years some kids have just waltzed into class, written their test answers on notebook paper, and sat back as their teachers filled in the correct answers on the little bubble forms. Then, clutching their students' miraculously improved test results and passing rates, teachers and principals got raises, promotions and general acclaim." About 50 educators are involved in the investigation and face possible dismissal.[102]

The United Federation of Teachers hired a private firm to evaluate the fairness and accuracy of the cheating report. The investigator, a former assistant district attorney, maintains, "critical exculpatory evidence was ignored, that children were questioned without parental permission, and that many of the teachers involved were never interviewed."

In response, Edward Stancik labeled the UFT report biased and incomplete and said that the "UFT can stick its head in the sand if it wants, but cheating is a problem here."[103]

Stats Vanish

A day after the Daily News reported that since 1998-1999 teachers accumulated 3 million absences, the city Education Department deleted the information off its web site. Department officials could not explain what happened to the data.[104] Is it so hard to figure out what probably happened?

Where's the Money?

In December 1999, the PTA held a fundraiser and raised $13,783, and it was expected that the money would be deposited in the PTA account with the intention to purchase science equipment. Instead, the check had to be turned over to the District Three Community Superintendent who had to be informed of checks over $2,000.

The check was never returned to the PTA, but the president later learned that the district claimed it used the money to pay for $11,000 worth of science items for the school and the difference would be returned to the PTA. However, based on her research and a payment warrant, she found that it was not clear that any PTA funds were used to pay for the items. She later filed a grievance charging the principal and a teacher with harassment and misappropriation of funding. A backlash caused her removal from office. As a result, she filed a $10 million lawsuit against the PTA review committee that recommended her dismissal from office.[105]

Sanitized Literature

Although education officials had promised to stop sanitizing and tampering with famous literary works on state exams, they got caught a third time. The first instance in June cut out references to Jews and Gentiles, and again in August the Regent's exam changed the words of several writers.[106]

North Carolina

Durham

A parent who was informed that her son hadn't completed all his work during the year became concerned because she had been told by the principal and other teachers that he was doing fine. After investigating, she found that his failing grades had been changed to keep him eligible for the school's football team. What she uncovered was "grade-tampering, grade-changing, grade-fixing (only athletes were afforded this privilege) and an institutional conspiracy to cover up willful and malicious acts of unethical and immoral conduct."[107]

Ohio

Akron

The schools are reneging on a contract with the community promising accountability that was put in place to appease voters before last year's successful levy campaign. Part of the contract was that spending by the district would not exceed 3 percent, but the district's spending went up to 5.58 percent or $14 million. The excuse for the increased spending was costs that could not be controlled.

One of the more interesting "uncontrolled" costs was money lost from students leaving the district to attend charter schools. This was a 22 percent increase amounting to $10 million.

However, knowing that the 3 percent limit could not be met, no effort was made to reduce costs other than cutting jobs through attrition. What's next? The district will be asking for a sales tax to benefit the schools.[108]

Columbus

Students at Eastgate Elementary School, who were praised for its test scores, said that adult tutors guided their pencils to the correct answers or calculated math problems while they took the mandatory state test.[109]

Pennsylvania

Department of Education

A report by the state Auditor General charged that the Department of Education showed a shocking disregard for sound business practices when it awarded a $2.7 million no bid contract last year to Edison Schools Inc. to analyze the Philadelphia School district.

"Education officials refused or failed to provide any evidence to prove their claims that Edison was the most qualified firm to conduct this analysis, that its multimillion-dollar fee was reasonable, that the contract was entered into lawfully, or that Edison's analysis was even necessary."

The Department claimed that no other single entity could have undertaken the study on the required timeline. This was interesting since Edison had never performed such an analysis before.

The AG report further stated that at least 75 percent of the topics Edison was required to address had already been addressed in at least one of 16 reports.[110]

Rhode Island

Statewide

Officials had to cancel five English and math tests because teachers had copies of the previous year's exams and used the tests, which have the same questions, to help students prepare.[111]

Texas

Statewide

Lower Standards

The State Board of Education approved a proposal under which the state would grade the new state test, Assessment of Knowledge and Skills, more easily for the next two years before requiring students to score higher to pass. The board departed from the recommendations of a panel of educators who favored tougher passing standards.

In part, the new test is designed to end social promotion and a passing score is required to graduate. However, even with the lower standards, field tests indicated that 40 percent of 10th graders would fail the math test and half would fail the science test.[112]

Again, the problem is that when either too many students fail or may fail, the standards are lowered rather than more effort to help students pass such as instituting Saturday classes, tutoring, summer school, etc.

Statewide Cheating

The Texas Education Agency has ordered 11 school districts (Clint, Dallas, Ector County, Fort Bend, Houston, Laredo, Midland, North Forest, Pharr-San Juan-Alamo, San Felipe-Del Rio Consolidated, and Wilmer-Hutchins) to review reports of excessive erasures on the state test. The investigation was prompted by reports from the state's testing contractor that identified schools with an excessive number of erasures and corrections on tests over three years.[113]

Dropout Manipulation

The National Center for Education Statistics report on dropouts indicated that the state rate is 5 percent, almost four times larger than the 1.3 percent reported by the state education agency. In all probability, even the federal figures may be too low.

The state does not count as dropouts students who finish all their required coursework but do not pass the state test to get a diploma, or students who leave and indicate plans to take the GED.[114]

Austin

Two former district administrators, a deputy superintendent and a central office employee, manipulated data from state tests to make it appear that some of the elementary schools did better than they actually had on the Texas Assessment of Academic Skills.

As the investigation unfolded, a grand jury indicted 18 school officials for altering student tests.[115]

The district itself pleaded no contest to a criminal conviction and agreed to pay a $5,000 fine. However, as a result of the test tampering investigation, problems were also found with the district's dropout-reporting system.[116]

Fort Bend School District

A principal and teacher resigned in the midst of a test-tampering investigation.[117]

Houston ISD

A Kashmere Gardens Elementary School teacher was fired for allegedly using an answer key to correct student forms, and two principals were reprimanded for not making the tests more secure.[118]

Sugar Land

Two administrators at George Bush High School, the principal and dean, resigned amid allegations that student records were manipulated to improve the school's rating on the state test.

The district investigated after receiving an anonymous letter with detailed allegations about the scheme. The investigation found that some students who might not score well were not allowed to take the test, and the test scores of other students were voided.[119]

Sharpston High School[120]

An assistant principal claims retaliation for reporting that the school faked student dropout records. The records were changed so that it appeared there were no dropouts. Yet, the 1000 freshmen class ended up in the senior year with only 300.

Why did this happen? Greed! A school's accountability is based on test scores and graduation rates that can lead to cash bonuses. Guess What? Sharpston employees split more than $100,000 in bonus money. How nice!

Utah

Some school district administrators want the state Board of Education to lower the score for end-of-year tests from 65-75 percent correct answers to 60-70 percent "to better represent the state's definition of student proficiency." In other words, too many students will not achieve the higher score standards, therefore, the districts want the proficiency score lowered.[121]

Of course, that is easier to do than teaching students so that they can pass the standard.

Virginia

Fairfax

A student journalist exposed a CheDe by school officials at West Springfield High School. Forty-seven students were corralled in the cafeteria amidst a group of security officers and told to "forge their parents signatures on a federal form 'or else.'" It should be noted that the school has an honor code. What a fine example of "honor" by school officials.[122]

Reston

A teacher at Langston Hughes Middle School was placed on paid leave, and 18 eighth graders were retested after they allegedly were prepped with questions that showed upon on their state test.[123]

International

Test tampering (cheating) is not just a U.S. problem. In Britain, 11 primary schools had their results annulled after investigations by officials revealed they could not be sure the pupils' work was their own.

One primary head teacher who had admitted altering answers in last year's national curriculum tests was allowed to resume her career after a severe reprimand for gross professional misconduct.

Experienced former primary school head teachers reported that cheating is quite common.[124]

Summary

Although there are teachers and administrators who embrace CheDe and who are even supported in their efforts, there are courageous teachers and administrators who try and maintain ethical and professional standards. Unfortunately, they are too often pummeled into submission by lawyers, boards, and even colleagues or, worse yet, circumvented by higher authorities.

The examples certainly illustrate why standards are being lowered, why accountability is shunned, why appeasement is accentuated, and why real achievement is on the decline. Clearly, CheDe is on the rise. It permeates every sector of school life, and it will increase sharply and significantly because the pain that follows honest attempts to improve schooling outcomes is too much for parents and society to bear. As test scores and graduation rates are linked to a school's reputation, job security, teacher raises, or performance bonuses, etc., the system will react accordingly and raise the level and degree of CheDe to new heights.

Once CheDe becomes ingrained in a school system or education agency, it follows that waste and mismanagement (WaMi) and fraud and stealing (FraSte) will find their way into the school culture.

Chapter Four

Waste And Mismanagement—WaMi

"When good people cease their vigilance...the evil men prevail." Pearl S. Buck

In every organization there is mismanagement and waste to some degree; therefore, it is unlikely that either can ever be totally prevented or eliminated. One of the problems is that sometimes it's not easy for everyone involved to agree on what is "waste" or what constitutes "mismanagement." There are books written for the business world on effective management of resources, and business also has a motivating force of bottom line profits that demands far more aggressive actions to eliminate and control mismanagement and waste. In addition, market forces involving changing needs and wants also forces management to adjust its practices and goals.

Those businesses that are not successful in managing change effectively and using resources more efficiently go bankrupt. It's a very simple and basic law of economics. It happens often with small businesses, but it also occurs with very large national retailers, manufacturing companies, financial services firms, and hi-tech companies. The Enron debacle and others like it certainly are shocking examples of gross mismanagement combined with wholesale greed. However, the vast majority of businesses are strongly motivated to control costs and meet market conditions because they want to remain in business.

<u>Governmental</u>

In governmental services (local, state or federal level) there is absolutely no such motivation to identify and reduce waste and limit the degree of mismanagement because there is no bottom-line to worry about; and, with very rare exception, there is no bankruptcy option. Oh, there is always plenty of talk about managing resources more effectively, but the rhetoric does not match the reality of what takes place. The underlying reason is that taxpayers are a continuing source of forced tax revenues to replenish the public treasuries.

What also must be added is that the voting public remains much too complacent and accepts the fact that there is and always has been corruption in the political arena of governmental services. That is why it happens and why it will continue. <u>Only when the public is aroused and demanding will wasted dollars be viewed as a resource to be salvaged.</u>

There are certainly examples of how activists can make a difference when attention is kept focused on such an issue. The zeal demonstrated by environmental and animal rights groups is a classic example. Sometimes even an individual can make a dramatic difference, as was the case with Ralph Nader who successfully shed light on car safety issues. Although there are some activist organizations for more efficient and ethical governmental services, they have been ineffective in achieving an apocalyptic impact. Studies, reports, and special commissions have repeatedly revealed that billions of dollars can be saved through better management practices, but little change occurs because too many self-interests are at stake.

An article, "Learning to Abandon What Doesn't Work" puts the problem facing education in sharp perspective: "Educators are much better at piling things higher and deeper and not particularly good at learning to get rid of what doesn't work.[125]

Part of the problem too is that the public is unaware of the extent of WaMi that does take place and this is particularly true regarding public education. So it's important to understand the issue of waste and mismanagement involved with public education dollars

It's staggering to imagine that systematic waste and inefficiencies "totals many billions of dollars annually."[126] It's tax dollars at work!

Of course, there are other factors involved: Outdated information systems, communication breakdowns, and either poor or no planning that can be described as pure, unadulterated malfeasance and incompetence. All these factors and others, however, are correctable and it does not take a lot of money. The fact is that resources are being spent lavishly and wastefully so that what is needed is reallocation of dollars and priorities.

School Governance

At the local level, town, city or county, school boards are the governing body and they are entrusted with the task and responsibility for safeguarding the treasure chests from the hogs who want to have unlimited feasting at the school buffet table. After all, the hogs (their identity is not always known) have absolutely no interest in controlling WaMi because it would then be much harder to feast on the school treasure chests and indulge their own wants at the expense of the taxpayers and the children.

What needs to be understood and appreciated is that not all WaMi is intentional. The fact is that seemingly innocent practices and policies provide the foundation for waste and mismanagement to be fertilized with good intentions.

The manner in which a school board meeting is conducted provides a good example. There are many boards that are anxious to have input before they make decisions and, as a result, allow individuals in the audience to participate in discussing any agenda items. However, it is not the purpose of a public board meeting to have a public hearing on every agenda item. A board must conduct its meeting as a meeting that the public observes and has some input, not ongoing input.

Well, what does this have to do with WaMi? Boards that allow the public to participate, react to, and discuss with the board every agenda item encourage small self-interests to dominate and influence its decisions that can prove costly. For example, a board may be considering the elimination or restructuring of a program that may be ineffective or costly but action may not be taken because a small group, often for self-interests, puts up enough of a stink that the board backs off from any decision. Or the reverse occurs, a small group wants a particular program such as a new sports team or athletic activity and demands board sponsorship. Should a handful of parents be decisive in adding more dollars to the treasure chest already overloaded with too many goodies? This practice occurs when board members are more interested in reelection rather than doing their job and when individual members want to show their influence and power.

WaMi is also encouraged when a board does not ask the right questions to the right people, or is reluctant to accept truthful answers that may force a reexamination of policies, practices and their own biases and beliefs. Boards must be trained in how to ask probing questions and how to seek honest input from staff. One way it cannot be done is to have a controlling superintendent who may prevent staff from expressing honest opinions. Also, it cannot be done when surveys are conducted that highlight problems, but the board doesn't accept the results.

This is not to say that what it may be told by staff is always accurate even though it may be truthful in the eyes of staff because of their personal biases and philosophy. The class size issue is a good example of this type of issue. Certified staff believes that small classes make a difference. Yes, it makes a difference in the workload of the teachers, but it doesn't necessarily produce better performance and this is confirmed by the research, as well as, actual practices. California has undergone an extremely costly effort to reduce class sizes and after six years the results are anything but encouraging. At the same time, the effort has resulted in fewer resources for building maintenance, addition of numerous temporary classrooms, and hiring thousands of unqualified teachers. Worse yet, the schools getting the most unqualified and inexperienced teachers are found in the urban districts where the most experienced and most qualified teachers are needed. This is WaMi at its worst with extremely high cost and nothing substantial to show for it!

In Florida where the voters approved class size limits, the reality of the cost and other problems involved are now being reexamined, and the governor is attempting to put it on a ballot again for reconsideration by the voters. The reality is that any school district would be hard pressed to show that the total added cost to adhere to small class size is justified by performance results. Admittedly, it is done for the right reasons even though it is based on faulty assumptions and self interests and without regard to the total costs involved, as well as, less expensive options to improve performance.

There are many other financial consequences in adhering to a small class policy. Many school districts are undergoing enrollment increases requiring new or expanded buildings. The smaller the class size, the larger the buildings have to be and more staff, furnishings, equipment and maintenance is required and all are extremely costly.

Changing building grade configurations is another costly WaMi. For example, billions have been spent on new middle schools that were vigorously touted to meet the needs of this age group. Well, what is now being advocated? The development of K-8 schools and that's where many school districts were at before the middle school concept. This will undoubtedly become another costly WaMi paid by uninformed taxpayers.

In the same way grade configurations are changed, so too are programs. Reading is a classic example going from phonics, to whole language, and now the federal push is back to phonics. This will be a very costly move in terms of materials, teacher training and confused children and parents. Another example was the costly and disastrous change from basic math to modern math and now the move back to more basic math.

Curricular offerings in the upper grades are still another potential WaMi. There are many optional course offerings provided beyond those that are required. There certainly is nothing wrong in providing some options, but studies have shown that in too many high schools the curricular offerings represent a candy store displaying every candy imaginable. Every course not fully utilized with cost effective enrollments are very costly to offer particularly when options are available either for distance learning or utilizing computer programs that can provide the same offerings at far less cost.

Not taking full advantage of what technology can offer in more efficient and effective administrative functions and classroom instruction adds to WaMi. For example, it's costly to maintain paper records that require floor space and files when there is a far more efficient option available to computerize the records requiring a fraction of space.

As indicated previously, businesses must constantly examine the changing cultural and marketing environment. For the same reasons, boards must ensure that there is a regular review process for all school programs and services so that adjustments can be made based on new research or changing needs.

A prime example demonstrating why such reviews are necessary is the bilingual program. First, there were no bilingual programs and then, based on changing demographics, it was thought that bilingual programs were needed. As usually occurs, the need grew to excess without any value-added benefits. Now there is enough new research to show that intensive bilingual programs for shorter periods produce better performance. However, with so many self-interests involved, it is becoming a bruising battle. In California the voters approved a change in the program, but the bureaucrats and bilingual lobby are trying to circumvent the will of the voters. That is not what a democratic society is all about, but the taxpayers foot the bill for the war and the WaMi costs.

The largest part of the budget (70-80%) involves personnel costs and it is the single and most critical source of WaMi. Therefore, part of the review process must look at how personnel are assigned and utilized. Any board that conducts such a review, openly, honestly, and intelligently, will find plenty of WaMi. Such a review must also look at workloads and student-loads of all certified and non-certified staff. The differences that will be found in teacher-student load—the number of students per class per day per teacher—would be an apocalyptic awakening.

Included with the personnel budget is the cost for professional development activities. More and more emphasis is being given to the need for professional development, but the fact is that too much WaMi is involved because most such activities are "one-shot" with no follow-up. There is a drastic need for much better planning to insure that the effort to instill new skills and techniques show up in the classroom.

Special education costs are literally going out-of-sight. It, like the bilingual program, was intended to meet some very pressing and specific needs. It's now in the excess mode and is virtually out-of-control. If a forensic comparison were made of what the laws originally intended to accomplish and what is actually happening in the name of special education, it would be like comparing two different programs. The WaMi in special education programs is really shameful, but it is such an emotional issue that few want to take up the fight to curb the abuses involved.

The preparation of the budget and the process for adoption is also important to understand because it is where WaMi begins. Typically, a new budget builds on the previous budget with increases for contractual commitments, program and staff changes. All other line items are then increased for "presumed" inflation." The problem with this approach is that the budget preparation begins with a very wrong-headed assumption that everything the district is doing in terms of programs, services, systems, and practices must be maintained as they currently exist (if a diet is not changed, the fat remains) and that inflation affects every line item. That's why the mantra is heard during every budget preparation and review process that the budget "is tight and just maintains the status quo." If more money just maintains the "status-quo," it reflects what is wrong with education: complacency, and complacency is never fat-free.

What the status quo means is that all programs and services are operating at 100% or near efficiency and effectiveness and none should be eliminated, consolidated or even changed. In other words, increases are demanded regardless of "productivity" (a blasphemous word in education). It's interesting to note that budget documents never indicate how performance has or will be increased because of more dollars.

Another mindless issue is the common perception that a quality school system has a low teacher-pupil ratio and small class sizes; however, both ratios are absolutely meaningless. For example, the reported teacher-pupil ratio in one district was 14.7 (total district) and 20.5 (high school); yet, the actual teacher-student loads (the number of students a teacher had during the course of the day) in the high school ranged from 36 students (for the entire day) or 7.5 students per class to 132 students or 26.4 students per class (no special classes were involved).[127] Obviously, tremendous disparities exist in teacher-pupil loads; some are justified, but rest assured that others are not. Using actual teacher loads and class sizes provide the reality of what is while averages simply hide the disparities.

It's also important to analyze how much free time each classroom teacher has during the course of a week. Such data is not reported. In one district, elementary teachers were free almost one-third of the day and this is not what you expect at the elementary level. In that district, five elementary positions were eliminated without changing class sizes and teachers were still provided with a preparation period.[128] Incidentally, the budget was also considered "tight," but it was not fat-free.

Department Chairs are usually part-time teaching positions. Although the non-classroom time is provided for supervision of the department and to handle department needs, schools would be hard pressed to document and account that the time is anywhere near productive and results oriented.

There are other certified staff positions that are non-classroom such as counselors, psychologists, social workers, speech therapists, etc. What is the student load of these specialists? More importantly, do the student loads make sense? How do they compare with other districts? These are critically important questions to have answered.

Are teachers scheduled and assigned in the most efficient and cost effective manner? In one district, two teachers were needed to cover the exact classes required by three schools, but the principals did not want to share teachers. They were asked: "What will you do with the unassigned time?" There was a profound reply: "We will find something for them to do." Such a forthright response deserved to be rewarded because the board voted, over the objection of the superintendent, to hire three teachers.[129] Was this a fat-free budget?

Therefore, it's absolutely critical to know how every certified and non-certified staff is scheduled and assigned, what student load teachers and specialists have, and how their time is monitored. In other words, how a district allocates and utilizes its personnel really determines whether it comes "fat-free."

What else needs to be considered? There should be a policy for evaluating programs, services and systems every 3-5 years. If there is no policy, the budget is probably getting clogged with cholesterol dollars. Incidentally, using internal staff alone is not valid because the foxes cannot be guarding the hen house. So what can you expect to find from such evaluation reviews?

A speech program was being reviewed and benchmarking with other districts revealed that there were three times as many speech therapy students even though the district was the smallest. After all students were re-tested by outside professional evaluators, the findings were shocking: two thirds of the students had no speech problem. Although this would appear to be a routine review process, a book could be written describing the tortuous eight-month battle the superintendent experienced not to renew the contract of the speech therapist.[130]

A review of an alternative program (not special education), found that students were attending the program only two hours a day (state law required a minimum of 4 hours). However, an attempt to improve the program by adding more time and establishing standards was vigorously opposed by the staff involved and an aggressive parent. Needless to say, the Board capitulated. Worse yet, the State Department of Education did not provide any written support for the superintendent.[131] This is an example that all reviews, no matter how negative, don't necessarily result in appropriate action.

A review of student activity accounts raised a red flag in one account. An audit revealed that the advisor was "borrowing" any cash received. Although a resignation and restitution followed, the superintendent was questioned as to why he had the teacher resign.

These examples (all based on the personal experience of the author during his experiences as a superintendent of schools in K-12 districts) explain why there must be a <u>constant and semi-independent review process</u> of all expenditures, programs, and services in order to keep line items from building up cholesterol. However, the harsh fact is that uncovering such program abominations is not encouraged or welcomed; yes, even by boards of education and other policymakers (the whistle blower syndrome).

Another important procedure for analyzing budgets is to compare the last completed budget year (by line item), the current year, and the proposal for the forthcoming year. This review should also include what was budgeted, what was actually spent, as well as, current encumbrances and expenditures.

Grant programs are a valuable source of additional funds so it would be important to know what specific grants were available, which ones were applied for, and which were approved. What also needs review is to look at how much grant money (if any) was returned because it was not spent. This is not an uncommon practice because it takes work and effort to spend grant money.

The impact of technology must be evaluated to determine if it has reshaped and redefined educational programs and practices in the same way it has made dramatic changes in the business world. Has it significantly increased productivity and school performance? If not, why not?

Of course, there are many other accounts that need to be examined carefully (substitutes, textbooks, travel, equipment purchases, consumable purchases, etc.), and financial practices need to be reviewed such as whether there is an inventory of all school assets.

The conclusions in <u>The 1999 Report Card on American Education</u>, bring many of the issues involved to a sobering reality "[132]

> "America's public schools are not serving our nation (or community) as well as we should expect and our leaders must be open to new and innovative ways to improve the quality of education…it is less important to increase the investment in education than it is to make the right investments.
>
> The study shows no evident correlation between conventional measures of education inputs, such as expenditures per pupil and teacher salaries, and educational outputs, such as average scores on standardized test.
>
> While there may be no specific policy prescriptions, more schools, more school districts, a low pupil-to-teacher ratio, high expenditures per

students, high teacher salaries, and federal involvement in primary and secondary education together do not improve student performance.

This study proves that the current path is not good enough, and that throwing more money at the problem is not the answer."

These conclusions are not new. The problem is that they are not generally accepted as being factual by too many educators. Of course, probably few people, including educators, have even bothered to read the report.

Therefore, the investment of taxpayer dollars must be monitored, protected and enhanced rather than squandered. Why isn't it being done more effectively? Simple! To put it in very blunt terms, there is no reward, recognition, or even thanks for doing so.

The reality is that the budget process is driven by the powerful "P's:" petty politics, personal priorities, pleading parents, predictive pandering, perplexed perceptions, picky personalities, proprietary power, and poor preparation. These are the fatty ingredients causing increased cholesterol that clogs the process for efficient and effective use of school resources. Is it any wonder that safeguarding the taxpayers' investment is a difficult and tortuous process?

However, the biggest whammy of all is yet to come, and it will hit like a bombshell particularly in the urban districts. A study released by a nationally recognized consulting firm to study funding in Connecticut schools has set the stage for a whammy of an explosion that will affect every single urban school district. The study will be used as a red flag to get more and more funding and the poor taxpayers will be the victims.

A column written by the mayors from Stamford and Hartford is the first "shot across the bow". They used the study to support virtually an unlimited amount of more money to solve the problem of low performing schools in their cities, and the punch line follows:

> "Those who are skeptical of the need for reform (financing) might question what it means to 'adequately' educate a child. The study, specifically defines 'adequacy' as that level of funding that will enable 94 to 96 percent of children in Connecticut schools to perform at or above the 'proficiency' level on the Connecticut Master Test and the Connecticut Academic Performance Test, as required under federal law."[133]

Translated, this means an unlimited amount of money will be required and, of course, even then the problems will not be solved. The reality is that no amount of money would significantly improve student achievement; it hasn't yet, even though it has been promised time and time again.

This is exactly what happened in Kansas City (see chapter 12) where the schools were given all the funds they wanted and the only result was unbelievable waste and fraud with no improvement in achievement. It is exactly what would happen in every urban district.

Consider one of the latest examples. In the Denver Public Schools, millions were spent on a literacy program and after three years, students in the poorest schools are not reading or writing better than they were before. According to the superintendent, "despite yeoman efforts to boost test scores...little progress has been made."[134]

However, there was a difference with students from affluent schools who did make gains, and the students in the lower socio-economic schools making no gains with some scoring even more poorly particularly in the higher grades. What this has to be saying is that socio-economic factors play a bigger role in student achievement than previously realized and this is one factor schools cannot really change. So pouring more money alone into poor urban schools will do nothing to solve the problem of low achievement. What can also be inferred from this is that there was little or no effort made to work with the parents. Until parents are made an integral part of literacy efforts, along with the neighborhood and community involvement, the schools efforts will be very limited.

There is no question that this is a very challenging and difficult agenda to implement, but it is the one factor that could make a significant difference.

Summary

All of the programs mentioned in this chapter have been fraught with WaMi. The dollars that can be recouped by eliminating the WaMi etched in every school and school district would fill its own treasure chest. These dollars could then be used for other pressing needs rather than asking the taxpayers for more and more dollars.

Until the taxpayers and parents realize that no matter how many more dollars are added to the school treasure chest, it is never considered enough nor will it ever be. Until this simple and plain fact is accepted, WaMi will continue without shame. In addition, until educators and policymakers understand this fact, improving low performing schools will continue to be illusive because the antidote of more money alone is the wrong prescription.

With thousands of schools identified as failing, and with more and more money pouring into the treasure chest each and every year, when will the money givers demand accountability in terms of better school and student performance? Until there is a constructive response from those who must be held accountable, WaMi will continue to fester.

CHAPTER FIVE

WaMi Examples

"Few men have virtue to withstand the highest bidder," George Washington

Every education dollar is a precious resource, and each dollar must be maximized by spending dollars wisely, efficiently and effectively. However, the real irony is that each part of a dollar squandered or wasted is not lost because taxpayers are simply asked to ante-up more dollars in the next budget cycle and sometimes even during a current budget year.

What must be hammered into every taxpayer's mind is that when a school district seeks more dollars and claims that it is a maintenance or status quo budget, it includes replacement of any wasted and mismanaged dollars.

One force that must also be considered in WaMi is the choke holds that "unions have on the operation of schools, allocation of resources, terms of employment, and efforts at reform…they are injurious to the public interest."[135] Consider the fact that they have $1.2 billion to spend! This makes them a powerful and extremely influential lobbying group, and the politicians know this only too well.

The examples of WaMi that follow will include the approximate time frame in which the incident was reported so that the reader will be able to place the event in proper perspective.

National

Title I

A U.S Office of Education report revealed that more than half of the Title I money to help the poorest children that is designated for certified teachers goes to hire aides.[136] Most states could not say how much improvement the more than $8 billion in grants had on the neediest of children. (9/12/2000)

A General Accounting Office report claims that many states appear to be in a poor position to meet new federal requirements for Title I funds aimed at improving the educational achievement of children at risk. The report highlights a recurring problem involving states' compliance with Title I, the largest source of federal funding amounting to $10.3 billion for K-12 education. As of March of 2005, 35 states were not in compliance with some of the 1994 requirements.[137]

Critics of the controversial program include former Education Secretary Rod Paige who have complained that much of the money has been wasted

Medicaid

Schools are missing out on between $1.5 billion and $2.3 billion a year in Medicaid reimbursements for coordinating and providing medical services to special education students from low-income families. By not applying for these funds, the medical services come from local and state school dollars.

It's estimated that only about 44 percent of the school districts are participating; yet, the law allowing schools to collect Medicaid for serving needy special education students has been on the books for 14 years. Participating schools did collect $648 million in 1999-2000 even though $1.5 billion in eligible costs were actually submitted. The problem is that schools have great difficulty in getting through the complex paperwork.[138] (5/8/2002)

Medicaid Scam?

A federal Medicaid report said the federal government had been improperly charged hundreds of millions of dollars for payments made for disabled children. States, school districts, and private companies made the overcharges. Some states kept as much as 85 percent of the payments intended for school districts for medically related services.[139] (10/30/2002)

Charter School Failures

More than two-thirds of the 86 charter schools that failed have resulted from mismanagement or other financial problems such as low enrollment.[140] (2/28/2001)

PTA Sugar Cure

In their zeal to help schools that can't pay for programs, candy sales and other sweetened products fill the funding gap. Coaches have been known to tie grades to meeting candy sale quotas or to threaten students with loss of the chance to participate in sports if sales fall short. Two years ago, investigators from the General Accounting Office visited 19 schools and found that merchandise sales helped finance programs like school assemblies, field trips, teacher training, and a variety of after school programs. It needs to be emphasized that the money raised through such sales is a common source of embezzled funds.[141] (8/21/2002)

Head Start

This $7 billion program prepares children for kindergarten has alleged and proven abuses of excessive salaries for directors to embezzled funds. In hearings scheduled for reauthorization of funds, a GAO report in March cited flaws of oversight.[142] (4/13/2005)

In a more scathing indictment of the program, columnist Laurence D. Cohen puts the program in perspective: "The GAO...unleashed the auditors from hell on Head Start programs and, to the surprise of no one, found all manner of programmatic and financial sins." An attempt to move the program from Health and Human Services to the Department of Education will likely not succeed because, "it has too many friends in the community-based social service world...it serves as an informal social service agency providing a haven for kids and jobs for their parents...every serious investigation and critical analysis of Head Start has come from the feds or independent researchers...The locals don't care whether it helps the kids as long as the payroll checks don't bounce." [143] (4/24/2005)

Alabama

Statewide

Few systems know exactly what they own. Fewer still know what's missing. The state's largest systems, Mobile County, Jefferson County and Birmingham, can't begin to show why equipment has been removed from inventory. Mobile and Birmingham track only equipment stolen as a result of burglary or breaking and entering. Jefferson County doesn't even do that. However, "few calculate theft from within because they have no faith in their inventories."[144] (12/3/2000)

Lessons are never learned. An investigation by the Birmingham News found that "money invested in public schools is often poorly guarded, misplaced and sometimes stolen."

- Many schools and systems don't have basic safeguards to deter thievery and misspending by employees, students or PTA officials.
- Theft and misuse of public money occurs regularly in school systems from the Tennessee Valley to the Gulf Coast. Those implicated are often among the most trusted people in education.
- Many systems fail to keep track of assets so they can't say for sure what they own, much less what is missing. The vast majority of 128 school systems don't know why computers and other equipment disappear from their inventory lists and can't say whether they were lost, traded in or stolen.
- At least 40 cases in the past decade were found in which school officials were charged in state or federal court with theft, corruption or fraud amounting to $3 million.
- Scores of court records, more than 100 Ethics Commission rulings, hundreds of school system documents and the most recent state audit reports for all 67 county school systems revealed that more than half had serious financial shortcomings.[145] (3/25/2001)

This is the fundamental problem: "The schools are funded and run by government employees with no motivation to stop the theft."[146]

Bessemer

Misuse of money by top school officials nearly drove the district to bankruptcy and led to a state takeover. "Enough money went into the pockets of people that over time it drove the system into the red…theft drove it under."[147] (12/3/2000)

A 1998-1999 audit found the following:

- An accounts clerk got unauthorized overtime pay and deposited checks to vendors into her personal bank account including a $20,500 check written to a utility company. She owes the district $135,000.
- A former superintendent filed improper travel claims, and his board credit card was used to charge insurance, car rentals and golf outings. He was ordered to repay $31,000.
- A payroll officer received unapproved overtime and cash advances totaling almost $40,000 (she repaid $8,766).

What this demonstrates is that the system had no effective monitoring system in place to track anything. How nice for the taxpayers!

Birmingham

Millions of dollars were overspent and millions more lost due to mistakes. To avoid bankruptcy, the district considered closing six schools and eliminating up to 535 jobs to erase a $42 million deficit. Although the former superintendent was blamed for the budget debacle, he claims that he left the district in sound financial condition and with clean audit reports.[148] (11/9/2002)

Jefferson County School District

Mismanagement, poor record keeping, and corruption has driven the system into financial chaos and state takeover this year. At least three people were convicted of conspiring to defraud the system and a long awaited state audit is expected to reveal hundreds of thousands of dollars in misspent money.[149] (12/4/2000)

Shelby

Although their method of tracking equipment is considered a model, $200,000 in equipment has "disappeared."[150] (12/3/2000)

Of interest, the state now requires superintendents to take a course in school finance. What were they taking before, monopoly? Is it any wonder there is so much WaMi?

Arizona

State Department of Education

Technology

Arizona's ambitious plan to provide its schools with more than 250 free software titles via the Internet was mired in confusion and conflict. Several districts cited problems with accessing and navigating the $27.9 million system. Accessing everything the system has to offer means districts will have to pay thousands of dollars more each month for faster connections. The eventual cost of the entire program system would exceed $150 million.

This costly system has inappropriate software, hidden costs, and questionable alignment to state standards. To make matters worse, the project's leader has resigned amid controversy over his alleged ties to one of the companies involved where he had been paid as a member of its advisory board. A state lawmaker has called for a special investigative audit into how the contract was awarded.

What is interesting is that the local school districts were never asked for any input on the project. As one district official stated: "It was kind of sprung on us."[151] (4/9/2002)

Charter Schools

This state that has the most charter schools (over 400) is cranking down on 31 charter schools that face fines and possibly closure because of late audits, ignored testing requirements, and financial fraud. The prior year, 55 charters missed their audit deadlines. Prior to that time, state officials were powerless to act.[152]

In other words, previous charters were granted without any oversight. Apparently, this was considered being prudent and responsible with taxpayer money.

Judge Slaps Legislature

The Legislature's $69 million dollar raid on a public school repair fund to balance the budget was ruled unconstitutional by a Maricopa County Superior Court judge. The fund is one of the three that lawmakers established to assure money is equitably distributed for constructing and maintaining schools.[153] (5/7/2002)

Building Fiasco

The School Facilities Board is broke and needs $970 million. Ironically, they wanted to use some of the money they don't have to sue contractors who have left behind millions of dollars in shoddy work. They have a novel means to get the money. It has to persuade 37 school boards to lend the state titles to 57 of their districts new and future buildings. The buildings would then be used as collateral in a 15-year lease-to-own program.[154]

It's certainly creative, and it's almost a guaranteed way to bury the financial mess further and further into the red.

Phoenix

Phoenix School District

The district is hoping to recover more than $500,000 in insurance premiums it paid to 239 employees in error.[155] (6/12/2002)

WaMi is so easy because it requires no real effort. The only requirement is laxity in doing one's job and that's not hard to do.

Wilson Elementary School District

The superintendent has been on suspension since March but continues to be paid his salary of $121,000 plus perks. He continues to receive his $750 monthly car allowance and to use the district gas card because he claims it is part of his benefits, and transportation is not limited to school business. The problem is that two board members who accused him of taking extravagant trips and running a self-serving administration want his resignation. The third member supports the superintendent and, therefore, he cannot be fired because a unanimous vote is required. His contract expired in June 2004; in the meantime, an interim superintendent has been hired at just $60,000 to run the district.[156] (9/27/2002)

It's unthinkable to provide transportation benefits not limited to school business, and to require a unanimous vote for dismissal; but it's only more taxpayer dollars for the WaMi parade. It also shows how easily some boards can be manipulated. The superintendent was finally removed, but the story does not end. The interim superintendent resigned a month early because he could not get along with the loan board member (the other two had resigned over the incident).[157] (11/26/2002)

Arkansas

Schools and colleges that received more than $50 million through a "monumental" accounting error will not have to pay back a dime. The money came from an education trust fund that is generated by a portion of the sales tax, but the fund was receiving about $8 to $10 million per year too much since 1991. In spite of the fact that "it was a monumental error that a 5th grader should not have made," the legislators agreed that trying to recoup the money was a bad idea and unnecessary.[158] (2/19/1997)

Only taxpayer money can be viewed as being "unnecessary" to recoup. It's easy to see how WaMi has such a merry welcome in every school district because no one will be held accountable.

California

<u>State</u>

Californians just passed the largest bond measure in state history in the amount of $13.5 billion for constructing new schools and upgrading older schools. This levy was passed in spite of the fact that "school districts have a long history of school construction boondoggles fraught with fraud and mismanagement (many examples will be found in this section).[159] (11/10/2002)

A study, "Where Is All the Money Going?" by two education activists revealed the following:[160]

- Approximately 40 percent of the state's education dollars are spent on bureaucracy and overhead rather than classroom instruction. The figures came from studies by the RAND Corporation and the Little Hoover Commission.
- Even though education costs increased 39 percent (inflation adjusted) between 1978 and 1999, textbooks are frequently unavailable, school libraries have been shut down, and art and music programs terminated.
- Four levels of administration run K-12 schools and act as though they were separate fiefdoms. They quarrel frequently and often and some disputes end in lawsuits.
- Interest groups, like the NEA, exert power over educational decisions; this, in large part, comes from their political contributions—$960,000 for the governor and $400,000 to the State Superintendent. That's why teachers have the best tenure law in the country receiving tenure after just two years.
- The power of local citizens has deteriorated because almost two-thirds of education tax dollars flow from the state.
- Spending statistics are "deceptive" because the study revealed that the state uses a per-pupil cost of $6,700, whereas the all-inclusive cost is approximately $8,500.

- The schools, once among the best in the nation, now lag behind almost every other state with the urban high schools becoming literally "dropout factories." The pay disparities among teachers means that the best paid teachers in 42 of the 50 largest districts work in schools that serve the fewest number of black and Hispanic students.[161]

How did such a spiral into self-destruction occur? When the reduced class size initiative was passed, it created jobs in the better schools and school districts. Who got hired? The more experienced teachers, of course, because they left the urban schools and this is where they were most needed. Yep, class sizes were reduced but who benefited? Certainly not the students who needed it most!

Since 1991, it has cost taxpayers $220 million to bail out seven public schools because of financial mismanagement (WaMi). Yet, despite such WaMi, school administrators actually suffer few consequences.[162] (6/1/2004) Is it any wonder why WaMi proliferates the landscape of Education America?

Despite all of the increased funding that is never enough, the schools now lag behind almost every other state. This conclusion by a number of organizations including the Rand Corporation, Education Trust-West, and the Harvard University Civil Right Project suggest that a combination of factors have contributed to an alarming degradation of the state's schools over time.[163]

State Department of Education

Double Trouble

Some of the mismanagement absurdities are absolutely comical. Two entities seeking $500,000 claimed to be running the same charter school. But don't blame them. A state official concedes that "the state oversight of charters is proving to be frustrating…and they don't know which charters are running which schools." Obviously, officials have no embarrassment in making statements that are so incredibly ridiculous. They grant the charters but they don't know what charters run which schools? Mickey Mouse could probably do a better job. Don't be surprised if they both receive the money. After all, what difference does it make when it's only the taxpayer's money.[164] (1/31/2002)

Misspent Fed Dollars

The departments agreed to repay the federal government at least $3.3 million in grants that were supposed to be used to teach English, but were allegedly misspent by community organizations. The grant money was distributed to community groups that sponsored English classes, but state auditors found a number of the groups could not document how they had used the money and had fabricated records of nonexistent programs.

It always gets worse. A former assistant superintendent of adult education said he was removed from his job after reporting the apparent fraud to a supervisor with the education department in 1996. He is seeking a whistle-blower's share of the settlement, but he may not prevail because a U.S. Supreme Court ruling bares whistle-blower suits against state agencies.[165] (9/20/2002)

However, in a stunning and rather shocking court verdict, the State Department of Education and former State Superintendent were slapped with a $4.5 million judgment. In addition, the jury found that the State Superintendent "acted with malice" in demoting the "whistle blower" to keep him from telling others.

Two consultants, who were also retaliated against for having told FBI agents about misuse of federal funds, settled their lawsuit for $160,000.[166] (12/5/2002)

There are few cases of education whistleblowers who are vindicated in their honesty and courage, too few, and that's part of the problem contributing to WaMi.

Alum Rock School District

The district has been described as the "abyss of mismanagement and turmoil" and where students post among the lowest test scores, and the highest staff turnover rate in the county. The problems are so deep and pervasive that four schools, no matter how well run, will not solve their problems.[167] (6/6/2002)

El Dorado High School District

Because of new computer software and human error, an excuse that is used repeatedly, there is a $2.3 million deficit in the current budget. It seems that some employees were left off of the balance sheet, so officials thought they had $2.3 million more to spend. How did these employees get paid? What's more fascinating, even the auditor didn't find the problem. However, despite the shortfall, no teacher layoffs are expected.[168] (9/11/2002).

Emeryville Unified School District (2001)

An assessment by the state's Fiscal Crisis and Management Assistance Team projected that the district with an annual budget of $8 million will be $1.4 million over by the end of the year. What is noteworthy is that yearly audits by the county department of education uncovered no problems. The County Schools Superintendent said her office reviewed Emery's budget yearly and found no problem. "The books were cooked," she said. "We're not fraud investigators." Really! Isn't part of a budget review to determine whether there are any red flags; otherwise, why bother to review a budget?

Parents had been telling the board that something was terribly wrong, but instead of asking questions, they (the board) did nothing. This is a Pontius Pilot phenomenon that could only take place with taxpayer dollars.[169] (1/10/2001)

But again, the story continues demonstrating utter incompetence. The superintendent had previously been fired from the nearby Compton Unified School District in 1992, and within a year the state had to assume control of that financially and academically failing district. In the same year, he was hired in Emeryville where the identical problem of financial mismanagement became so serious that the state had to intervene once again. The county superintendent's office must have known about this previous problem and should have been more sensitive and careful in its audit in Emeryville.

How is it that with so many applicants for a superintendent's position a school board manages to pick the one with a financially mangled past from next door? This is really WaMi at its best and deserves some type of Oscar for the worst decision of the decade.

Los Angeles

Contaminated Land

The board spent $25 million to purchase another (it wasn't the first time) environmentally contaminated site and district staff continued to proceed with condemnation of additional parcels even after being warned about open-ended environmental problems.[170] (3/1999)

It is hard to imagine how warnings, no matter how serious, are ignored in so many instances of WaMi.

What's Next?

U.S. Corps of Engineers has been called upon to build 150 schools. The military must now protect the taxpayers from the terror of fraud, mismanagement and corruption of public officials. Thousands of school boards build schools without the assistance of the military. The local Congressman instigated this unusual answer.[171] (12/16/1999)

Lease Waste

An investigation regarding a building lease determined that a report and Certification of Safety was not obtained. The district expended $368,000 in lease and property tax payments but never occupied the building. The actual cost to the district to fulfill its obligations under the remaining term of the lease was $574,000.[172] (2001)

Now get this! The Inspector General, who is employed by the school district, dropped dozens of cases of possible abuse and fraud because of severe budget cuts.[173] (11/2/2001)

It seems more prudent to see taxpayers' money wasted rather than spending it where it can do the most good. Stopping abuse and fraud would certainly more than pay for itself, but common sense is not so common at least not when it concerns taxpayer dollars.

Bond Fund Mismanagement

An audit of a $2.4 billion bond issue for repairs and improvements involving 12,495 projects found that $600 million was wasted. There was no system in place to identify where projects were, their cost, and how they were being managed. The fact is that officials betrayed their promise right after voters approved the measure by ignoring recommendations from an oversight committee. Maybe Enron used Los Angeles as their corporate model.

Of course, the money went somewhere, it was spent, and it certainly wasn't all cash. There had to be paper trail somewhere. Part of it was even spent on a new school that was not included in the bonding.[174] (11/29/2001) These WaMi stories are certainly perplexing! How is it that officials can be so incompetent and yet still retain their jobs?

Literacy Program Scam

The school board claims it was misled in purchasing a $6.7 million literacy program. The company they thought was awarded the contract was not the company that got the award. Instead, it went to a start-up firm with only three employees located in a law firm with close connections to the state Senate Majority Leader.[175] (3/16/2002) No mention was made of who "misled" the board.

Inspector General Power

A bill was introduced in the legislature, supported by the unions, to give independent power to the IG to investigate reports of corruption, conflicts of interest, unethical conduct and other misconduct. He would get "unfettered access" to all documents and reports. In the past, the superintendent and the board have considered proposals to bar the IG from initiating investigations without board approval and to require that all reports be kept confidential. In fact, the IG's office has been pressured to lay off financial audits of educational programs. Therefore, it should not be surprising that the superintendent strongly opposes the bill seeing it as an intrusion on is authority to perpetuate WaMi.[176] (4/7/2002)

Therefore, it should come as no surprise, that in spite of scandal after scandal, the legislators decided to scale back proposed legislation to expand the powers of the Inspector General; nevertheless, the position will continue until 2015 because it's probably good public relations. The superintendent vehemently opposed the expansion of powers saying the IG would not be accountable to anybody because it would be taken out of control of the school board.[177] (9/17/2002)

The reality is that is exactly what is needed if an IG is to function free of local politics and influence. It's this type of political cowardice that explains why WaMi really whams every school district. No one really wants to get rid of WaMi because it is too lucrative as will be seen in the FraSte examples.

Law Firm Sued

A legal battle that pitted the district against one of Los Angeles' oldest law firms has been settled for $3 million. The district sued the firm for allegedly ignoring conflicts of interest and giving poor advice on one of the most expensive schools being built on an abandoned oil field that contains potentially dangerous gases. The half-finished $175 million high school will now be completed.[178] (4/10/2002)

Jumping the Gun

Even before the public had voted on a $3.3 billion bond program, the superintendent hired a consultant to oversee the project. Although he has excellent credentials, critics of the decision claim it was payback because he was responsible for resurrecting an abandoned $200 million high school.[179] (6/18/2002)

Lottery Dollars Mishandled

In its annual report, The Los Angeles grand jury stated that the LAUSD failed to comply with state law in how it spent $1.3 billion in lottery revenues over nearly two decades.[180] (6/29/2002)

Specifically, it mishandled $27 million for instructional materials. The chief financial officer said the district did nothing wrong: "The whole report has to do with esoteric accounting issues, not whether the money was spent properly."

The report said the district should take $27 million from its general fund to reimburse two special-purpose accounts for instructional materials.[181] (6/29/2002)

The grand jury did not view the issue as "esoteric accounting," but rather as a clear violation of law.

Audits Rips Bonding

A state audit found that school officials deceived voters in winning approval in 1997 for a school bond measure, paid exorbitant private management fees, and improperly spent $90 million on employee salaries, consultants and legal settlements. "There was exaggeration and an inflated expectation for what it could accomplish." The district was originally accused of lying deliberately to voters but that was toned down to making statements that turned out to be false.[182] (6/30/2002)

It would be nice if someone could explain how a statement deemed to be "false" is not a "lie." But this is the type of double talk and educational jargoneese that prevails when WaMi is uncovered.

History Hotel

The 81-year-old Ambassador hotel, a plaster-peeling hulk of a building popular with stray cats that was closed in 1989, was purchased by the school district for $105 million. Of course, they don't know what will be done with the building: restore the neglected grounds to their former splendor, preserve a few choice parts, or raise every last cabana and start from scratch. Yes, it's historical. A senator from New York was assassinated there, the Rat Pack played there, and seven American presidents slept there.

"Students often feel that history doesn't have any use to them so touching base with a building that experienced everything from prohibition to the assassination of a presidential candidate could be a way to pique their curiosity."[183] (8/4/2002)

Conflict of Interest

An investigation by the Inspector General found a blatant conflict of interest involving an outside law firm that played a key role in a $5 million contract won by a real estate firm that employed the same lawyer.[184] (9/11/2002)

High School Building Halted-Restarted

Further work was abandoned on building a $200 million high school, the nation's most expensive, because it was being built on a former oil field and environmental hazards had not been fully addressed before ground was broken in 1997. Although school officials had information about the risks involved, they did not share the information with the board.[185] (3/2000)

The school board voted to revive the project and to conduct a thorough inspection to see if its environmental problems could be addressed. In the process, inspectors determined that the half finished school might be sitting on top of an active earthquake fault line.[186] (9/27/2002)

The story of the Belmont school complex is like a soap opera in that it goes on and on without end. A 220 page report representing 2 years of work by the district attorney's office concerning the Belmont Learning Center concluded: "A public works disaster of biblical proportions, but the evidence fails to establish the existence of any felony violations."[187] (3/4/2003)

The Board has now voted to put $115 million more in the $175 million it has spent thus far for this unfinished boondoggle of a school construction project. Of course, the environmental study must still be completed. The new plan calls for the demolition of 2 unfinished buildings, and the four remaining buildings would be completed.[188] (5/23/2003)

It can be a lot easier

It is no secret that school building projects take too long and are usually over-budget, but it doesn't have to be that way. California law allows homebuilders to provide new schools in lieu of impact fees. In Corona, developers used the law to build a 9-acre, $7 million school in just 13 months. If the school district had to build it, it would have taken an estimated 7 years.[189]

The LAUSD officials actually considered the creation of a program that would turn over the financing and construction of schools to private developers. Needless the say, the plan was never implemented. Why not implement a plan that would save time and money and be far more efficient?

Examples of public-private partnerships can be found in a number of districts. In Niagara Falls, NY, Honeywell Inc., built an $83 million school for the city to lease, allowing the city to avoid any tax increases or debt. More importantly was that Honeywell was able to erect the school for $15 million less than it would have cost the district. Houston, TX also formed a partnership to construct two new high schools under a lease-purchase arrangement. The schools were completed a year earlier than would have occurred and cost $20 million less than the original school estimate.[190]

Private-school partnerships are feasible under the provisions of the federal Economic Growth and Tax Relief Reconciliation Act of 2001 allowing private companies to use the proceeds of tax-exempt bonds to build and repair schools and then lease the facilities to school districts. So why aren't more schools taking advantage of this law?

Double Dipping

A former top administrator, who was bought out at a cost of $100,000 because he mismanaged the most expensive high school in the country, was retained by the superintendent at a cost of $58,000. His job was to improve procedures in the accounts payable department. Interestingly, the district just finished paying two accounting giants to audit and improve business operations. The superintendent is empowered to enter into such contracts if they are below $250,000. Rewarding incompetence seems to be part of the culture by school administrators.

However, the school board president terminated this secret contract.[191] (10/30/2002)

Retroactive Contracts

Retroactive contracts—contracts that are handed out by school officials but not approved by the board—are part of a long-standing pattern of staffers trying to circumvent board oversight. With $10 million more handed out just waiting for board approval, after the fact, the board warned the superintendent: "This is the last time they agree to large contracts that officials sign without approval...in the future such agreements will not be honored and disciplinary action will be taken against staffers who violate the policy."[192] (11/11/2002)

Consultant Craze

In 2002, the district paid 663 consultants $71 million from voter approved bond funds for its crash program to build or expand 150 schools. It would have cost one-half as much to hire its own staff. The consultants represented

30 percent of the Facilities Services Divisions 2,300 staff, and 80 percent of the 423-person work force.[193] (1/29/2003)

Oakland Public Schools

The state's Fiscal Crisis Management and Assistance Team, the state's troubleshooters for failing districts, released a scathing assessment of the district for mismanagement, poor student achievement, and serious financial problems that date back over a decade. The audit states that it is in need of immediate and dramatic management assistance.[194] (2/9/2000)

With a Fiscal Crisis team available, why did it take so long for action to be taken?

It seems that "poor accounting practices" including no accounting for a 4,300-student drop in enrollment exacerbated the problem. It is really hard to understand how such a monumental error could be made. The county finally appointed a state financial expert to oversee the budget when more accounting discrepancies revealed $27 millions missing (this is a made-for-TV movie project).

According to the superintendent, "nothing coming from the budget office seemed to indicate that we were on a collision course." Incredible to say the least and WaMi at its best! Such performance should be considered criminal. It isn't and that's part of the problem, no real consequences for malfeasance and incompetence.

The school district finally went bankrupt in 2003 and a state administrator was put in charge.

The Oakland WaMi saga continues. A June 2004 audit could not determine if in 2002-03 the district had properly complied with scores of state and federal mandates. Where were the state and federal officials that are supposed to monitor such mandates? The district could be forced to repay $163 million to the state and federal governments. Additionally, bonds worth more than $322 million might be in jeopardy of losing their tax-exempt status.[195] (9/1/2004)

The mayor added more pizzazz to the story: "It's a crisis that has been going on for decades." So again why was nothing done sooner? Consider just one fact: Fewer than half the freshmen who enter high school graduate (48 out of 100). The dropout rate still hasn't changed despite the millions of dollars being spent.[196] (4/12/2005)

This is another WaMi that is not understood by the policymakers and the taxpaying public: spending more dollars, getting more dollars, changing governance, etc. does not mean that there is a corresponding effort to get better results. It also means that officials don't respond appropriately to warnings. Whistleblowers were at work in Oakland to no avail. They warned of one

WaMi concerning a tax levy that was approved in 2001 for vocational and special education; instead, the money was being used to help pay for construction of a new $29 million headquarters building. The headquarters was obviously a far more important priority for dollars rather than improving the graduation rate. In addition, $40 million was not set aside to pay for the loan.[197] 2/9/2003)

This horrendous story is but one example of how WaMi weaves its culture throughout every fabric of school finances, operations, and practices.

Orchard School District

Mismanagement

This 800-pupil school district purchased a $400,000 phone system without competitive bidding required by the state's Public Contract Code. It also sold a $40 million bond program to the community without conducting an independent study on how fast student enrollment was growing. According to a report, "it does not appear that the district accurately projected future enrollment to determine the need for another school prior to passing the bond."

The school superintendent resigned after seven months of controversy about his leadership and free-spending ways. He purchased a $79,856 BMW, and traveled to England and Cuba all at taxpayer expense.[198] (1/1/2002)

In December, the county superintendent declared the district in a state of "fiscal crisis" with non-existent internal accounting controls and little or no oversight on the use of credit cards. "At almost every level, in almost every endeavor, the district was grossly mismanaged."[199] (4/11/2002)

Ravenswood

The districts' leadership, in a letter to a federal judge, said it would not object to paying a $10,000 fine and attend 4 hours of ethics training for submitting fraudulent petitions to a federal court.[200] (2/23/2002)

A court order required the district to provide a written explanation any time it does not follow the monitor's recommendation on a hiring decision affecting its special education program, which was the subject of a class-action lawsuit. The court was not provided with an explanation for hiring a principal against the recommendation of the court-appointed monitor. As a result, the superintendent will be required to appear in court to show why she should not be fined or exposed to other sanctions.[201] (8/23/2002)

Richmond

The school district had to seek bankruptcy protection because of "unsound management practices and unjustified budgeting techniques" by the superintendent. The grand jury exonerated the superintendent and the board because "there are no legal penalties for failings of either the superintendent or board." However, the grand jury concluded that the bankruptcy filing "was the culmination of several years of failure by district's board of education to exercise effective and prudent control of financial affairs." The primary motive of the board members was to influence their reelection.[202](6/19/1991).

Incompetence and malfeasance without penalties are hard to understand, but such behaviors are what allow WaMi to spread its tentacles far and wide in school district after school district. Pity the poor taxpayers!

Sacramento City Unified School District

The federal Department of Education conducted an investigation and found that $7.5 million of Title I monies were misspent. An original complaint was filed by a group of parents six years prior and the complaint remains "open." What's really very interesting about this is that by keeping the complaint open, the parents cannot file any appeal. This is how the U.S. Department of Education responds to complaints, appear interested, but do nothing.

"The district is depriving children and their parents of their Federal right to education and betray the taxpayers whose trust they mock."[203](6/24/2002)

San Francisco

A Chronicle investigation found that school officials misspent and mismanaged ten's of millions of dollars for school repairs and modernization projects. More WaMi was added because the facts were hid in order to win voter approval for more funds.

This is no surprise since there has been a 13-year practice of using voter-approved bond and tax funds to pay employee salaries. Since 1988, $68 million out of $337 million in such funds was diverted from promised projects to pay salaries and benefits of non-teaching employees. The investigation found mishandling of the funds, money was moved between accounts without proper authorization, key management positions were empty, undisciplined accounting practices occurred, and purchasing policies for real estate were ambiguous.[204] (12/5/2001) Is that all?

There were plenty of prior warnings about the mismanagement of the funds. Complaints from citizens began in 1995, and a Citizens Advisory

Committee, appointed by the school board to monitor the voter-approved funds, repeatedly complained to school administrators about the incomprehensible spending reports. When the committee sought to hire an auditor to track the expenditures, it was rebuffed.

City officials including the mayor's office, the Board of Supervisors, the treasurer and the controller took a hands-off approach.[205] (11/12/2001)

No one was disciplined in any way for this gross WaMi that can only be described as deliberate and planned deceit. How can WaMi be stopped or reduced with there are no penalties to the perpetrators who betray their trust?

Now that these practices have been uncovered by the newspaper investigation, officials have promised to adhere to the regulations governing bond and tax funds. Can anyone believe this?

Network Nonsense

School officials found that a $68 million networking project by a private company would have cost $18 million less if done by district technicians.[206] (5/28/2004)

Colorado

Jefferson County School District

The school board has hired a psychiatrist and a licensed professional counselor to improve "difficulties" in working together. To date this largest state school district has paid over $13,000 for a series of private group sessions during just two months. At the same time, the district is laying off teachers because of overspending. The counseling sessions apparently did not prove helpful because board members left the last session because "we realized we weren't going to go further."[207] (4/23/2002)

Elbert County

The superintendent gave himself a $54,000 raise and treated himself to lavish dinners.[208] (1/3/2003)

Englewood

The 2002-03 budget of $28 million failed to account for all staff positions resulting in a shortfall of $478,000.[209] (1/8/2003)

St. Vrain Valley School District

The district (22,000 students and 38 schools) overspent its budget by $13.8 million because of accounting mistakes such as leaving 150 employees off the books.[210] (12/19/2002)

It should be noted that state lawmakers in 1993 created an interest free loan program to carry districts through. The law says the state is to give the money to any district submitting a request without even signing a single page request sheet.[211] (1/3/2003) What an invitation to WaMi and FraSte—come one, come all and dip into the taxpayers' treasure chest.

But there is more! The school board knew as early as December 2001 that the district's fund was too low, but took no action to prevent a $13.8 million shortfall.[212] (1/9/2003)

Why should the board do anything with such state largesse at its disposal? Who should be held accountable, the board or the loony legislature?

Connecticut

Amity Regional School District

A scathing investigative report included a recommendation that nine of twelve Amity School board members resign for "gross mismanagement" of the district's finances involving $2.8 million. A special tax levy was required to cover the shortfall. No one has resigned and the district responded by proposing one of the largest budget increases ever.[213] (5/6/2002).

The anger and frustration of the communities involved surfaced with a vengeance when the proposed budget was rejected with a landslide vote. Voters said they voted against the budget because "they thought the Amity school board couldn't be trusted with their money."

The board had been warned of the $2.7 million shortfall 10 months before it was made public and an investigation found there was nothing to indicate the board acted upon being notified."[214] (5/8/2002) Silence is golden!

The Attorney general stated that he has not ruled out the possibility that criminal prosecution or civil penalties might result from his ongoing investigation. "The issues are certainly serious and significant involving both illegal and improper conduct." Many of the issues now flagged as problems had previously been raised by a state education auditor.[215] (10/4/2002)

Budget referendums have been attempted and all have failed because 5 of the original 9 members of the board still refused to resign.[216] (4/7/2003)

In WaMi incidents, there is a strong pattern that warnings do not lead to any corrective action. It is far more important to protect the incompetence and the incompetent, and CheDe is the way to do it.

Hartford

Lease Rip-off

School officials say they were "held hostage" and were locked into a ten-year lease for a school building it did not want to house the central office. They didn't want the building because the price tag was too high at $13 a square foot plus incidental expenses of one million dollars. No parking was available so employees would have to ride a shuttle bus from a nearby parking area costing $800 per day, plus lost work time riding the shuttle estimated at $300,000. What needs to be understood is that this is a cash-strapped school district with one of the highest per-pupil costs in the state and, yet, is one of the lowest test scoring districts.

The fact is that the school district had been offered a building at below market rates ($10 a square foot) along with 200 free parking spaces in a secure lot. To sweeten-the-pot, structural improvements worth $2-3 million would also be included. However, since city hall was empowered to negotiate for the school system, it refused the deal.

Why turn down what was obviously a much better deal? The reason for the refusal was easy to understand. The two owners of the building were politically connected and the chairman of the school trustees works for the law firm representing the building owners—what a sweetheart deal. It's all legalized pillaging of the school treasure chest and another classic example of WaMi at work.[217] (2/3/2002) Although it was perfectly legal, ethically and morally it was shameful!

Bloated Payroll

The city, facing a $50 million projected deficit, has 500 more board of education employees than a peer city with the same number of enrolled students. Total city positions have increased from 11 per thousand residents to 15.8—it has more employees now than it did in 1950 when there were 53,000 more residents.[218] (4/7/2002)

This is what happens when programs and staff become entrenched. Even when there is a precipitous fall in enrollment, there are no reductions; however, there are always additions to the budget when enrollment increases.

District Of Columbia

Convicted Felons OK

In 1994, auditors found that school officials had hired thousands of people arrested or convicted of crimes including one-quarter of the security staff.[219] (10/25/95)

Status Quo Shake-Up

Over 1,100 pink slips were given to employees because getting rid of dead weight is required to break the status quo.[220](6/17/2002)

Whose perception?

Although three superintendents, school boards and the courts have said that special education programs are better today than ever, some parents still don't agree. "The bureaucrats running the show may be different, but not much else has changed."[221]

Good Thinking?

The facilities department has been revamped five times in recent years and at one time it was even run by the U.S. Army Corps of Engineers. New janitors and engineers were hired, new boilers and air-conditioning installed, and new roofs and windows put on dozens of old school buildings. The problem is that the new janitors and engineers don't know how to operate the new systems.[222]

No Difference

Fifteen troubled schools that are on the "transformation" list are not much different from the average D.C. school with low-test scores and low parental involvement. In fact, reform advocates urged school leaders to place one-third of the districts 146 schools on the list.[223]

Special Education Scam?

Lawyers are not exempt from legally gorging the school treasure chests. A DC lawyer who represents special education clients helps to determine if they need further diagnostic testing. And if necessary, he then refers them for private school placement. Sounds typical of what is happening in every school district. However, there is one itsy-bitsy WaMi in this scenario: The lawyer involved is also president of the testing company typically charging far more than other providers, and the private schools charging on average the highest tuition rates have corporate ties to the law firm. So far, it amounts to a ten million dollar rip-off.

City officials are simply "disturbed" as to the extent to which private entrepreneurs are able to take advantage of special education requirements without careful oversight by school officials. School officials were reportedly "upset" to learn how much this has cost. To try and limit such excesses, the DC Board is trying to set up more school programs for special education students. What must be understood is that the district had a cost overrun of $63 million, so why didn't they determine much sooner that special education overruns could be reduced with more in-school programs? Obviously, no one seemed to care that the "financial pot was boiling over." Why bother, it's only the taxpayer's money.

Interestingly, although it's legal, it may not be ethical according to the DC Bar Association. Ethics rules require disclosure to the clients of the law firm's relationship with the testing company and the schools.

The story gets more interesting. In at least 16 cases, Superior Court judges appointed this same law firm as "education advocates" for children in need; and in at least some of the cases the firm persuaded the judge to send the children to one of their schools.

It gets worse! The lawyers involved cannot really be faulted because they were thoroughly trained in the entire process by the school system where they all worked for years. One served as the school board's general counsel, and another had worked for 20 years in special education in DC schools. They were the rare individuals who learned something in the DC school system.

On and on it goes! What is more astonishing is that two members of the firm that were involved in this practice had been stripped of their law licenses in unrelated cases in the 1980s, but they were reinstated in 1994.[224] "Education" certainly pays along with the right connections! (2/18/2002)

Charter School Debacle

The Techworld Public Charter School that was shut down for financial mismanagement awarded $60,000 in bonuses to about a dozen staff including the principal. School officials also tried to auction off the furniture and other equipment.[225] (6/30/2002)

Falsified Enrollment

Several charter schools over-reported student enrollment figures that provided a total windfall of over one million dollars. The money received by charter schools comes from the school budget. One of the charter school employees testified "the enrollment had been padded to defraud the public school system."[226] (4/1/2002)

No Oversight

Auditors examined payments to private special education providers and found that of $69 million paid out in a 28-month period, $67 million of the bills were paid without being properly reviewed. Payments were being made to ineligible students, and the district overpaid after it was billed several times for services provided only once. The city's chief financial officer admitted that it does not have control over the problem, but they are working to fix it.[227] (9/3/2002)

Did anyone wonder why the chief financial officer had no control over the problem?

How Nice!

There are no funds in the budget to pay about 650 employees who are on the DC school payroll. This helps to explain why per pupil costs are over $10,852 in comparison to the national average of $7,280, and why the ratio of school employees to students is 6 to 1.[228] (3/31/2003) This is a district that has an absolutely dismal record of student achievement and high school graduates.

Florida

Statewide

OPPAGA

The Florida Office of Program Policy Analysis and Government Accountability (OPPAGA) is a special staff unit of the Legislature created by state law. OPPAGA examines agencies and programs to improve services and cut costs when directed by state law, the presiding officers, or the Joint Legislative Auditing Committee.

Since its inception in July 1994, OPPAGA has made recommendations having a potential fiscal impact of $2.5 billion. Of these potential savings, $1.9 billion would come from school districts over a five-year period. Of course, the savings can only be realized if school districts implement the recommendations that they are not required to do.

Board Gets Paid

The state is one of the very few that pay board of education members. For example, in Duvall County, members are paid $34,682. In Northeast Florida, the range is $28,053 to $21,785.[229] (4/1/2002). What ever happened to public service?

Non-Ed $

State law or tight budgets have not stopped schools from using taxpayer dollars for non-education expenditures. Some examples follow:[230](4/26/2003)

- Miami Edison Senior High in Dade County spent $25,000 on a trip to Busch Gardens (located in Florida).
- Oriole Beach Elementary School in Santa Rosa County spent $6,000 on a gazebo.
- Stark Elementary in Bradford spent $2,000 on a trip to Universal Studios (located in Florida)
- Webster Elementary in Sumter County spent $200 to hire BoJo-the-Clown for a school celebration.
- William Turner Tech Arts High in Dade County spent $30,000 on bonuses for 32 custodians.

Performance Audits

The following are examples of performance reviews simply to indicate the savings that can be realized if report recommendations are implemented. What the reports also indicate is that the amount of savings that can be realized is money that was and is being wasted and mismanaged.

Brevard County School District

A performance review indicated that if the recommendations are implemented, the district could experience a positive fiscal impact of $5,895,000 over five years and it could attain the Seal of Best Financial Management in two years if it votes to implement the report action plans.[231] (August 1999)

Lake County School District

A performance review indicated that if the recommendations are implemented, the district could experience a positive fiscal impact of $557,900 in fiscal year 2001-02 and $5,114,000 over a five-year period.[232] (12/2001)

Brooksville

A new finance director found that the district, in financial turmoil, did not know how much money was available for daily operations and longer-term accounts. What she also soon discovered was a $3.3 million windfall—the money had accumulated for years in an overlooked account.[233] (6/20/2002)

Broward County

Tech Woes

Overhauling the technology system, estimated to cost between $65 million and $136 million, will be closely scrutinized because of growing accusations of waste and mismanagement. Among the problems cited were:

- The purchase of an e-mail system for $500,000 that was left on the shelf and the following year another e-mail system was requested.
- A computer company was paid $489,054 for maintenance contracts on computers that had been removed nearly two years earlier.
- Technology companies complained that only one firm could fill bids and proposals.[234] (3/19/2002)

Grand Jury

A grand jury ripped the district's building programs in a report five years ago citing waste and sloppiness. [235] (8/21/2002)

Duval County Public Schools

The district was investigated by the State Auditor General regarding the expenditure of $2.5 million of Title I money set aside for schools with students from low-income neighborhoods. The money is supposed to supplement funds the schools already receive, but the audit shows it was used to supplant state and local money at five schools.

In another case, $600,000 allocated to reduce class sizes was used to hire 18 teachers who didn't work in classrooms.

Board members spent most of 2001 debating which companies should bus 60,000 students. The board followed the advice of attorneys and approved new contracts. Two weeks later, the board ignored legal advice and rescinded its vote. As a result, one contractor withdrew its bid, and the next best bid cost the school system an extra $1.7 million.[236] (3/30/2002)

Coral Springs

Officials paid one million dollars for a track at Coral Springs High School estimated to cost $500 thousand[237] (9/27/2000)

At Piper High School, 193 items valued at $328,000 could not be located.[238] (9/27/2000)

A district inspector refused to approve a mold and mildew clean-up project at Riverside Elementary School. She found that insulation was being placed over wallboard that hadn't been fully cleaned, windows hadn't been properly sealed, and water was still entering the school's cafeteria. The inspector was pulled off the job "temporarily."[239](8/21/2002)

Hernando County School District

Missing items valued at over $111,000 including computers, video cameras, musical instruments, film projectors, generators, mechanical work benches and a golf cart were "struck from the books." The two schools where the mischief or misplacement occurred were at Hernando High School ($33,000) and Springstead High School ($24,000). The only explanation given was that both schools had extensive renovations in recent years. When renovation and relocation occurs, so do the districts assets.[240] (6/24/2002) Admittedly, a novel answer, but since they know that this happens, why wasn't a system put in place to track the assets?

If every school had an up-to-date inventory control system, very few do, the loses that would show up checking the inventory each year against each item would be shocking. The lack of a current inventory of assets is a guaranteed WaMi in every single school district.

Hillsborough County School District

An audit by Ernst and Young found that the district was loose in hiring outside contractors, spent too much for construction services, and failed to document and oversee an array of goods and services. This district spends over $1 million per day on school construction.[241](6/6/2002)

Miami-Dade County School District

Land Ripoff

A state audit revealed that the district overpaid for land in 11 out of 14 cases amounting to $7 million. Interestingly, two of the land office administrators are on a two-year leave working as private consultants. Among their clients are two municipalities and a private company that are developing charter schools in Miami-Dade.[242] (4/7/2001)

Millionaire's Greed

A millionaire board member pocketed more than $1 million in rent payments from public funds, money meant to benefit a program for at-risk children. Although he headed a non-profit agency that won school funding for the program, he did seek a legal opinion, abstained from voting, and stripped his title of "President" from the agency. He said he received no benefit from the agency or school contract. Yet, his wealth doubled while he served on the school board.

However, an investigation showed that he received more than $1 million over two years, 100 percent of it from public contracts. Interestingly, he was elected in 1996 claiming: "This era of improvement begins today."

The recommendation to support the agency came from the superintendent whose administration was faulted for poor management of school money, costly land deals and chronic overcrowding. Although he was fired last year, his buyout package was reportedly worth $800,000.[243] (9/21/2001)

The greedy gluttons never tire of devouring the school treasure chest.

Millions Wasted

A phone book size report that analyzed the district's business practices claims "the district could save millions of dollars by correcting many poor business practices."

Millions are wasted because "no one takes into account the cost of something. They're not running the system as a business, just allocating dollars without weighing things out. There's no frugality." Of course, this could probably be said about most school districts.

"Controlling costs simply has not been a management priority…performance expectations relating to cost are rarely articulated and systematically tracked."[244] (12/16/2001)

This is one way to insure that WaMi and FraSte will run rampant in any school district.

Wasted Testing

About 60 percent of the 16,000 students sent to undergo a battery of evaluating tests at a cost of $4.8 million to see if they should be eligible for special education did not need it.[245] (12/16/2001)

Transportation Pothole

The $90 million dollar transportation office responsible for moving 70,000 students twice a day was criticized for a "fundamental deficiency" of almost complete absence of a system of accountability based on measurable goals and objectives." The report estimates that simply improving routing procedures could save $20 million.[246] (12/16/2001)

Questionable Contracts

The fourth largest school district in America, with a budget of $2.4 billion, doled out millions of taxpayer dollars for questionable contracts that sometimes had little to do with helping the 365,000 students in the district. Instead, the money benefited lobbyists, contractors, property owners and former school officials.[247] (4/7/2002)

Failure Pays

In 1995, the district contracted with Edison Schools to manage E.S. Reeves Elementary School. An evaluation by the district's Office of Evaluation and Research found that Edison "failed to comparatively improve the students' academic achievement." The district still renewed the contract for another five years.[248] (4/7/2002)

Apparently, the district wanted the failure to continue.

Lobbyist Influence

A lobbyist has major influence on how money is spent, and the clients he represents have won nearly $300 million in business from the school district. On just one health benefits contract, he earned $4 million. His most important allies in winning contracts are the school board and a powerful union chief. This same lobbyist has held fundraisers for six of the nine sitting board members.[249] (4/9/2002)

Taj Mahal High

More than $75 million was paid to build the "Taj Mahal" of public schools, Northwestern High School. It was only $47 million more than original estimates and four years over the estimated completion date. School inspectors have now discovered "life safety" repair problems that could cost $1 million to fix. No one should be surprised at the results because the board hired an architectural firm that had no previous experience in performing this type of project, hired a foundation contractor with slim experience that eventually could not finish the job and has since dissolved, and it accepted a bid that was $19 million more than estimated.[250] (4/11/2002)

Maintenance Waste

A district audit found that the maintenance department was plagued by wasteful practices, a huge work-order backlog, soaring overtime pay, and a lack of basic management controls over productivity. As an example, the district pays $8 per square foot to maintain its facilities. It's the highest in the state and about $3 higher than private industry.

What was also uncovered was that as rising expenditures put pressure on the operating budget, more than 100 staff support jobs were reclassified and moved to the maintenance department. This change allowed salaries to be paid from capital funds that are meant to build, renovate and maintain schools.

A proposal to privatize maintenance work at 27 schools could save millions, but the unions are opposed since it would mean the loss of over 200 workers.[251] (5/14/2002) Translation: There are 200 more workers than are needed.

Tower of Money

Two offers to build an $11 million broadcast tower for virtually no cost was turned down by the school district, not the board who claims to have had no knowledge about the free offer. Instead, it gave the contract to a private company to build the tower even though the bid was $3 million more than the district had planned to spend. The company had never built such a tower before. The lobbyist representing the company was the same one indicated in the prior example.[252] (6/16/2002)

Audit Pounding

The Florida auditor general "pounded" the district in a report on its construction department saying it paid contractors for uncompleted work, wasted millions of taxpayer dollars, and put unqualified people in top jobs.

The district's internal auditors were more much more lenient in that they said: "Delays are an area of concern and the system may not at times receive the quality of work from construction, design and building communities." They are also rather lax in collecting fines. A contract entitled the district to recoup $341,000, from design firms that made mistakes, but the district staff only collected $16,000.[253] (6/28/2002)

In June, auditors assembled 650 pages of documents to support an April 2004 forensic audit revealing more than $100 million was wasted in the school facilities program.[254] (9/1/2004)

It should be pointed out that the critical term is "forensic." All audits should be forensic audits because this is how to uncover WaMi and FraSte at work. Normal audits are really cursory in nature and usual do not discover such problems.

Cypress Bay High Costs

School auditors questioned costs in connection with the new $38 million school. Among some of the questioned items was $23,000 for a lobbyist that helped to secure the contract, $19,500 to a search firm to find a manager to run the construction site, and even an espresso coffee machine with $1,600 worth of Colombian coffee. In all, the contractor billed the school district about $1.6 million for so-called reimbursable expenses.[255] (5/9/2002)

Hope?

The school board unanimously approved an inspector general position. The district is the first in the state to take advantage of legislation permitting the IG of the State Department of Education to have a local office to investigate corruption.[256] (9/22/2002)

Wasted Millions

The district wasted millions of the $980 million bond fund approved 15 years ago for school building construction. Added to previous funding, $1.6 billion was available to build 44 new schools. Of those, 39 went over budget to the tune of $117 million. In fact, $250 million was used just to manage the building program.

The school board repeatedly failed to control costs, and made decisions that went against staff recommendations. After 15 years, the district can certainly be recognized for building the most expensive schools in Florida along and having legal and administrative costs of $34 million—four times the state average.

Half the money spent to build Paul Bell Middle and Miami Edison Middle went to architects, lawyers, consultants and others—not to the builders. [257](2/9/2003)

Miami Beach High School opened with anticipation four years ago. However, what no one expected was rain pouring in the building, and lockers that could not be used. This is just one of 19 new buildings that have deficiencies and problems. [258](2/11/2003)

After a devastating series of articles by the Miami Herald (at least someone was doing its job), it concluded:

> "The train wreck, otherwise known as Miami-Dade County school district, can't be salvaged by state oversight; a battalion of prosecutors are needed. The waste on school projects is so routine and institutionalized that random incompetence must be ruled out. It's impossible to believe that any group of bureaucrats could be so collectively and consistently derelict over the course of 15 years."[259] (2/23/2003)

Sadly and tragically, this same conclusion can be made of many other school district construction projects. Such WaMi dereliction certainly does put students and employees in harms way, but that doesn't seem to matter as long as the greedy gluttons can feast themselves on the largesse of taxpayer's money. Again, it's all legal. The bottom line is that there is no crime for being incompetent or exercising poor judgment.

St. Petersburg

Excellence Academy, one of the states 545 registered providers for educating handicapped children, is an estate in foreclosure with broken windows, overgrown vegetation, no electricity or water, no license to operate a school, and citations for housing code violations. The woman who answers the door denies she is running a school, but the state has paid her double or triple the amount than for other voucher schools.

There is a McKay Scholarship law that was passed to "provide a genuine private alternative for disabled students." However, its language is so loose that an operator only needs to fill out a two-page form and check a box to "affirm" the school has a surety bond or letter of credit. The teachers don't have to be certified, and they don't even need a high school diploma.[260] (11/13/2002)

Charter School Turmoil

St. Leo's, in Ocala, and Deerwood Academy in Port Richey, both charter schools, were two schools in chaos with missing money and haphazard administration. What the two schools had in common was that the same director moved from St. Leo's eight years ago to Deerwood.

Even after his abysmal management was exposed, some co-workers at both schools staunchly defended the director. They said he was targeted for the misdeed of others. No one at either campus claims that he pocketed school money, but the degree of his mismanagement has baffled superiors and associates alike.

He did come highly recommended for both jobs, but even he admits to doing "some boneheaded things."[261] (10/27/2002)

Palm Beach

An audit revealed that 45 staff members were overpaid by $34,000 during the 2000-01 school year. The overpayment occurred because the staff members doctored time sheets to make it appear they had been working when they weren't. The money used was earmarked for after-school and child care programs. [262](12/7/2002)

Apparently, the 45 staffers needed more care than the children; but that's what corruption is all about, take care of yourself first, last, and always.

Georgia

State

Six state department of education employees were fired because the agency's payroll was $900,000 over budget in July. If the payroll bleeding was not stopped, the payroll budget would have had a deficit of $12 million. Five of the six employees had been in jobs eliminated by the General Assembly, and all five had been contributors to the State School Superintendent's campaign to run for governor. When the funding for their positions was eliminated in June, the State Superintendent put them in new positions, paying them $51 per hour. She questions the board's findings and the timing of its actions, yet her own budget director did not dispute the board's findings.[263] (8/17/2002)

The State Board of Education voided more than $500,000 in contracts it said the State Superintendent authorized without its approval and without competitive bidding, and they voted to recoup the money that was already been paid. State law requires competitive bidding on technology purchases over $2,500. The finance director stated that the process used to award the contracts was unusual because checks typically are not cut until after services are provided, and payments are usually made every month or quarter, not in one lump sum.

The board said the departments designated to receive the services from the contracts did not require or need them. One of the contracts involved the use of a software program that did not fit the schools' need. In one example, only 60 of 110 high school students might find a use for one of the programs, but the department paid for software licenses for 320 students.[264] (11/15/2002)

State auditors are looking into the legality of the deals, and the state attorney general's office also has started an investigation. It's nice to see that once in a great while appropriate action is taken against WaMi perpetrators.

Hawaii

The Department of Education Contracts Specialist attempted to award all autism service contracts to an agency where his mother was the lead psychologist. He is now involved in another controversy in which a "bogus contract extension" for autism services specifically limits the free speech of medical professionals...and the Department of Education has admitted to the blacklisting of providers who advocate for children's needs.[265] (9/5/2002). It certainly is a nice, cozy relationship.

A charitable trust responsible for operating the Kamehameha Schools has reached a settlement with the attorney general's office that five ousted trustees should reimburse the estate for millions of dollars they allegedly mismanaged. The estate's insurance company will pay $20 million.[266] (10/4/2000)

Idaho

State School Superintendent

While supervisors in the office of the state school superintendent had to approve travel requests, actual expenses were never reviewed; after all, the amount was only $336,000. Employees paid more than necessary for airline tickets ($22,000), charged personal side trips in rental cars, and rented expensive full-size cars instead of more economical mid-size cars.[267] (9/7/2000)

Illinois

State Department of Education

An investigation by the auditor general's office concluded that there was a "breakdown in the fundamental principle of administration" of the agency's multi-million dollar operational budget. It cited 45 examples of mismanagement including inadequate monitoring of federal grants, personnel, and contracts.

Added to the list was "deficiencies in control" for travel and other expenses by the State Superintendent.

The audit was described by a legislator as: "It's the worst audit I have ever seen in my 20 years around here...it was very poor management...I've never seen an audit that bad, ever." Nevertheless, the Governor and state board supported the State Superintendent responsible for this "worst audit." [268] (3/26/1997)

Obviously, the standard for accountability is set low enough so that mismanagement practices can be considered routine and normal.

Chicago

Inspector General

A former FBI agent, experienced in probing public corruption, was appointed to the newly created post of Inspector General created by the legislature. The IG is responsible to investigate allegations of fraud by employees and businesses under contract with the school board. However, the Chicago Board of Education has criticized the position claiming it costs too much. That's probably the first time the board claimed something cost too much.

The IG opened ninety-two cases in the first six months. [269](4/27/1994)

Overtime Fraud

An investigation of school engineers and maintenance assistants by the Office of Inspector General (IG) found that the district spent almost $1.5 million in overtime pay and that a "staggering" number were suggestive of abuse, waste, and possibly criminal fraud.

The report went on to say: "The district suffers from a persistent lack of accountability that saps the strength and efficiency of the entire system." [270] (1/11/1995)

Employee Misconduct

Chicago school officials announced plans to fire or discipline 44 district employees as part of their effort to rid the system of corruption. Among those fired or disciplined were 14 teachers and four principals with some facing criminal charges as a result of the investigations. Some of the incidents included a security monitor who was convicted for stealing three television sets from a school which he used to trade for crack cocaine, a custodial worker who was captured on video taking money from a teacher's desk, and a principal at a city high school that had numerous financial irregularities. Additionally, there are 100 other investigations of employees under way.[271] (1/31/1996)

Professional Development Fiasco

A $250,000 audit of $200 million used for teacher training and funded by outside donors found: "More than $123 million was used without any overarching strategy for improving instruction. Individual schools spent $71 million with unclear and highly variable results, and little proof of improvement was demanded." In fact, the president of the teachers union said most teachers would agree with the audit's major findings.

The president recalled an institute day when teachers were herded into the school auditorium to attend a team-building seminar organized by the principal. The leader of the team, the principal, never attended.[272] (11/15/2002)

Overtime Jackpot

Three of the highest paid teachers in the system accrued overtime pay ranging from $63,000 to $88,000 in addition to their salaries that hovered around $80,000. Although the Inspector General is reviewing each case, there doesn't appear to be any wrongdoing.[273] (11/28/2002)

What is not understood about WaMi is that it is not a question of wrongdoing alone, but rather what is ethical, reasonable, cost effective, and mismanagement free. Otherwise, WaMi is accepted as the cost of doing business in education and that's wrong.

Renaissance?

In an attempt to remake city schools, Renaissance 2010 was created with strong support from the business sector. It called for shutting down the worst schools and reopening 100 small schools free from district controls. However, the power struggle among unions, parents, and reformists is strangling the initiative.[274] (4/10/2005)

Belleville

The first lawsuit in Illinois history to stop a school building project was filed to prevent further construction of a $64 million high school. The suit claims that the land was priced substantially above market value, the county had no plans or a budget to provide access roads, water, sewer, electrical, and phone service until years after the school was scheduled to open, and construction contracts were let without bid, bond, or cost caps.[275] (3/2000)

Naturally, there are no consequences for those who planned this fiasco of a construction project.

Hazel Crest

The district needs a $4 million bailout just to keep meeting its payroll after November 22nd. Even if it gets the cash infusion, it may be dissolved at the end of the year. The former superintendent warned in 1997 that the district was headed for financial disaster. Independent audits revealed that the district was overspending its budget as far back as 1986.

How is it possible that no action was taken during all the years of overspending? Was everyone asleep?

A Tribune review of nearly 20 years of records, along with interviews with former and current officials, shows that the district helped dig itself into a hole with free spending, lax financial controls, and inept financial management.

The district has had nine superintendents in nine years, and four business officers in the last five years.[276] (11/11/2002)

Turmoil in a district always multiplies the corruption.

Iowa

Iowa has an Office of the State Auditor that has among its responsibilities to conduct audits of school districts and agencies.

Department of Education (2001)

The School Improvement Technology Program, a $150 million program, was audited and some findings included:

- A district purchased $329,000 of computer equipment to give to teachers who completed 72 hours of software training. These computers were not included on the district's fixed asset listing and are considered to be the personal property of teachers.

- At three school districts, a total of $19,000 was spent for phones and cellular phone charges. Of the total, $15,000 was the first installment of a five-year lease purchase agreement for a $67,000 phone system for one school district.
- A district spent $12,000 for two fireproof safes.
- A district purchased twelve binoculars with graduated microscopes and eighteen student microscopes for over $9,000.
- A district purchased a digital piano for $3,000.

"The reports filed with the Department of Education do not provide consistent, useful information to assess overall improvement in technology made by the schools." [277](2001)

Des Moines

Federal grant money amounting to $340,000 was misspent for no-bid construction work, done by an employee's son, on office furniture and other items that included purchases of champagne, cakes, taco bars, photo albums and a hair dryer. The grant money was intended for remedial math and reading programs. How these items could be justified for use in these programs is hard to imagine. Yet, the supervisor of the district's title office claims that the program is audited annually, and questions have never been raised on how grant money was spent.

Clearly, audits do not uncover fraud, unauthorized expenditures, or even if grant money is properly monitored

Why was this investigation started? The district office received complaints that the construction work involved failed to follow state bid requirements, and that the title office had hired relatives of employees to do the job, a violation of the districts' nepotism policy.

Remodeling office space to the tune of $48,354 was a violation of federal grant policy that prohibits expenditures on building construction-related items. State law requires sealed bids for contracts exceeding $25,000, but there was no bid process, and $100,000 was spent to refinish and repair furniture. Another issue with these expenditures was that the contracts were given to the son of the title office's administrative assistant. To make matters worse, $58,000 was spent on new office furniture and equipment without seeking bids and $8,000 worth of equipment could not even be located. Three relatives of employees in the title office were hired part time for other work, a violation of district hiring policy.

If this wasn't enough, $91,000 was paid to former employees to work part-time that was at a higher rate than they had been paid during their employment with the district. Yet, the supervisor of the office stated: "I haven't done anything wrong."

This helps to explain why such WaMi takes place because it is not considered "wrong" to waste and mismanage taxpayer dollars. Obviously, it must be viewed as an entitlement to gorge on the treasure chest.

The fact that the nepotism policy was violated was not new. It was the second time in six months that the district had investigated allegations that the policy had been violated. In other words, policies mean nothing unless they are monitored carefully and often, and unless swift and decisive action is taken the first time a violation occurs. [278](2/14/2002)

$ Errors

An outside auditor found accounting errors amounting to $9.1 million. The schools' auditor, business office, and financial consultants were not able to uncover the errors that took place over a long period. [279](12/20/2002)

Again, there were no consequences for those individuals who failed in being accountable and responsible.

Rockford

The district is only one of two to lose federal money earmarked for improving reading. This is a very unusual action on the part of the feds, but it was caused by the superintendent who turned away monitors who were there to see whether the money was being spent correctly.[280] (4/5/2005)

This district has serious shortcomings in student performance, and it has financial problems. To turn away $681,000 because the monitors did not give advance notice is shear madness. If the money was being spent properly, why fear the monitors' review?

Kansas

Because of a budget shortfall of $750 million, lawmakers are taking a second look at consolidation. Of the 303 school districts, two-thirds are losing students, and fifty districts have less than 50 students. Trying to maintain so many small districts is WaMi at work.[281] (2/5/2003)

Kentucky

Since the Kentucky Education Reform Act of 1990, the Commissioner of Education has filed charges against 22 school board members and eight superintendents.[282] (9/3/1997)

Kudos for the Commissioner!

Louisiana

New Orleans

Board Stupidity?

The school board, in this poor and minority district, bought out the superintendent's contract because of "unyielding academic shortcomings, alleged test tampering, and missing candy money and equipment." However, a lawsuit instituted by the district attorney is charging that the school board violated the open meeting law when it approved the $210,000 settlement. The board had a real classic response: "His problems are no different from those of other urban districts"[283] (2/25/1998)

In other words, such behavior is considered normal for urban districts. Can the bar be set any lower? Probably!

No Controls

An insurance investigation is underway involving $70 million in annual expenditures because "controls are so loose as to leave ample room for less than honest acts." One gross example was that state auditors instructed the district not to pay a construction contractor because he was unlicensed and under investigation, yet a check for $300,000 was issued.[284] (6/18/2002)

Maryland

Baltimore

The district is faced with a $31 million deficit complicated by a budget failure to account for expenses of a $10 million human resources computer system that could have caught other financial irregularities.[285] (1/8/2003)

The excuse of "computer errors" is a common retort for financial WaMi. There is an adage that says: Junk in, junk out. Doesn't anyone use live human resources to double check what gets dumped in and what gets spit out?

Prince George's County School District

Unsubstantiated Expenses

An audit found unsubstantiated expenses by school board members amounting to over $9,800. This county is one of the very few that provided an expense account for school board members. A hearing was conducted after the audit before the Maryland House Appropriations Committee. Although the board chairman indicated that members would give up their credit cards, three members refused to do so.[286] (10/4/2000)

Is there no recourse by the rest of the board members or by the voters? Why couldn't the credit card company have been notified to stop any charges on the cards? Perhaps that was too easy.

Over-budget

The county overspent its budget by at least $7.5 million, but the total could reach $10.5 million. This fiasco was due to the principals who hired about 200 per diem teachers without proper authorization.[287] (10/11/2002)

School officials acknowledged that they were aware of the financial troubles as far back as a year ago. It received regular financial reports, but the reports didn't shed much light on the financial state of the system because the technology was outdated.[288] (10/17/2002)

Although the excuse was that the technology was outdated, didn't the principals who hired without authorization cause the problem? Their decisions had nothing to do with outdated technology, but rather with a WaMi system that was out of control.

Anne Arundel County

A task force has been established to study the "staggering" increase in school construction costs. The latest example is the price to rebuild Marley Elementary School for $20 million. That's nearly as much as the cost of the senate office building ($22 million), which has three levels of underground parking and even a Tiffany skylight. It's also twice what the county was paying for a new school just a few years ago.[289] (5/9/2002)

Owings Mill

The president of the PTA was asked to resign because she could not account for $4,000. There was no evidence to "say anything was done illegally—very sloppily, but not illegally"[290] (2/5/2003). So where did the money go? On a slippery, sloppy, slope!

Massachusetts

State

No Audits

An attempt by the governor to have an independent office audit state-aid-to-school expenditures amounting to $4 billion failed. Ironically, the legislature also failed to provide funds for the Educational Management Accountability Board, the current audit agency.[291] (11/2000)

This incomprehensible action sends a clear message to every district that the legislature has no interest in having school districts audited to see how funds provided by the state are spent. Only one conclusion can be made: They must be afraid of what effective and independent auditing would find in their districts. Shame on them!

Consultant Largesse

A state audit concluded that the Department of Education paid eight consulting companies $14.3 million to pay the salaries of 126 consultants "who operated without the necessary department oversight…all in all, the department may have wasted at least $9 million." [292](10/30/2002)

Dollars Wasted

A study by Beacon Hill Institute, "Getting Less for More" studied the impact of the state's Education Reform Law, which has poured $7 billion of additional dollars into the schools. It concluded that raising teacher pay, hiring new teachers, and reducing class size either failed to improve or worsened test scores.[293] (7/26/2002)

The president of the state teacher union said: "The findings contradict what is taking place." However, the fact is that the report used the state's own statistics. So who is "fibbing"?

Construction Probe

The state plans to investigate billions worth of school building construction for budgets far beyond originally approved, and extravagant spending on routine items. The audits will include 600 school projects since 1989 and the responsibility has shifted from the Education Department to the Treasurers' Office. The state has had a long history of school construction problems. For example, a middle school project in Arlington doubled in cost since state approval. Part of the problem has been blamed on lack of audit staff and funding. [294](3/31/2005)

Let's get this one straight! The legislature did not approve an independent audit office or funding, billions are spent without audits, and when it has determined that massive waste of taxpayer dollars have occurred, the audits begin. Wouldn't it have been more prudent to approve an independent audit agency particularly since there was a history of construction problems? This probably makes too much sense; but then again, there doesn't seem to be much of it around in Education America.

Lawrence

The superintendent of this chronically under-performing school district was fired on August 7th amid allegations of mismanagement, wasteful spending and patronage."[295] (9/3/97)

Nashoba Regional School District

Accounting mirages hid a $1.4 million shortfall from last year in this district of 3,000 students. "Mysterious transfers had been recorded. Money that students raised from bake sales and car washes went to district operations, and financial statements given regularly to the School Committee didn't match anything in the actual accounting ledgers." Thus far, 20 teachers have lost their jobs.

What is interesting is that the present superintendent replaced a superintendent who himself grappled with a $1.4 million deficit.[296] (9/9/2002)

Didn't anyone question how the administration could spend student money to fund district operations and whether it was legal? When there are no consequences, WaMi is encouraged.

Higher Ed "big whammy"

Although this book concentrates on public school dollars, it is important to understand that higher education is also a paradise for WaMi. A study by a group of business consultants appointed by the governor "portrays public higher education as a wasteful bureaucracy consuming $1 billion a year with little to show for it."[297] (3/25/20003)

This is not only true of higher education in Massachusetts, but the same can be said of most such institutions of higher learner supported by tax dollars.

Michigan

Statewide

A private company, Standard and Poor, hired by the state to analyze school data, found that central administration costs have risen more than twice as fast as instructional expenses, including teacher salaries over the past three years.[298] (Spring 2002)

Detroit

School Supplies Stolen

School supplies were delivered to "a convenience store, a gas station, and just about anyone with cash in hand," and it's no small deal. Over $250,000 in school property was stolen since 1990. Most of the thefts are alleged to be "inside jobs."

What is interesting about this case is that the school systems chief security investigator finally went to the media to expose the thefts because "he could not get anybody's attention." He described the culture very vividly: "If we lose, we just buy more." This is the reality of how taxpayer dollars are viewed.

It's estimated that over $4 million could be saved by overhauling the way it buys, stores, moves, and tracks its property and supplies.[299] (3/30/1994)

Bonding Mismanaged[300] (3/2000)

An audit in December 1999 revealed that the business practices used in the district are far below standards; however, it did not audit a $1.5 billion dollar bond issue for school improvements. It took an investigation by The Detroit News to conclude: "Incompetence, mismanagement, and cronyism by school officials, employees, and contractors, and a system with inadequate safeguards, have devastated the project."

Although a bond issue was passed in 1994 to repair 263 public schools and build more than a dozen more, "little work has been done to date, and only $134 million has been spent." One reason why the repairs didn't get done should be in Ripley's Believe It Or Not: "There was no master plan to spend the money."

Since there was no master plan, how was it determined what was needed in dollars for bonding? This sounds more like a tale for an old-fashioned radio show called, "I Love A Mystery."

One million dollars was wasted designing or building additions that weren't needed, $343,000 went for a computer system that was never used, and $518,051 was paid for land that was appraised at $85,000.

High Schools Misspend

An audit revealed that 29 high schools misspent almost $1 million, money from athletic events was not accounted for, and money was improperly spent on flowers, fraternity dues, and employee lunches. [301](1/31/2001)

Start Over

In a series of articles by The Detroit News, it recommended that the budget crunch was an opportunity to "tear up school budgets and start over with the mission of squeezing every available dollar for classroom instruction."[302] (3/3/2002) It will never happen!

Plenty of PR

While 700 staff members were laid off and schools cutting expenses by 10%, the board was paying out $1.5 million to public relations firms to promote the schools.[303] (7/23/2002)

Dusty Supplies

For years, the district has allowed thousands of school supplies to go unused and gather dust in a huge warehouse. The inventory covers 385 pages, identifies 426,103 items, and the estimated value is $3.8 million. The supplies have piled up over the years because administrators ordered too much or changed their minds and never returned unneeded supplies. [304] (8/6/2002)

Plagiarized Purchases

Five schools paid a vendor $36,300 for computer equipment and office furniture that wasn't delivered and overpaid for the equipment they did receive. One school paid $3,200 for 32 computer chairs when quotes from other companies ranged from $735 to $1,212.

Payments also fell short of $10,000 meaning the service did not have to be approved by a supervisor or secured through competitive bids. For example, a $19,521 payment was split into two payments. This is a common procedure to avoid competitive bidding.

To clean up years of financial mismanagement, audits were ordered of all schools and principals were required to attend a workshop on proper bookkeeping procedures. In the past two years, auditors uncovered nearly $2 million in missing or misspent money.[305] (11/15/2002)

Administrative Glut

The increase in administrative expenses is most evident in this district. Last year, eight employees were promoted to executive level positions and received pay increases between 11 and 48 percent. This was occurring while staff was being cut.[306] (Spring 2002)

Roaches—No Charge

At Rosa Park Middle School the physical plant is shameful. Heating is extremely uneven, classes dimly lit because there were no replacement bulbs, and the carpeting had no padding. When the carpeting was pulled back it revealed "one of the worst roach infestations anywhere." Staff claimed their requests for relief were met with indifference.[307] (12/6/2002)

Perhaps the roaches were tolerated so that they could be used as part of the student count.

No, No $

Here's another one for the Ripley Museum. A retired entrepreneur wanted to put up $300 million into urban education; but the lawmakers and education establishment didn't want it. Why? He wanted it tied to performance: Open a charter high school, graduate 90%, send them to college or other training, and he would give the city a new building for one dollar.

Another entrepreneur offered $200 million to build a university, but officials would not change zoning (so he built the university on 750 acres in Naples, Florida). [308] (2/24/2003)

With a district in such financial and academic distress, how could it refuse such a gift? Obviously, they felt they couldn't deliver the performance required; besides, it wasn't worth the effort.

Title I Shambles

Officials are investigating allegations of cronyism and misspending in the Title I office. This is a $140 million federal program earmarked for low-income children. Allegations include exorbitant fees to consultants, temporary workers to provide redundant services, and that the head of the office hired his mother and other relatives for jobs for which there were not qualified.[309] (4/9/2005)

Minnesota

Minneapolis Public Schools

A newly appointed finance director, an outsider and non-educator, found himself $30 million in the red. By using his business skills, he negotiated wage freezes, instituted a spending freeze, required every discretionary spending request to come to his desk, restructured the central office, cut transportation by increasing the walking distance, and reassigned students to neighborhood schools. He closed the budget gap. What surprised him was that he expected to find a bloated bureaucracy, but he discovered that central office was, in fact, too thin particularly in the finance department.[310] (6/17/2002)

Missouri

Missouri has an Office of the State Auditor that reviews school districts' financial procedures and operations. The listing below is an example of some audit findings of waste and mismanagement.

Lonedell R-14 School District (1999)

In 1999, the district purchased 25 acres of land for $98,900 ($3,833 per acre). Although there were no formal plans on how the district was going to finance the construction and operation of a new school building, school officials indicated the land was for a future middle school. However, an appraisal of the land was not obtained prior to the purchase. According to the Assessor's Office, the land was appraised at $28,000 ($1,100 per acre). At the time of purchase, the district's financial situation was poor enough to be placed on the financially stressed list. The lesson learned is that when a system works, no matter how unethical or corrupt, use it.

Howell School District (1999)

During the two years ended June 30, 1999, the district received and spent over $6 million in basic state aid to which it was not entitled. This was caused by an error in the reporting of average daily attendance data. The district did not correct the attendance reporting errors when detected in October 1998, and it continued to be overpaid.

Columbia 93 School District (1999)

Various schools and offices maintain petty cash funds ranging from $100 to $2,500. During the last year these funds totaled $128,000. In several instances, it was found that petty cash reconciliation's had not been performed; as a result, there was no documentation supporting the petty cash balances.

St Charles R-VI School District (1999)

The district leased modular units for temporary classrooms. Had the district lease-purchased or purchased the units, it would have saved between $101,000 and $203,000 on a second lease.

Kansas City 33 School District (2000)

The district closed the textbook depository warehouse in December 1998 that had an inventory of $1.5 million. In May 1999, the district contracted with Follett Education Services to provide textbook procurement, warehousing, and inventory management, but it did not solicit proposals from other vendors. In addition, it did not monitor the terms of the contract and, as a result, the district was overcharged $32,000 in fulfillment fees and $141,000 in freight costs.

Reorganized School District No. 1 (2000)

The central office receives cash and checks from various sources on a daily basis. The largest source is from the cafeteria. For the two years ended June 30, 2000, over-the-counter receipts were approximately $440,000. The receipts are not deposited intact and receipt slips are not reconciled to the bank deposits. In addition, the cafeteria does not compare actual meals served to receipts.

It's a recipe that is served in many school districts so that WaMi and FraSte could take place.

Fox C-6 School District (2000)

District policy requires purchase orders be submitted for all purchases which are not specifically exempted by the School Board. Thirteen out of seventeen purchases reviewed either did not have a purchase order, or the purchase order did not agree with the amount of the vendor's invoice. Overpayments to vendors were not discovered on a timely basis. A contractor submitted four invoices totaling $74,000. The district generated two checks totaling $129,000 for these invoices. The district did not detect the overpayment of $55,000; the vendor did and refunded the money to the district. It's nice to know that there are some honest vendors. Another contractor submitted two invoices totaling $47,000. Again, the district submitted two checks totaling $58,000, overpaying the contractor by $11,000.

St. Louis Schools[311] (2/12/2003)

The district had thousands of dollars not accounted for, poor control of finances, and risked losing federal dollars for having unqualified teachers.

A bookkeeper at Central Visual and Performing Arts High School made two cash withdrawals totaling $7,631; the money is unaccounted for and the bookkeeper resigned. However, the bookkeeper claims she was following the orders of the principal.

Nebraska

A consolidation effort, started a decade ago, has dissolved 330 districts leaving 517.[312] (2/5/2003) This is a vivid example that WaMi was clearly at work by operating far more districts than was justified. Financial constraints finally forced policymakers to face reality and practicality, otherwise, the WaMi would have continued.

Nevada

Clark County School District

Legislative auditors were ordered by a law passed last year to conduct a preliminary study of the school district and one other, Washoe County, to determine whether they properly maintain buildings, recruit new teachers, transport students and manage employee health plans. Auditors reported that in

Clark County, 18 percent of the 1,521 credit cards given to principals and administrators had been lost or stolen.

However, a full audit was not ordered because the district would have to pay for the audit, and it does not want a rehashing of the audits that were already done.[313] (9/11/2002)

What a system! The district must pay for an audit, so if it refuses, as it did, nothing happens. It's like asking a criminal to pay for his own trial; if he refuses, he goes free.

What minds dream up such idiotic laws?

New Hampshire

Claremont

This city and four others sued the state in 1991 arguing that the heavy reliance on property taxes discriminated against children in poorer towns. The state Supreme Court ordered the Legislature to adopt a fairer school finance system.

Claremont received $20 million in state assistance in the past three years, "but some city leaders say the money has produced neither significant improvement nor long-term relief for local taxpayers." One board member responded by saying, "there still isn't enough money to reach adequacy."[314] (5/20/2002)

There never is or will be. More money doesn't improve performance, or much of anything else, unless it is used effectively and efficiently and for the right purposes.

Raymond School District

A top school official in this district of 1,800 students said his decision to send 13 Raymond staff members, including himself and a member of the school board, to a four-day literacy conference in Hawaii was simply part of a continued effort to improve the district's teaching staff. The school official defended the $19,000 four-day trip, because it came from a federal grant, not the local budget.

Whether or not federal or local dollars are involved, all such funds come from the same taxpayers. It's this kind of warped thinking that perpetuates WaMi.

Previous trips included a high school conference in Nashville for $2,875, a technology conference in Monterey, CA for $11,294, a safety conference in Reno, NV for $11,187, a middle school conference in Providence, RI for

$3,374, and a curriculum development conference in San Antonio, TX for $2,690.[315](8/12/2002)

The school budget for 2002-2003 includes $90,000 for staff development, a very rich pot for such a small district, but a nice cozy pot for WaMi.

Happy vacations—courtesy of the poor taxpayers!

New Jersey

State

The state inspector general reported that the $8.6 billion school construction program was riddled with questionable spending and management practices that may have wasted tens of millions of dollars. A wide range of internal weaknesses makes the New Jersey Schools Construction Corp., vulnerable to mismanagement, fiscal malfeasance, conflicts of interest, and waste, fraud and abuse of taxpayer dollars. One particular egregious example was the spending of more than $67 million for land that was already publicly owned.[316] (4/22/2005)

Camden

A state review of this poorest school district in New Jersey that spends $10,307 per pupil found: (1) It spends between $315 and $393 per student more on administrative costs than comparable districts (2) It has too many employees and could save more than $8 million by cutting staffing (3) It has 336 more food-service workers than necessary and (4) 3,714 staff receive too much extra pay and overtime beyond contract salaries amounting to $7.2 million. Interestingly, 87% of the districts $197 million budget is provided by the state.[317](10/30/1996)

The district will get $35 million in state aid to keep operating, but the school board must approve a budget for 2002-2003 school year that will require tough choices including job cuts. About $36 million needs to be cut from the $298 million budget. This comes on top of earlier cuts that eliminated over 500 jobs.[318] (6/19/2002)

Because of the state pressure, the board approved a plan to slash $25 million involving 242 job cuts. The cuts include a variety of non-certified and certified positions but, interestingly, there will be no cuts in administrative positions. (6/22/2002)

New Mexico

Hondo Valley School District No. 39 (1997)

The former business manager's employment contract amount was altered to reflect a $2,524 salary increase without obtaining required approval from the Board.

The district established an "Administrative Account" within the student activity funds that is restricted to account for "those resources owned, operated and managed by the student body...for educational, recreational or cultural purposes." Interest earned on the account balances belong to those funds; instead, interest earned was allocated to the Administrative Account. This account was used to pay for Board Members lodging expense for a conference.[319] (1/9/1997)

Is there no shame for using student monies to attend a conference?

New York

Statewide

Career School Scandal

"Fraud and abuse are pervasive among state trade schools which do little to help students." The indictment of virtually every aspect of proprietary trade schools was prepared by the N.Y. Interface Development Council, Inc. The schools are too free from impunity in which they defraud the city's poor. Loan defaults by proprietary students total $27.6 million. All this despite a 1986 state law aimed at strengthening controls and oversight.[320] (3/15/1989)

Middle Schools Fail

A status report given to the Board of Regents said most of the middle schools are not making needed changes and, as a result, are still turning out too many students at risk of failing. Scores on the state's English and math tests in Erie and Niagara counties were worse than in 1999. The problem is not just in troubled city schools, like Buffalo since even normally high scoring districts like Orchard Park "stumbled."

Although state officials said that middle schools should not remedy their academic problems with drills or by spending too much time on preparing for tests, superintendents disagreed and said that they will support teaching to the test more than ever as the focus on test scores continues.[321] (6/18/2002)

New York State Board

Over $9 million is spent on programs provided by outside consultants to assist students in low performing school districts. Interestingly, the consultants were allowed to analyze their own performance. A state audit found that some of the programs were not effective; in fact, students at schools without the programs performed better. [322](11/2000)

New York City

Mismanagement

City investigators minced no words in their report. "The School system's inability and unwillingness to enforce its own rules has resulted in system wide mismanagement and corruption. It does not know how many of its teachers are in the classroom or are performing administrative duties, a $42 million extracurricular-pay program for teachers is routinely abused, the board's failure to monitor contracts with private companies has deprived the board of the very services for which it has contracted, and the school system has shown it is incapable of addressing any problems that relate to fraud and corruption."[323] (9/19/1984)

It's incredible to think that so many highly educated and highly paid bureaucrats can be so incompetent and so uncaring.

False Diplomas

A former official of a New York City trade school pleaded guilty to defrauding the U.S. Department of Education of $25 million by creating false high-school diplomas for students so that they could obtain federal grants and loans. [324](3/15/1989)

Corruption Probe

The mayor named a five-member commission to investigate the drug and corruption scandals over the past two months. Allegations have been made that school board members and employees have been engaged in illegal drug sales and abuse, trading jobs for political favors, and the theft of equipment and supplies. [325](1//11/1989)

What better evidence to demonstrate the betrayal of the children and the public trust!

Election Fraud

A 10-month investigation found widespread corruption of the 1993 Community School board election and resulted in five school officials being arrested on charges of ballot fraud. The 32 boards set policy and control budgets in excess of $100 million. In some areas, anyone could vote, often multiple times, but many parents were not allowed to vote. In some districts, teachers and staff were pressured into supporting a candidate. [326](5/1/96)

Asbestos Fraud

In 1993, the opening of schools was delayed to allow time to inspect schools for the presence of asbestos. The reason for the inspections was the discovery that many of the inspection reports had been falsified.[327] (10/25/1995)
Not even the safety of children and staff is of concern to the corruptors.

No Credibility

In 1998, the Chancellor "found" $63 million in the districts cash-strapped budget.[328] (11/1998) There was no mention of where the money was found.

Easy Diplomas

The Board revoked the diplomas of 62 former high school students from Eastern District Academy in Brooklyn because they were given credits for running errands for teachers and answering phones at a travel agency.[329]

Enrollments Padded

A state commission investigating attendance fraud found that dead children were listed among those reporting to class each day and some of them even received report cards. The parent of a dead child went to the school and told the appropriate personnel of her child's passing, but he was kept on the roster for another year.
Students are worth money whether alive or dead!
In 1998, the New York Post described how the "wholly unreliable" enrollment figures generate a half-billion dollars in "cooked school books." An examination of the attendance tracking system revealed that 40,000 class sheets that should have been fed into the system were not. One high school even recorded 100% perfect attendance for every Friday of the year.[330] (12/13/1999)

Construction Fiasco

A state commission investigating a $2 billion shortfall in the capital budget for school construction recommended that it be taken out of the hands of the Board of Education. It seems that the board failed to acknowledge that its own decisions on the size and location of new schools caused many of the higher costs, and had not complied with a state law requiring formal amendment of the capital plan. Of course, no one is disciplined for such gross mismanagement.[331] (7/27/2001)

Building Costs Excessive

NYC spends 414 percent more to build a high school than the rest of New York ($657 per square foot) with costs exceeding that of the most expensive new office buildings. In 1999, the costs to build high schools ballooned 90 percent over original estimates, and 70 percent higher to construct elementary schools.[332] (2/5/2002

Splendor in the Board Room

The seven members of the New York City school board received pay and perks amounting to over $580,000 each for part-time work. How is this possible? It's easy when you have a huge treasure chest to feast on. It begins with a stipend of $15,000 per year and a staff of 30 getting over $100,000 per year. Then add an office, cell phones, high tech pagers, and luxury cars with lights and sirens. Of course, chauffeurs are needed to drive the limos and this only adds another $327,000 to the yearly tab. There is no monitoring of limo usage because there is an honor system. Honor seems to come with a huge price tag.

A state Assembly plan to revamp the school system would strip city board members of more than $500,000 in expensive perks.[333] (5/2/2002)

A total of over $4 million dollars is spent for these seven part-time overseers of one of the most educationally deprived school districts in the country. In contrast, the trustees for the City University of New York are unpaid and neither do the Port Authority's commissioners.[334] (2/12/2002). Is it any wonder why the Mayor wants to abolish the Board of Education?

Retreat Questioned

School officials spent $40,000 to send 100 bureaucrats on a two-day retreat at a lavish Long Island estate so they can discuss recruiting new teachers. Officials claim that they do not have a meeting place big enough for 100 people.[335] (3/5/2002)

No space big enough in the Big Apple? How much more absurd can it get?

Grant Bonanza

The Chancellor proposed to spend $2.7 million for private consultants to write grant applications over three years because school staffers can't do it—they don't have the time and expertise needed to effectively plan and write proposals.[336] (4/23/2002).

One can only assume from such a statement that no grants have ever been written (since no staffer has the expertise). Rather an asinine assumption to say the least. How do the other thousands of school districts write grants with far less staff, but NYC schools with thousands of employees and a massive bureaucracy does not have staff with time or expertise is beyond comprehension? Sounds like a lot of hogwash!

Cushy Cafeteria Jobs

The Board of Education plans to hire more than 1,000 teachers for a summer program to monitor the cafeteria at $33.18 per hour or a total of three-quarters of a million dollars a week. Yet, teachers are needed for the summer program to help students who flunked during the year. What's interesting is that teachers are not allowed to monitor the cafeteria during the school year.[337] (5/9/2002)

The union representing school aides charged that $4 million is being wasted. School aides perform this duty during the regular year and are paid $12.33, but they were not offered the positions. Teachers would get paid over $6,000 for the summer, but aides would only cost $2,200. The aides are trained and experienced in monitoring school cafeterias whereas teachers refuse to perform such duties during the school year. Saving only $4 million when faced with a $5 billion deficit doesn't seem to be important.[338] (5/11/2002)

Where Are The Teachers?

The district employs about 80,000 teachers. While the student population increased by 8.8% over eight years, the number of teachers jumped by 23%, but there has been no appreciable change in class sizes. How can this be? About 1,000 teachers earn their salaries in district offices or board headquarters where there are no students."[339] (6/25/2002)

Classroom Costs

A state panel reported that the cost of constructing a classroom in the city was three times ($432 a square foot) the national average ($146 a square foot). Part of the reason is that contractors routinely add a 20 percent "aggravation tax" to their bids to offset the bureaucratic red tape. Other reasons cited include lax oversight, poor communication, and backbiting between the two agencies that are responsible for building schools, the Board of Education and the School Construction Authority.[340] (8/30/2002)

Students Pushed-Out

According to Advocates for Children, 160,000 students were "discharged" from schools from 1998-2001. Although there are legitimate reasons to discharge some students—moving, transferring, and not being in attendance for 20 consecutive days—some are forced out because they're behind in credits. It's important to understand that students who are discharged are not counted as dropouts (CheDe at work).

Some parents have even signed forms agreeing to the discharge because schools tell them to leave and that they have no choice.

The officials claim that this is not true. "The department has always been and always will do everything within its power with every available resource to give students a traditional high school diploma."

Obviously, something is happening because classes for the alternative general equivalency diploma report a huge increase in the number of 16 and 17 year old applying for their classes, and in one center the enrollment has doubled. [341](11/9/2002)

If students were discharged for poor performance, why is it that they then enroll in a GED program?

Bilingual Butchered

The Lexington foundation conducted a study of 58 bilingual programs and found that administrators consistently waste time and money on planning and extracurricular activities. A school that had a $175,000 grant did not use a dime of it on teaching. Creative reporting also seems to be practiced such as a school bragging about its rising test scores but only reporting results from 104 of the 136 participating students.

The shameful report was substantiated by another study made by the Puerto Rican Legal Defense and Education Fund.[342] (11/29/2002)

Expensive Move

It cost $529,000 to move a portable classroom about 4½ miles even though the original estimate was less than $200,000. However, rather than public bidding the project, it was sent to only six pre-qualified firms. The highest bid was over $1 million.[343] (1/27/2003)

Frustration

A former corporate executive hired to train principals from inside and outside the system came close to quitting two times because of the "system enervating bureaucracy." [344] (5/23/2003)

Nassau

The Huntington school district has more than $10,000 of unused social studies reading textbooks. Similar purchases were discovered in Lawrence.

"By not following proper purchasing and inventory procedures, districts invariably pay more than they should."[345] (9/9/1992)

Niagara Falls Fallout

In 1955, a new school was opened on land that had been sold to the board by Hooker Chemical Company for $1.00. Although Hooker wanted a provision in the transfer that the land would only be used as a park, the board refused. Instead, it built a school on the property and sold the rest of the land to a homebuilder for development.

It all sounds like a good deal, but there is a very shameful punch line. The homes built on the land later became known as "Love Canal," a devastating environmental disaster because of the hazardous and deadly wastes buried on the land.[346] (March 2000)

Port Washington

The district attorney indicted a construction company involved with a middle school project for filing fraudulent certified payroll documents. Although two board members questioned the paper work submitted, they were greeted with contempt by other board members who stated that they rely on the administration, the architect, and consultants to manage projects. This in spite of the fact that a few years earlier the district lost substantial sums of money in another construction project, and even though a previous educational consulting firm official pleaded guilty to extortion.[347] (12/24/1999)

Again, warnings and expressed concerns over possible corrupt activities seem to fall on deaf ears by those who are seemingly responsible for monitoring the taxpayer dollars. Such refusals to heed "red flags," can only be interpreted as suspicious to say the least.

Nassau County

An audit revealed that taxpayers have been paying for some phones that have not been used in a decade and others listed in buildings that no longer exist.[348] (3/20/2002)

Roosevelt School District

The district has historically experienced financial problems and it is one of the poorest performing districts in the state. It's been under oversight for years. In spite of the fact that more state resources were provided, problems persisted. The State finally ousted the school board clearing the way for a state takeover of the small school district located on Long Island; it would be the first such action under a recently adopted law providing for state intervention. The State contends that the district failed to correct deficiencies in its academic performance, building maintenance, finances, dropout rate and teacher turnover. [349](5/7/2002)

North Carolina

Brunswick County School System

At least nine Central Office positions were filled without the positions being posted, promotions and/or salary increases were granted to persons who had not been evaluated in the last two years, and supervisors and directors received "extra duty pay" for undocumented extra duties.[350] (1995)

Iredell-Statesville Schools

After a hearing, the board found that the superintendent culpable for a $1.8 million deficit in one school year and a $3 million shortfall in still another school year. The board then voted to dismiss the superintendent.[351] (3/13/2002)

Ohio

State Department of Education

A state audit criticized the department's oversight and monitoring of 92 charter schools that cost the state $131 million, and recommended that it should be stripped of its authority over charter schools. Among the findings that led to the recommendations were: (2/7/2002)[352]

- By His Word Charter School, with two schools in Columbus, owed more than $1.2 million in taxes, benefits and funding for students who were not enrolled.
- Riser Military Academy Charter School in Columbus owed the state more than $5,000 in misspent funds, and owed $11,000 to the teachers' retirement system and $3,600 in federal taxes.

Youngstown City School District

As a result of its precarious financial situation, YCS has become the first school district in the State of Ohio to be placed under fiscal emergency. It has an operating debt of over $28 million with no plan to pay it, and a current operating deficit of $12 million.

Average daily attendance is down from 14,400 in 1992 to 12,000 (a 17% drop), and a further decline to 10,000 is expected by 2006. Although enrollment has decreased significantly, building closings and reductions in the size of the workforce have not kept pace resulting in underutilized buildings and a high number of employees per student.

While revenues have remained flat, expenditures per student have increased significantly from $5,300 (1992) to $7,300 (1996) that is considerably higher than peer districts. Maintenance and operational costs are 24 percent higher than peer district average.

Student teacher ratios in the middle and high school are out-of-line with 161 classes having fewer than 15 students.

A report concludes that the current financial crisis is severe and is worsening and projections to 2005 indicate the crisis could reach $203 million. This report contains 138 recommendations that provide a framework within which decision-makers can initiate the required corrective actions necessary to revitalize the district.[353] (12/20/1996)

Cleveland

One of the grandest weeklong retreats that was held in 2001 came with a bill of $56,000 and it was paid through grant money. Of the amount, $24,000 was spent on speakers and $12,000 on books that employees were told to read.[354] (8/12/2002)

Columbus

The state's biggest charter school that uses home-based computer instruction must repay the state $1.6 million to settle a dispute involving enrollment data. Although the school said it enrolled 2,270 students in September, records show only seven students logged onto one of the school's computer systems. Nevertheless, the school received funding for all its students totaling $932,030. It also was unable to retrieve over 400 computers from students who left.

This problem "is not an admission that anything was wrong...there existed no standards.[355] (4/11/2002)

If this duplicity isn't wrong, what is the standard of ethical and financial behavior?

Maple Heights School District

The cost of "retreats" has come under question because, although the total amount of $15,000 seems modest, it easily surpasses what some suburban districts spend. The meals of choice for one retreat included $29 filet mignons, $27 New York strip steaks and $23 Chilean sea bass.[356] (8/12/2002) What, no flaming deserts?

Oklahoma

Statewide

The Office of the State Auditor and Inspector does audits of school districts.

Jenks School District

The district found that it owed the state $500,000 after counting its half-day pre-kindergarten children as full days.[357] (1/8/2003)

Oregon

Double Dipping

Former retired school employees return and continue to work in their same positions thereby collecting a retirement check and a school paycheck. Some of the retirees bring home more retirement under this system than in their previous positions.

Yep, it's legal because the retiree is paid less than a regular employee. Well, since it is legal why doesn't the retirement system disclose the dollar value of benefits that are included? They haven't as yet.

Employees with 31 or more years had a retirement check on average between 96-104 percent of their final year's salary. What a bonanza, and it's all at the taxpayer expense. (1/30/2003)

Pennsylvania

State

Audits

The Pennsylvania Attorney General's Office is very active auditing school districts not only for fraud but to insure that school districts receive their proper allocation of state funds.

Voluntary performance reviews conducted by the AG's office identified more than 250 recommendations to help 16 districts reallocate millions of dollars to the classroom for teaching and learning. The should be called the "WaMi Watchers."

No Tutor Takers

The state allotted $24 million for grants up to $500 to parents whose children in grades three through six scored less than "proficient" on certain tests. The "Classroom Plus Program" requires parents to use the money for tutoring designed to boost their child's reading and math knowledge. Of the 100,000 eligible children, only 11,450 received grants because the other parents did not make application.[358] (7/24/2002)

Rebuilding Program Fiasco

In 1998, the Supreme Court ordered a state-funded school-rebuilding program in 30 poor cities, but so far not a single new school has been built. Only about $44 million of more than $600 million in planned emergency repairs have even begun. According to school officials the delays are due largely to a state bureaucracy that has moved too slowly.[359] (5/13/2002)

It's interesting that the bureaucracy never moves too slowly to demand more funds.

No-bid Edison

The Department of Education showed a shocking disregard for sound business practices in giving a $2.7 million no bid contract to Edison Schools, Inc.[360] (11/20/2002)

Duquesne City School District

An investigation found that as the financial condition of the district was deteriorating in the late 1990's; district officials and school board members were spending tens of thousands of tax dollars on restaurant meals, out-of-state travel, electronic equipment, and <u>convention related necessities like room service, pay-per-view movies, and cocktails</u>.[361] (2/14/2001)

Mismanagement Potpourri[362] (2/14/2001)

- From 1996-1999, the district's former superintendent and former business manager charged nearly $55,000 on district credit cards and receipts could not be provided for $48,000.
- In 1999, six school board members, the former business manager and assistant superintendent attended a conference in San Francisco that cost taxpayers $25,000.
- The district made purchases totaling over $658,000 from a technology services company with no written contract and no record of board approval.
- Problems were identified with the student activity funds resulting in a loss of revenue for the various club accounts. However, AG recommendations to strengthen the student activity funds were not approved by the board. Why should they, its all-free money.

What good does it do to have oversight of one-kind or another and audits whose recommendations fall on deaf ears?

Construction Overrun

An investigation of a building construction program found that estimated project costs of just over $16 million actually cost over $23 million, and there was a failure to obtain prior approval for change orders.[363] (8/2001)

Trailers Unnecessary

During construction, 12 trailers were purchased at a cost of $384,848 and an additional $47,000 was required for installation. "There is no evidence that the trailers were needed at that time or at any time since. There was no competitive bidding and only inadequate records exist to justify the purchase."[364] (2001)

Isn't this great? WaMi is found big time, but so what? There are no consequences of any kind.

Luzerne County Intermediate Unit

The former executive director misused nearly $55,000 in federal special education grant funds and inappropriately reimbursed a nonpublic school $129,000. The special education funds were used to establish a computer lab for graduate courses offered by Wilkes University. There was no record or evidence that the lab was used for special education courses or projects.

The director and two staff also obtained personal financial benefits from the misuse of computer equipment by receiving $56,542 from the University for teaching the courses.[365] (11/2/2001)

Apparently, such WaMi is legal. Of course, ethics is not a consideration; it never is when it comes to WaMi.

Philadelphia

The district plans to hire an inspector general to investigate suspected wrongdoing and file suit against companies and individuals who fail to fulfill contracts.[366] (1/16/2003)

Attendance Scam

The district received over $20 million between 1993-1996 for 14,605 days of attendance for students who were listed on the rolls but never attended the city's schools.[367] (3/2000)

Consultant Payoffs?

This financial distraught district, while under the sole control of only one reform commissioner, paid out over $3 million for eight no bid contracts. In addition, the contracts went to politically connected consultants and law firms including two public relations firms that had a spending cap of $150,000 but were paid over $700,000.[368] (6/24/2002)

It's a good example of how reform efforts are, too often, a sham to placate the public.

Reynolds School District

An investigation by the Attorney General's Office concluded that the superintendent misused school property, violated state law, filed an inaccurate annual report, and misspent special education dollars.

Auditors found unallowable special education expenditures that included picture framing and $2,300 for drapes. "Children with special needs deserve to receive the full and direct benefit of access funding…this money should never have been used to redecorate a conference room."

The district responded by saying: "The questioned expenditures do provide a direct benefit to special education program students and families." This response means that a Raider Mascot wall hanging costing $875.00 provides a direct benefit to special education children and families. Did anyone bother to ask how the wall hanging is a direct benefit?

The superintendent was punished with the option of five days of suspension or forfeiting accrued paid vacation. [369](12/15/2000)

This is how WaMi is dealt with, a slap on the wrist.

Brookville Area School District

An investigation found that the teacher advisor did not manage funds of the ski club properly. Funds were co-mingled with the teacher's personal funds, non-eligible persons participated in ski club activities, the advisor signed the ski club treasurer's name to blank check request forms, and he received perks benefiting his family. Up to $12,000 was involved.

Although the teacher's conduct was a serious breach of school policy, the real issue is that the "district itself did not have adequate procedures and controls in place to monitor the handling of student activity funds" even though previous audits indicated "improper student activity fund practices."[370] (7/2001)

The repeated patterns of warnings without action in district after district, time and time again, is a stark reminder that there is no accountability, no ethics, and that too many school officials have no conscience. When this happens, as it often does, it means that "the children and public be damned."

Harrisburg City School District

Renovations for three schools amounting to $570,000 violated the State Public School Code requiring competitive bidding where work exceeds $10,000. The district had no records of competitive bidding or the bid quotes it received. Investigators found that much of the renovation work was divided into individual jobs costing less than $10,000 in spite of the fact that the Public School Code prohibits such practices.[371] (10/12/2001)

Hazelton Area School District

An investigation found that the district had misused hourly rate contractors by failing to seek competitive bids or price quotes involving $187,000.

Purchases of $26,637 were made from a business owned by a board member.[372] (9/4/1999)

Morrisville School District

An audit found that because of poor oversight and disorganized management, it looked like the district was playing favorites with a financial and technology services company after awarding nearly $150,000 worth of contracts. There were no written contracts, payments were made without detailed invoices, invoices were paid before work was completed, and grant money "may" have been spent for work not performed.[373] (9/22/1999)

Northern Tioga School District

A school board member violated the Public School Code and board policy when he sold $78,000 worth of yearbooks to the three district high schools and received commissions on the sales.[374] (5/28/1999)

North Penn School District

An audit found improprieties in the districts financial management between 1995-1997. It paid almost $200,000 in investment fees than it should not have, lost the use at $1.4 million reimbursement income, lost over $180,000 in potential interest earnings, and forfeited over $670,000 in future state aid.[375] (8/26/1998)

Punxsutawney Area School District

An audit uncovered a questionable relationship between a district official and a bus contractor causing the district to forfeit over $70,000 in future state funding. "In the last decade, officials have consistently failed to properly manage and oversee the operation of its pupil bus transportation contract."

Among the findings was that 8,000 gallons of tax-exempt fuel was used by the bus contractor for its other business vehicles, and that vehicles were provided at no charge to the business manager and former superintendent for personal use.[376] (9/26/1998)

Chester Upland School District

This troubled school district was ordered to pay a local charter school the money it owed and to pay it on time in the future. The district claimed it did not have the money. It faces a deficit of $5.5 million this school year and a shortfall of millions more next year (2002-2003). The district stated that the court had no authority to order the district to pay. [377] (6/22/2002)

It's nice to know that school officials can disregard court orders with impunity.

South Carolina

Statewide

There is a State Grand Jury whose purpose is to investigate and uncover white color crime and public corruption.

Clarendon School District

This district is the third to be referred to the State Grand Jury in recent years (the others were Sumter and Fairfield).

Tennessee

Memphis

A private foundation, Parents in Partners, has yanked funding for the schools until leaders can show they spend wisely. The decision was based on a consultant report recommending 65 actions that could save $114 million over five years.[378](1/8/2003)

Texas

TSPR

The Texas Comptroller of Public Accounts initiated the Texas School Performance Review (TSPR) in March 1991. Eleven Agency divisions spend $8 million annually to conduct many different types of monitoring of more than 150 different state and federal programs.

The program began as a pilot program for management and performance audits of select Texas school districts to promote better education through improved school district management and cost efficiency. Since 1991 TSPR has recommended more than 5,500 ways to save taxpayers more than $628 million over five years in just 63 public school districts. A follow-up review in 35 of the districts indicated that 90 percent of the recommendations had been implemented for a savings of $103 million thus far.

The Agency is responsible for monitoring more than 1,200 school districts' and charter schools' use of $14 billion in state and federal funds to educate 4 million students.

What probably makes this program so powerful is that the Comptroller is a former teacher and school board president.

The TSPR was one of 10 winners of the prestigious 1999 "Innovations in America Competition" awarded by the Ford Foundation.

The next 8 examples are just a sample of the performance reviews conducted by the Comptroller of Public Accounts. It should be noted that references to money that can be saved means that money is currently being wasted and mismanaged.

Austin Independent School District

Austin was selected for a performance review because officials had manipulated student dropout data and the results of the state-mandated student achievement test, and by its escalating property tax rate.

The audit developed 163 recommendations to improve operations and save $70 million by 2004-2005. Its budget in 2001 was $579 million. Eighty-nine of the recommendations have been implemented, 67 are in various stages of progress, and 7 have not been addressed as yet.[379]

Beaumont Independent School District

An overwhelming conclusion drawn from the community input and other on-site activities was that the board of trustees had not been effective in leading the district. Too often board decisions appeared to consider ethnic and cultural issues rather than doing what's best for the children.

Total savings of more than $21 million could be realized over the next five years (1995-2000).[380]

Bastrop Independent School District

Bastrop's school population will grow at double the growth rate of the rest of the state. The performance review indicated that only 46 cents of every education dollar found its way to the classroom.

Sixty recommendations could result in net savings of more than $3.9 million over the next five years.[381]

Christoval Independent School District

Forty-three recommendations could result in net savings of more than $295,000 over the next five years (student population is only 379) [382]

Dallas Independent School District

Dallas is the second largest school district in Texas with almost three out of every four students living in poverty. It has 28 low-performing schools, the highest number in the state.

The review determined that the district needed to address six major challenges:

1. Inadequate focus on education
2. Lack of accountability

3. Leadership instability
4. Board turmoil
5. Poorly planned and managed contracted services
6. Failure of core business functions

The 193 recommendations could save $69.9 million over a five-year period.[383]

Eagle Pass Independent School District

The performance review was made to help hold the line on costs, streamline operations and improve services.

The 64 recommendations could save nearly $12 million over the next five years.[384]

Galveston Independent School District

Galveston has dramatically improved over the last four years with more than 75 percent of its students passing the state test compared to only 45 percent in 1994-95. However, the gains are overshadowed by various administrative and financial problems. The Board of Trustees became the first school district to request a performance review.

The 130 recommendations could result in savings of more than $4.3 million over the next five years.[385]

Lasara ISD

The district provides grades pre-K to 8 and has a 95% Hispanic population with 89% disadvantaged. The 37 recommendations could save $810,000 over five years.[386]

Lyford Consolidated School District

This district encompasses 300 square miles and is 95% Hispanic. The 42 recommendations could result in savings of over $600,000 in the next five years.[387]

If every state had such a process in place, millions and perhaps billions of dollars could be saved. Congratulations to Texas for this novel and effective process. However, why is it that the local districts could not come up with the same recommendations or be trained in how-to-do-it?

State

Texas Education Agency

The State Auditor's Office faulted the TEA, responsible for monitoring $14 billion in state and federal aid, for not efficiently monitoring federal programs such as special education and bilingual education. It's rather shocking that more than 40 districts have not had a special education review in at least 10 years, and 63 have not had a review in at least six years. The TEA visited only 36 of the 180 highest risk educational entities. "It is rather ironic for the TEA to be out of compliance since it is the Agency that is constantly hounding local school districts to follow every dot in federal guidelines."

The TEA was also faulted for utilization of staff resources. "For example, 20 monitors were sent to each of two districts even though one district had less than 150 students and the other district had more than 10,000 students." (5/2/2002)

After all, they have to be kept looking busy.

An audit concluded that the agency could not easily provide comprehensive monitoring information because it does not compile or consistently track monitoring results, and on-site monitoring processes may not ensure an accurate assessment of a district's compliance with state and federal requirements.

Trust Fund

The management of the Permanent School Fund, a trust fund of $19 billion, is being investigated for impropriety. Last year, the House General Investigating Committee obtained documents that allegedly detailed a company's plan to make money by using its influence with board members to obtain contracts.[388] (8/22/2002)

TCMAC Audit

The Texas Curriculum Audit Center is a complete management system that gives administrator the means to design and improve curriculum. The Texas Association of School Administrators offers it to school districts, and a number of them have had complete curriculum audits.

Dallas Independent School District

Abuses by building principals involving student-activity funds increased 31 percent (794 incidents) last year. The funds amounted to over $15 million a year. This is not a new problem. In 1998, five schools were investigated after more than

$89,000 turned up missing from activity funds. According to Dr. Moses, "we actually saw more schools with more problems this last year after I had already talked about it...when you see that blank checks were pre-signed by principals in 79 schools, the message is not coming through."[389] (4/12/2002)

This is one of numerous examples cited in which student activity funds have been raided by administrators for expenses not related to the activity funds. What is mind-boggling is why this is not considered theft since the funds are not part of the school budget or other tax dollars. Yet, in none of the cases has anyone been subjected to any civil or criminal charges.

Ft. Worth School District

An audit sharply criticized the maintenance department's handling of $6.5 million to a local contractor who was awarded contracts based only on oral price estimates, and allowed him to define the nature and scope of his jobs. The department then paid him without verifying that the work had been completed. The FBI is investigating. The audit thus far has cost almost $400,000, and potential overcharges amount to $4.8 million.

Texas law generally mandates that construction projects costing $25,000 or more be advertised for bidding. However, the top two managers of the maintenance department circumvented the bidding process by telling the contractors to break up large jobs into series of invoices under $25,000. [390] (1/28/2003)

This technique is used repeatedly to avoid bidding, and why not, there are no consequences.

Houston Independent School District

Charter School Stink

The superintendent of the Prepared Table Charter School was given a $235,000 buyout package just before a state hearing convened to decide if the financially troubled school should close. The school is accused of misusing federal funds, inflating student attendance figures, commingling public funds with church funds, and paying exorbitant administrative salaries. A catering company was hired to provide 2,500 meals a day even though the school had just 1,500 students.[391] (7/16/2002)

Family Ties

The superintendent of Alphonso Crutche's Life Support Center hired more than a dozen relatives who collected over $1.2 million in state funds. It included $130,000 to his sister who was living in Ohio.[392] (11/5/2002)

For Sale

"The Taj Mahal" administration 24-acre building complex sitting on prime city real estate is up for sale at an estimated price of $40 million. One of the trustees said that it was the "epitome of bloated bureaucracy." It cost $6 million to build the complex in 1967 and this was done even though a bond issue was rejected. To balance the budget, expenses were cut such as kindergarten classes, language classes, counselors and special education. [393](8/9/2002)

San Angelo Intermediate School District

Two indictments were obtained against the executive director of support services. The indictments allege that he knowingly presented a falsified document to the grand jury and provided official bid information that was not public to another bidder.[394] (2/13/2002)

Wilmer-Hutchins School District)

The Comptroller's Office issued a scathing report charging that the district had "displayed a pattern of disregard for law and needs a full-time state master to oversee its activities." Its test scores are among the lowest in the state, the number of district employees had increased despite a decrease of 6% in student enrollment, it has four times as many central administrators as the state average for its size, and it has no idea how many computers are in the high school.

The district is disorganized, disregards regulations, and its leaders seem to have little control over what goes on. Board members told the review team that they did not understand the budget or the financial statements they were supposed to evaluate.

The report makes 98 recommendations that would save the district, with an annual budget of $19.9 million, $7.3 million by 2007.[395] (3/29/2002)

Virginia

Arlington

Tuckahoe Elementary School, in one of the wealthiest districts ($12,000 per student), does not provide soap for its kids, band-aids, tissues, and pencils. Yet, these are all required items for students to bring to school. [396](9/1/2002)

Virginia Beach

A special grand jury has convened to examine why the district ended the last fiscal year $12.1 million in the red. "Spending just wasn't controlled…they were moving the money around like a shell game."[397] (11/22/1995)

Five board members resigned after a grand jury declared some board members were fiscally irresponsible and unfit for further service. "The evidence overwhelmingly demonstrates an attitude of fiscal unconcern amounting to recklessness." [398](3/13/1996)

Washington

State Office of the Superintendent for Public Instruction (OSPI)

Ethics investigators are looking into a two-day workshop sponsored by a publishing company and OSPI. The former assistant state school superintendent in charge of special education contracted with the publishing company for the two-day workshop after she had accepted an offer of employment with the company. The company cleared over $40,000 on revenues of $66,000 for a 60% profit. The former assistant also signed 40 OSPI purchase requests for a total of almost $14,000 to the publishing company.[399] (4/8/2002)

Mukilteo

The superintendent was paid $320,000 to leave his position because he was romantically involved with a district employee. There is no district or state policy forbidding relationships between school administrators and their subordinates. However, the board was concerned about "perceptions." The payout enraged teachers and the community. [400](11/13/2002)

Romance does pay well!

Seattle

Wasted Dollars

The school board sank $14 million into an unused postal service building it likely will never be able to utilize. On top of this looming debacle was $25 million wasted on "dumb lawsuits." In addition, an 8.2 percent pay raise was given to administrators including those "who are grossly incompetent and even dishonest."

Mismanagement apparently is an acceptable school practice because according to the Seattle Weekly, "the state auditor doesn't even seem to care about the district's financial affairs." To make matters even worse, a school board member was quoted as saying: "If the superintendent was doing a lousy job, she wouldn't tell him because that's not her job.[401] (10/19/1999)

Then whose job is it, Snow White and the seven dwarfs?

Budget Abuses

Auditors found that schools failed to properly account for some payroll costs, student-activity funds, lunchroom money, and travel payments. Some problems were a repeat of previous years findings, and it was the sixth year in a row the auditors pointed to weak cash-handling procedures involving $4 million in student money. In one school cafeteria, auditors found cash sales were consistently higher when substitute employees rang up sales. According to an auditor, "it is difficult to enforce rigorous cash-handling and accounting procedures in a large district where individual schools have much of the fiscal authority."[402] (9/6/2002)

This is how such budget abuse prepares the groundwork for FraSte to flourish.

Budget Blunder

Due to accounting glitches and computer problems (here we go again), the district found it was short $21 million from last year, and $12 million from this year for a total of $33 million. Last year, $7 million was counted twice, another $5 million in costs from 2000-2001 school year were accounted for in the 2001-2002 school year, and $7 million in salaries and benefits didn't get reflected in last year's budget. The same budgeting practices were carried over to the present budget. "Some of the problems came to some people's attention, but not the right people's attention."[403] (10/5/2002) There are, of course, no "right" people around (perhaps they ought to hire some).

The budget saga never ends. Administrators discovered that accounting problems also involve erroneous accounting of spending by individual schools. The schools were notified not to spend cash carried forward from the last school year until it is determined that the accounts are accurate; instead, some schools carry-forward accounts that are not accurate. [404](10/12/2002)

An independent auditor was hired to analyze how the district ended up with a multi-million dollar deficit. The core of the audit will try to figure out why the problem was discovered only recently when the blunders took place a year ago.[405] (12/19/2002)

The fact is that district staff knew about key elements of the deficit for more than a year, but no one told the school board or the public (CheDe at work).[406] (10/23/2002)

This problem is happening more often and boards always seem surprised. What they should be surprised about is their own ineptness in not being able to competently monitor school finances in a variety of ways rather than just depending on the school superintendent.

Is it any wonder that mismanagement and waste litter the school landscapes? The parents, students, and taxpayers pay the price and the public trust is betrayed without shame, and the betrayal goes unpunished. Wow, what a system.

Wisconsin

Milwaukee Area

Over 30 school administrators do not hold up-to-date licenses from the State Department of Education. State law requires valid licenses, "but it is up to the local districts to ensure compliance." However, districts can lose state aid, but it has never happened.[407] (4/1/2002) That's why this practice continues.

International

WaMi is not unique to the U.S. In Britain, the Department of Education has been condemned for "serious failings" in a training fraud that cost taxpayers millions of pounds. In 2000, Individual Learning Accounts were started as a training grant for all adults. It was so easy to defraud the system that a single fraud involved 80,000 accounts representing 16 million pounds. Accounts were being opened at the rate of 10,000 per day. Over 2.6 million accounts were opened, but it was not clear how many were legitimate. An investigation did find that criminals were selling thousands of ILA account numbers. "It was a license to print money."

Even though the Department of Education was warned before the program started that it was vulnerable to fraud, the system was kept open for another 8 months.[408] (5/1/2002)

They too have a deaf ear when it comes to warnings!

Summary

It is extremely hard to believe how well educated school officials and highly paid administrators believe that they are entitled to make decisions about how tax dollars are to be spent no matter how foolishly, and to mismanage resources so arrogantly; clearly, it has nothing to do with helping children that they betray with such ease.

What is also obvious is that ignorance or lack of ability may be responsible for some of the problems. However, these explanations cannot explain the numerous examples where warnings of corrupt problems were given and routinely ignored. Any responsible thinking person can plainly see why it occurs (arrogance and personal benefit of some sort) and how WaMi occurs (lack of effective monitoring). Unfortunately, there is no motivation of any kind to prevent or expose WaMi other than a sense of personal ethics and public trust; unfortunately, these seem to be rare traits in Education America.

It is absolutely no secret that school construction and/or remodeling, use of consultants, purchasing procedures, school activity funds, allocation of human resources, etc. are ripe targets for WaMi and worse. So why isn't there better oversight?

Why are Boards of Education, State Departments of Education, the U.S. Department of Education, legislators, educational associations, and even auditors seemingly so ineffective in uncovering and, more importantly, preventing WaMi from proliferating the educational landscape? How could it be that there is so little caring for taxpayer dollars, and even less for providing available resources to serve children more readily and effectively?

Why are repeated failures rewarded with continued support? Why are court orders ignored with seeming impunity? Why are regulations and policies so easily shredded in performance of one's responsibility? Why are warnings not heeded? Why is lip service given to reforms, but in reality little of anything changes for the better? How can incompetence be practiced so easily and accepted as part of a school culture? How can WaMi continue day in and day out with no real consequences?

There is only one incredible answer to all of the questions. School boards and staff members, as well other education policymakers, who have the power to prevent WaMi, have abdicated their responsibility and the trust that they were given by a trusting public.

One of the most important and obvious questions is why there isn't any education and training for school personnel and policymakers to understand the devastating effects of WaMi and how to prevent its occurrence? Where are the seminars, workshops and training materials? Where are the educational associations in providing conferences and information about WaMi?

There is only one undeniable answer to these questions. Discussing corruption would be an admission that it could or does exist and that is simply unthinkable to imagine. It's easier to ignore than admit.

The questions can go on and on, but the bottom line is that, as hard as it is to believe, those involved would rather betray the trust placed in them by the parents and public rather than openly face the factual existence of corruption. Why there is such willingness to betray the public and children is beyond this author's ability to comprehend. It's absolutely baffling because this is not why people enter the education profession. The system seems to inoculate even seemingly honest educators from any sense of responsible and ethical behavior when it involves the children they are dedicated to serve and their obligation to spend taxpayer dollars most effectively.

An article by Linda Shrock Taylor adds another rather sobering explanation:

> "Parents and taxpayers complain, but schooling officials have been well trained to ignore all criticism; all anger; all common sense. Not only do schooling officials ignore all controversy, they actively seek to shut-up, remove, even destroy truthful and honorable employees. No threat to the status quo is ever tolerated, at any level."[409]

Agree or not with the statement, it is a rather candid issue to consider as part of the overall problem.

There is a final, but rather meager explanation to help answer many of the questions raised. The public and even those within education have really no idea how pervasive WaMi is because there is no national attention to it and no support groups advocating its elimination. In fact, this is why this book has been written—to inform and raise the threshold of knowledge about school corruption and the devastating effect it has on the education of children.

There is a final question: When will there be enough of a public outcry not to take it anymore? Only then will action begin to deal with this insidious plague.

If the WaMi examples have proved unbelievable and demoralizing, the worse is yet to come. FraSte examples will prove even more shameful and obscene for anyone with a sense of ethical and moral values.

CHAPTER SIX

Fraud and Stealing—FraSte

"Discovery consists of seeing what everybody has seen and thinking what nobody has thought." Albert von Szent-Gyorgyi

It is hard to understand and even imagine why professional educators and other school employees, and employees of agencies supporting public schools would steal, jeopardize their careers, and betray the children and the public trust. The fact is that it happens, it continues unabated, and it seems to be getting worse. In the corporate world, corruption has been described as "a growth industry" and, sadly to say, the same can be said about Education America. The difference is the corporate world admits it is happening, in Education American there is stark silence about corruption.

There are, of course, many reasons why it happens and why it persists. One reason is the fortress mentality surrounding any reality or even perception that Education America is corrupt and corruptible.

Another reason is that whistleblowers are stigmatized rather than being recognized for their courage and rewarded for their vigilance. For example in New York City schools, "Harassment, intimidation and, in some cases, termination are the consequences faced by a growing number of teachers who've stepped forward to blow the lid off school corruption." One teacher found a rat in his school mailbox. Another discovered her personnel file suddenly filled with complaints. Yet another stopped receiving his paycheck. A former dean at Martin Luther King Jr. HS who helped The Post show how some city high schools fraudulently collect taxpayer dollars for no-show former and non-existent students by doctoring attendance records, lost his job.[410] (6/21/1999)

Yet, when the teachers' union urged the school chancellor to set up a "waste watchers" telephone hot line to expose corruption in the school system and help identify wasteful and inefficient practices, the offer was declined. A spokesman for the chancellor stated "we have a system in place for parents, teachers and community to get involved."[411] (11/8/2002) He forgot to add "and get pulverized in the process."

Any district that refuses help to identify corruption, particularly from those who are on the firing line, clearly indicates the fortress mentality that there is no priority or even concern for preventing corruption. Maintaining the façade of "all is well" is their first and only concern.

When a district doesn't place a priority on uncovering corruption and instituting policies and procedures to prevent FraSte, it gives a clear message to staff to literally ignore or compromise the system's internal controls supposedly designed to safeguard school dollars.

<u>The fact is that in the vast majority of school districts, financial internal controls are very loose, unsupervised, poorly monitored, and uncoordinated.</u>

The fundamental problem, therefore, is that attitudes and perceptions need to be changed for those who are responsible for monitoring school finances and the myths must be eradicated from their minds:

Myth: Embezzlement can't happen in our school or district.
Reality: It can happen in any school or district.

Myth: The finance office takes care of the financial details.
Reality: Most finance offices have no effective procedures for protecting all school dollars.

Myth: Central office staff and building principals are responsible for monitoring school finances.
Reality: They are often the perpetrators or too concerned with protecting the district from bad publicity.

Myth: Audits are too expensive.
Reality: Audit dollars are far less expensive than embezzled dollars.

Myth: Employees are trustworthy and won't steal.
Reality: Employees steal whenever and wherever administration makes it possible because of poor oversight and practices.

Myth: Procedures are in place to identify fraud quickly.
Reality: Without proper security procedures and without <u>forensic</u> monitoring practices, embezzlement can go on for years.

So one of the most critical, no-cost and really simple means to help stem the tide of FraSte is for the right tone to be set at the school board table and in the office of the superintendent. This means that they must handle financial and policy matters with utmost honesty and vigilance, not by words, but by their deeds.

Having an ethics policy followed up by education and training is a simple first step. Unfortunately, it seems that too few boards make such an effort. There are probably three basic reasons for this. First is the fortress mentality to protect the system at all costs. Second, many boards simply don't believe corruption could take place in the system. Third, they would rather have a loose system so that corruption can take place (school board members who may take offense at this statement need only read the many examples in this book).

It's also important to understand that FraSte is certainly no stranger to the business world and some of their studies are very informative and should be heeded by all school officials.

What's rather shocking is that international statistics report that internal and external auditors combined detect only 19 percent of all fraud cases. Management accounts for 58 percent of all fraud cases.

The lesson here is that audits conducted in most schools will usually not uncover FraSte nor are they designed to do so. This is an extremely important lesson for all school officials and even town officials to learn. What also needs to be understood is that school management is not interested in publicly exposing FraSte or other corrupt acts.

It should be rather obvious, therefore, that one of the most important prevention strategies is to properly train auditors, administrators, managers, supervisors, directors, staff, and school board members about the extent of the problem and how to look and where to look for FraSte. The examples in this book will show where FraSte happens, how it happens, and who does it. Such knowledge should then provide the basis for designing far more effective financial management systems that would reduce much of the FraSte. What must be understood is that prevention is far more cost effective in dollars and human resources.

A study conducted by the Association of Certified Fraud Examiners[412] (a 33,000 member organization) revealed some interesting data about the business sector and it's directly applicable to the education sector.

1. Losses from fraud caused by managers and executives were 16 times greater than those caused by rank and file employees.

2. Losses caused by men were 4 times greater than those caused by women (this could be because more men are found in the higher positions).
3. Losses caused by people over 60 and older were 28 times those caused by people 25 and under.
4. Losses caused by people with post-graduate degrees were 5 times more than those caused by high school graduates.

These studies should serve as a real wake-up call for school boards and superintendents to institute more aggressive financial controls and provide more comprehensive monitoring procedures.

There is another critical reality that needs to be pondered. An interesting study found that 10% of the people would never steal under any circumstances, 10% would steal at every opportunity, and the other 80% would steal given the right motive.

Therefore, a critical need in any prevention strategy is to understand why employees commit corrupt acts, and why are they so easily tempted to steal. There are many reasons and, although greed is at the heart of most FraSte, there are other motivating factors.

Employees who feel cheated, unappreciated, used, overworked, and/or who feel that they have been or are being treated unfairly, or as bonded servants will, eventually, find a way to retaliate or get revenge in some way. FraSte is a perfect way to get back at the system. "Getting even" provides a lot of satisfaction and sometimes the only satisfaction.

The Association for Certified Fraud Examiners provides an explanation for the corporate world but it's certainly applicable to Education America.

"One element common to most occupational fraud offenders…is that almost none of them took their jobs for the purpose of committing fraud."

So how do good people become corruptors? A 20-year old Hollinger and Clark study of 12,000 employees found: "Nearly 90% engaged in 'workplace deviance' which included behavior such as goldbricking, workplace slowdowns, sick time abuse and pilferage…and one-third actually had stolen money or merchandise…The researchers concluded that the most common reason employees committed fraud had to do more with motivation—the more dissatisfied the employee, the more likely he or she was to engage in criminal behavior."[413]

This behavior is, of course, one of rationalization that justifies the fraud, but there are other reasons as well. Pressure caused by personal hardships can certainly cause someone to commit fraud, but it is probably not a major cause in education. The major reason for fraud in education is that of opportunity because it is so easy to do.

The repeated fraud events, year after year, in the same school districts are a stunning example of how lax school officials are in preventing fraud. One of the common elements in the examples is that only after the discovery or revelation of theft are steps taken to correct the obvious flaws in the financial system; and, as will be seen, even then fraud often continues.

Therefore, the reason for detailing the numerous examples is not intended to highlight the negative but rather to indicate that stealing from the school treasure chests is far more prevalent than anyone realizes. By examining the incidents and how the dastardly deeds are perpetrated, it is hoped that the need to question, review and improve financial management practices and systems will become the number one priority of all those who are involved in or affected by schools: educators, school boards, town leaders, politicians, parents and parent organizations, seniors and all members of a community.

Unfortunately, and sad to say, is that the real lesson to be learned from the examples is that school boards are simply not qualified or able to be responsible for spending and monitoring school dollars because they do not have the education, knowledge, training and skills to perform this crucial responsibility. In addition, there are those who are not ethically and honestly endowed to resist the temptations inherent in the job.

Regardless of the reasons, school boards need independent, mandatory state oversight and a handful of states do have such a practice in place. Unfortunately, state oversight alone is not enough because all such oversight is aimed at uncovering corruption rather than preventing it from happening. There must also be independent oversight at the local level and an easy no-cost method to do this will be found in the conclusion. In addition, boards need to be held legally responsible for their actions if they have not been prudent or have not followed legal advice or state laws and regulations.

The bottom line is that the taxpayers should not be burdened to pay more taxes for the incompetence of school boards or for employee incompetence or fraud particularly when advice and warnings have been given and ignored, and when prevention measures are so easy to implement.

<u>Until there are severe enough consequences and penalties for failures to protect the school treasure chests, FraSte will continue on its relentless, shameful and inevitable path.</u>

CHAPTER SEVEN

FraSte Examples

"A man who has never gone to school may steal from a freight car; but if he has a university education, he may steal the whole railroad." (Theodore Roosevelt)

What is absolutely clear and undeniable is that no taxpayer dollars in the education treasure chests are immune from being plundered and pillaged by Robin Hood Hogs who steal and embezzle in the most devious, interesting, and creative ways. This means that no school district is immune from the ravages of these greedy predators. Further, it means that if a school district looks for it, FraSte will rear its ugly head. This is the cold, hard, reality that every single school and school district must accept. Unfortunately, it does not even register as a glancing thought.

The fact that some states are missing from the examples should not be construed to mean that fraud has not occurred. It is far more likely that there is no aggressive process in place, such as required independent state or local forensic audits, to uncover fraud or that some schools and districts are more effective in hiding corruption. The examples will certainly demonstrate that no school or school district, regardless of size or wealth or location, is free from FraSte.

To list all of the cases uncovered would fill a set of encyclopedias. The ones that follow only represent the tip of the iceberg. There is no doubt that any district that aggressively and competently looks for FraSte will find employees who have betrayed the children and the public trust.

Another important issue that should not be minimized is that the betrayal of the public trust does not just rest on the shoulders of those who perpetrate FraSte. It is also on the shoulders of those who are responsible for monitoring school dollars because they are not fulfilling their responsibility as guardians of the school treasure chests. Still worse is their failure to accept or understand that they have been given a sacred covenant when taxpayer dollars are turned over to them to be used for the children and not for greedy or selfish ends.

National

Collusive Practices

Federal and state officials say schools appear to be especially vulnerable to illegal conspiracies among their suppliers and the evidence of such practices is growing. Bid rigging in the sale of products to schools seems to be pervasive nationwide. According to the Department of Justice, schools are being victimized by bid-rigging schemes on a large scale.[414] (9/22/1993)

Book Scam

The nation's largest book distributor was accused in a federal lawsuit of cheating public schools (libraries, universities and government agencies) out of more than $100 million. Baker and Taylor Inc. deliberately overcharged the institutions for discount books by intentionally misclassifying books so that they would not be eligible for the deepest discounts.[415] (2/12/97)

Diploma Scam

An FBI investigation named Dipscam (diploma scam) searched 29 so-called degree granting "institutions" and found that thousands of public school educators bought bogus masters and doctorate degrees from the non-existent universities. Interestingly, no charges were filed against the individuals who bought the bonus degrees (it would overburden the federal courts). However, the names were to be turned over to local and state authorities for appropriate action.[416] (5/25/1983)

Milk Contracts Rigged

Three dairies were indicted on charges that they participated in an alleged conspiracy to fix prices for school milk contracts. These indictments brought to 40 the number of dairies charged with such offenses. "The incidents of collusion have been epidemic in the dairy industry." The investigation has spread to 16 states and 38 defendants have been sentenced to jail. Fines and damages alone amounted to $21 million.[417] (9/4/1991)

However, uncovering such fraud does not put an end to the corruption. As of last month, the Justice Department's investigation of the dairy industry had led to criminal cases being filed against 53 corporations and 66 individuals in 13 states. To date, 46 corporations and 48 individuals have been convicted and have paid a total of $46.3 million in fines and $8 million in civil damages.

Thirty-two grand juries in 21 states are continuing to investigate the dairy industry.[418] (9/22/1993))

School Bus Price Fixing

Six Michigan companies are accused of violating antitrust laws in the sale of school buses and school-bus bodies to school districts. Companies in Iowa, Montana, Nebraska, North Dakota, and South Dakota also have been charged with illegal price fixing and bid rigging in the sale of school buses. Twelve corporations and 16 individuals have been convicted.[419] (9/22/1993)

Technology Theft

Nationwide, law-enforcement officials say thefts of schools' technological equipment, from computers to videocassette recorders, is a growing problem. Schools are becoming a more frequent target as they add new technologies that can easily be sold on the so-called gray market.

The National Alliance of Safe Schools claims "theft of school property is nothing new...it's just that we've increased the spoils of stealing." The bottom line is that schools are poorly equipped to prevent theft, and most school theft can be traced to employees and students.

Yet, no one, including the FBI, tracks such statistics nationally.[420] (6/5/1996)

With millions of dollars being spent on technology, it is absolutely shameful that no real effort is being made to protect such precious assets. It is a shocking example of how the children and the public trust are betrayed.

National Education Association

The Landmark Legal Foundation filed a complaint with the Labor Department that the NEA concealed its use of million's of dollars in tax-exempt teachers' dues and fees for political activities, primarily for Democratic candidates and causes. It did not inform its 2.7 million members that it spent the tax-exempt revenue to recruit and support candidates running for local, state and federal office since at least 1994. Federal labor law requires the union to tell the truth about its political activities and expenditures.[421] (4/23/2002)

The National Faculty

This Atlanta non-profit organization, a provider of professional development for teachers since 1968, has closed its doors and filed for bankruptcy after the discovery of an apparent embezzlement of $400,000 by the accounting and personnel manager. The Agriculture Department, private foundations and school districts provided funding of its $5 million annual budget.[422] (9/5/2001)

Apparently, the Agriculture Department is not only interested in growing better crops but also in growing staff trainers for education. How considerate of the Ag Department!

Free Lunch Is Costly

The federally subsidized school lunch program is full of abuse and even fraud because the process to qualify comes down to parents self-reporting their income. Advocates claim that the worst that happens is kids may get a free lunch. Not true! The problem is that the number of free lunches also determines Title I funding because it is based on the percentage of students that participate. Free lunch numbers are also linked to other local, state and federal funding streams. So any fraud in the program is quickly multiplied and that's why many schools work hard to sign up students. In fact, many schools offer free ice cream and other tokens to kids who return their forms even if the students aren't eligible. In addition, some schools over-report their school lunch data to get more school aid.

There are other ramifications. For example, New Jersey districts that have more than 20 percent of their students on free lunches are supposed to begin providing full-day kindergarten and half-day pre-school.[423] (3/14/2002)

One of the breeding grounds for establishing a culture leading to school corruption is program manipulation. It is almost impossible for fraud to occur without cheating and mismanagement laying the groundwork.

E-Rate Raiding

A GAO report verified that the $2.5 billion e-rate program providing subsidies for Internet services has been fraught with fraud and abuse.[424]

Alabama

Examiners audit the 67 county school districts on a rotating basis, and the most recent audits pointed out failings in more than half. Although school systems are required by law to address auditors' concerns and develop plans for correcting the problems, they frequently respond with empty promises.[425] (12/4/2000)

And why not, it always seems to work; besides, there are no consequences when promises are not kept.

"School systems across Alabama have been plagued by theft, financial impropriety and incompetence in recent years"[426] (2/2/2000)

Why is it that so many school employees feel entitled to shed their responsibility for protecting the school treasure chests from being plundered? It's really disheartening to know that they have no conscience when they betray the children and public.

The Birmingham News examined scores of court records, more than 100 Ethics Commission rulings, hundreds of school documents and the most recent audit reports from all 67 county systems. More than half of those audits found serious financial shortcomings. The investigation found 40 cases in the last decade in which school officials were charged in state or federal court with theft, corruption or fraud involving schools. Prosecutors pinpointed a minimum of $3 million siphoned from schools, but investigators believe the actual total is far higher.

State auditors uncover 10-15 schemes involving theft and misuse of school money each year, and probes into school employees make up the biggest slice of all the Alabama Ethics Commission's investigations. "Law enforcement officials believe those caught are a tiny fraction of the guilty," and state auditors report that "what we see here is the tip of the iceberg…probably three or five times or more than what we actually know is going on out there."[427] (12/3/2000)

This statement by law enforcement officials is certainly not limited to Alabama, and it should be etched into the minds of every school official, policymaker and taxpayer; instead, it is completely ignored as an issue or problem in schools.

One of the most far-reaching cases occurred in the 1970s and early 1980s involving bid rigging. A supply company used phony bids to make it appear the bid law was being followed and regularly made kickbacks to school officials. Twenty-three schools reaching into 13 county school districts and two city systems were part of the scheme to steal hundreds of thousands of dollars. Two of the officials from the supply company received three years of probation.[428] (12/3/2000)

Mobile

A former school board president and an architect were convicted of federal racketing and extortion charges involving $500,000 covering a 1977 to 1984 period. They received prison terms of 12 years.[429] (12/3/2000)

Bessemer

Three employees stole thousands of dollars from the system. Among the corruptors were the superintendent who made unauthorized purchases of $30,000, the payroll officer who paid herself $39,000 for overtime and cash advances, and an employee who wrote checks to herself totaling $130,000, waited for them to clear, and then altered the payee's name.[430] (9/6/2000)

Birmingham School District

School air conditioners were stolen and found to be cooling the businesses and rental property owned by former school board employees. [431](2/13/1994)

A former foreman in the service center was indicted by a federal grand jury on 15 counts allegedly spearheading several schemes to defraud the schools out of more than $70,000 that included money laundering, embezzlement and mail fraud.[432] (2/13/1994)

The former operations and maintenance director, considered one of the most trusted of all employees, was found to be one of the most corrupt. He masterminded a scheme in which phony companies billed for thousands of dollars in work that was never performed. More than $150,000 in checks that were written to vendors wound up in his bank account. In all, eight people were involved.[433] (12/3/2000)

It's rather startling in looking at these and many examples to follow, how the "Robin Hoods" of education seem to find so many willing accomplices.

Dallas County[434] (12/4/2000)

The district, one of the poorest in America, didn't know it paid $74,000 for anti-drug books and pamphlets that it never received. The drug-free school counselor was pocketing the money for over six years.

Keith High School

Auditors found checks deposited into a bookkeepers account. She pleaded guilty to forgery charges, received a 10-year sentence and repaid $11,000.

FraSte Revelations

The Birmingham News reported the following cases of FraSte:[435] (12/3/2000)

Decatur School System

The Board of Education president, a former policeman, pleaded guilty to the theft of $50,000 from the band's booster club when he served as treasurer. He was sentenced to three years in prison.

Elyton

An elementary principal pleaded guilty in 1999 to charges of embezzling almost $20,000 from school bank account.

Eufaula School District

The superintendent of schools was suspended after being indicted on felony charges of conspiracy and theft in 1995. He was accused of taking $1,800 in school system funds and giving the money to three unnamed people for political purposes.

Harvest

A Sparkman High School teacher and coach were charged with stealing televisions and VCRs from the school.

Huntsville

A Mastin Lake Elementary PTA officer was charged with embezzling $35,000. A Williams Elementary PTA officer ordered more than $8,000 worth of computers with school money, but kept the money instead. He was so distraught when police charged him that he committed suicide.

Montgomery County Schools

A trusted payroll clerk earning $20,000 per year used "daring and guile" to embezzle more then $337,000 over the past decade. The court ordered her to make restitution, but she has repaid less than $400.

Northport School System

From 1993-1997, $25,000 vanished from the vending machines at Northport Junior High School. The principal resigned and stated "she did nothing wrong…I don't know what happened."

Prattville

A former cheerleading sponsor, who is now an assistant principal in another county school, awaits trial on charges she took thousands of dollars from the cheerleader fund at the junior high school.

Talladega County Schools

A janitor, considered loyal for 29 years, awaits trial on charges of burglarizing an elementary school. He was videotaped taking money, tools and appliances.

The Problem

The Alabama Tax Watch really crystallizes the issue: "All of these problems stem from one root cause, the schools are funded and run by government employees with no motivation to stop the theft."

Although this is a harsh indictment of school employees, it's easy to understand why they have arrived at such a conclusion.

As will be observed in all the cases to follow, this can be said of just about any school system; otherwise, such corruption could not be occurring so consistently and systematically.

Arizona

State

An investigation by the Attorney General's office resulted in charges that education officials at the state and local levels stole hundreds of thousands of dollars over eight years. The AG has characterized it as "one of the biggest cases of fraud involving public money."

A former school superintendent was charged with bribery, theft, and fraud in connection with the misuse of $500,000. There is an interesting punch line in the criminal complaint in that it was conducted under the direction of a former deputy superintendent in the state department of education. The school superintendent received over $400,000 for "fictitious book sales." Of course, the state official then got a "kickback" from the "super" hog.

Other fraudulent activities involved a professor from Northern Arizona University who owned a publishing house that gave $15,000 to the school superintendent as part of the scheme with the state official.

As if this wasn't enough, investigators also found that some projects circumvented state and local bidding procurement requirements resulting in fraudulent expenditures. One such project was "Study Skills in the Classroom" that was influenced by state department officials who chose the vendors and decided how the money was spent. As a result, almost $60,000 was spent on publishing costs for the project, but no goods or services were received for the expenditure.

The Robin Hood Hogs always have their merry band of bandits. It's just so surprising at how creative and clever the scams are. However, what is more shocking is how the dastardly deeds went on for so long. Were the auditors on vacation for eight years? Of course, the response is always the same when such scams are exposed: "There was a lack of accounting and management controls and…safeguards are now in place" to prevent a recurrence.

So why was there a lack of controls and what makes anyone think that a new system cannot be circumvented? Increased vigilance and controls help to make it more difficult to defraud, but no system is safe from being circumvented.[436] (9/19/1990)

Amphitheater Unified School District #10

An investigation by the Auditor General found: (1) The district failed to solicit sealed bids for construction involving over $500,000 and (2) The district paid unauthorized charges for construction services. A recall petition was successful in removing a majority of the governing board. [437](11/2000)

Deer Valley

A parent called for an investigation into the use of district-owned vehicles by the superintendent and other administrators because he believed that they were "triple dipping." The parent claimed that four of the five associate superintendents receive annual car allowances of $3,500 specified in their contracts, but they also use district cars and gasoline from the district-owned pump—neither is permitted in their contracts. The superintendent "resents the accusation that he or the associate superintendents have misused district money or vehicles."[438](8/15/2002)

This type of attitude can only come from those who feel a sense of entitlement to the largesse of school treasure chests.

The superintendent was placed on administrative leave pending an investigation by the Maricopa County Attorney's Office. His contract salary was supposed to be paid in 26 equal installments, but he was paid 28 times in one year.[439] (10/10/2002)

Mesa

The Franklin East Elementary School PTO treasurer admitted he embezzled $15,000. The treasurer did return the money. What is most surprising is a statement made by the president of the PTO Magazine, "Embezzlement is quite common among PTO's and other non-profits."[440] (4/22/2003)

The owner of Arizona Southwest Prep Academy (a charter school) was indicted on two counts of theft and one fraud charge. He was accused of using $3,000 for personal use, $9,000 in federal grants, and falsifying the number of students enrolled.[441] (3/22/2002)

Mobil Elementary School District #86

A governing board member was charged with "personally misusing $2,322 of the District's resources involving travel and cellular phone use."

The governing board member reimbursed the District prior to the conclusion of the investigative report.[442] (11/27/2000)

Phoenix School District

The Maricopa County attorney's office reviewed an allegation concerning the superintendent's financial management. He spent $20,000 in district funds on promotional materials circulated at the American Association of School Administrators annual convention in 2001 where he was elected president. He also had some of his salary taken as two balloon payments not authorized by the board.[443] (10/16/2002)

A former PTO president of the Magnet Traditional School admitted taking $18,000 of the group's money; although she denied using the money for gambling, bank documents link the ATM card to local casinos. She was jailed, but she did repay the money and apologized.[444] (11/21/2002)

Scottsdale District #48

An investigation by the Auditor General concluded: (1) District administrators fostered a climate of disregard for the proper use of public monies (2) Administrators and employees ignored or circumvented required school district procurement rules and (3) Administrators and employees accepted favors from preferred vendors

The investigation was hampered and delayed because the Superintendent of Schools, contrary to law, "refused to provide certain records."

As a result of the investigation, a 25 count civil complaint was made by the Attorney General's office against the school district for financial misfeasance and personally profiting from their official business dealings. The complaint was also seeking penalties of over $14 million.[445] (11/1998)

When a culture of fraud exists, it's hard to change it even when there are court ordered judgments. The Auditor General had to conduct another investigation that found:

"District officials failed to comply with the terms of its October 1998 consent judgment by failing to charge a charter school $101,378 in rental fees…and that a governing board member failed to disclose that he was employed by the charter school."[446] (11/2001)

Window Rock School District

Former school officials and local contractors have been accused by state and federal investigators that they had colluded to defraud the district of hundreds of thousands of dollars. Some of money was used to pay for parties at topless bars and at a brothel. [447](9/25/1991)

Arkansas

State

The state's former education director conspired with an influential former state senator, and the former executive director of the Arkansas School Board's Association, to defraud the Association out of thousands of dollars involving self-insurance for workers' compensation fund.[448] (9/12/2001)

Little Rock

Two former test proctors were among nine others indicted on fraud and conspiracy charges for allegedly helping prospective teachers cheat on their licensing exams. According to the indictment, the proctors accepted payments to let people take the test at locations other than the designated location, were given assistance on the exams, and allowed extra time for completion.[449] (9/20/2000)

California

Statewide

The state implemented a Fiscal Crisis & Management Assistance Team (FCMAT) accountability program. It is based upon a commitment to a standards-based, independent and external review of school district operations. FCMAT has noted positive differences between an objective standards-based approach versus a nonstandards-based approach. When standards are clearly defined, reachable, and communicated, there is a greater likelihood they will be measured and met.

Every standard is measured on a consistent rating format, and every standard is given a scaled score from zero to ten as to their relative status of completeness. It is from this comprehensive standards-based review of all data that the recommendations for school district improvement and enhanced student learning are provided to the district.

Alum Rock

A senior accountant in the school district embezzled nearly $1 million over six years. Such fraud was not limited to the school district funds, but also to the Alum Rock Foundation, a volunteer group that raises money for the East San Jose district.

Her fraud was accomplished simply by writing out checks in small increments. An investigation found that she had several bank accounts and that some of the stolen money was used to purchase several homes in the United States and Mexico and to support relatives.

She was sentenced to six years in prison and has made $170,000 in restitution payments.[450] (6/11/2002)

Fresno

The Fresno Unified School district Board revoked the charter of Gateway Academy because of a reported $1.3 million debt. The State Attorney's office raided the headquarters and seized more than 100 boxes of records and 60 computers. It's alleged that the school was inflating attendance figures, withholding money to its schools (it has 11 locations) and employees, and withdrawing large amounts of cash from school-related accounts.[451] (2/27/2002)

Los Angeles Unified School District

This school district is only one of a handful that established its own Office of Inspector General in 1999 to conduct routine and investigative audits.

The embattled IG resigned after six years. He had received much criticism for his critical reports. Apparently, revealing FraSte is viewed as being "critical" of the district.[452](4/8/2005)

Some of the citations included in the 2001 report follow and it is an excellent example of the results obtained when there is an Office of Inspector General:

Embezzlement

- A school administrative assistant admitted to charges of embezzling $7,500 part of which was altering payroll records for overtime totaling $4,500.
- Another assistant embezzled $9,000 from the student body accounts.
- A former school administrative assistant misappropriated $12,000 by submitting duplicate invoices and by forging and negotiating checks for which she received personal benefit.
- A cafeteria manager deposited cash and checks collected from meal sales to her personal bank account by instructing parents to make checks payable to her or cash.
- An administrative assistant accepted cash for the Student Body Fund but did not control the money causing thousands of dollars to be missing from the account.

Bribery

Employees complained that they were asked or required to pay a supervisor a sum of money to gain or retain employment. Other allegations involved nepotism and payroll fraud charging the supervisor placed relatives on the payroll although they did not provide work or services.

Unlawful payments

An investigation revealed that a high-ranking administrator accused of mismanagement and inappropriate actions had arranged or permitted payments to select employees for secondary assignments with no additional work performed.

Policy violations

An investigation determined that a principal accepted inappropriate donations from entertainment film companies and failed to deposit the donated funds, allowed school facilities to be used by the film companies, provided false information to an administrator who was conducting an inquiry, violated the nepotism policy by employing relatives, and forged the signatures on a document.

Misuse of Assets

An investigation determined that teachers who were assigned to work at teachers' centers were selling merchandise during work hours without authorization. The operators had formed a nonprofit corporation and accumulated bank deposits of $10,000 and more than $10,000 in materials and supplies.

Contract fraud

An investigation determined that a vendor providing Constructability Reviews (CR) for construction on school sites had subcontracted the CRs to an individual who was also a district employee. The employee/contractor in turn used the names of two individuals as part of the team that provided the reviews except, when interviewed, the two individuals claimed they had not been involved.

Record Falsification

An assistant principal, with the knowledge of the principal, routinely changed grades to reward or punish students. In addition, unsanctioned proficiency tests were administered to seniors who needed to pass the test for graduation, and then false passing results were entered on their records so that they could graduate.

Payroll Fraud

- Two teachers were being paid for hours they did not teach; they signed for hours at a school at which they did not even appear.
- A school administrative assistant utilized illness and vacation time but had never deducted the time from he accrued leave balances, and also submitted timecards for unauthorized overtime pay.
- A senior office assistant received improper overtime pay in the amount of $11,824, but based on the response of the principal, the amount was

reduced to $8,655. The employee then transferred to another school where she confessed to taking $2,300 from the student body fund.

- An official in the Division of Adult and Career Education requested and approved teaching assignments at offsite locations for department employees that never went to the locations to perform the work.

Nepotism

A school principal was found to be hiring unqualified relatives of other administrators for teaching positions. One individual was paid a teacher's salary while assigned to a non-teaching position, and a second individual held a part-time counseling position without the proper credentials.

False Claims

Several schools entered into a $200,000 contract with a technology vendor for the purchase and installation of computers and software, as well as, to provide training and support services. The vendor was awarded the contract because of his association with a district principal. Invoices totaling $31,000 were paid although the vendor failed to deliver all equipment and services as specified by the contract.

The above examples are typical of what is uncovered when there is an active effort to find FraSte activities. Such efforts will always bear fruit that is spoiled and rotten in the education treasure chest.

Falsifying Credits

Criminal charges of grand theft were brought against 43 teachers who received salary increases based on fraudulent college credits. The teachers are accused of receiving salary increases averaging $3,000 annually for college-extension classes they never attended.[453] (3/17/1982)

Embezzlement and Theft

Auditors discovered that more than $300,000 in federal earthquake recovery funds for one school could not be accounted for. Four big screen TV's purchased with the funds were missing, and the district was billed for over 2,000 hours of work that wasn't done. [454](8/21/1998)

The internal auditor stated: "My gut feeling is that for every dollar, 20 cents is wasted or embezzled."

More Bloat

The district planned to buy a 29-story, $153 million edifice to house its central office headquarters. The 928,000 square foot structure is 50% larger than needed. However, apparently it's not a problem. Even though it has already been accused of having a massive and bloated bureaucracy, a school board member remarked: "This will give the bureaucracy plenty of room to grow." This is happening at a time when the district is doing without music and art programs and can scarcely afford to maintain an adequate supply of books."[455] (8/6/2001)

The greedy gluttons always serve themselves first and the children come last.

Inflated Enrollment

Although the district inflated enrollment figures that provided an additional $120 million in state aid, the governor allowed the district to keep the money. The record keeping and other controls were so lax that officials couldn't verify whether students had excused absences. The district responded with finger pointing, denial and the threat of litigation.[456] (12/5/2001)

It certainly sends an interesting message to those schools that play by the rules.

Embezzlement

A Westlake High School bookkeeper was arrested on suspicion of embezzling more than $150,000 from the Associated Student Body accounts to support her gambling problem.[457] (2/14/2002)

A former district employee pleaded no contest to a charge of embezzling nearly $30,000 in public funds by redeeming rewards checks the district earned through its long-distance phone company. She agreed to pay $29,700 in restitution.[458] (4/3/2002)

Activity Fees

The United States Justice Foundation filed suit against the district alleging that schools illegally charge activity fees. For example, Mt. Gleason Middle School requires the purchase of physical education uniforms that bear the schools logo, and students are told that their grades will be lowered if they do not wear the uniform. Interestingly, the uniforms can only be purchased at the school. Money from such sales, as will be seen in many of the examples in this chapter, is a rich source of embezzled funds.[459] (4/27-28/2002)

Newport-Mesa School District

An ex-school finance officer admitted to embezzling $3.5 million (the largest such theft in California school history) over an eight-year period (1985-1992) was sentenced to six years in prison. He hid the money in an old insurance account from which he wrote checks to himself. As a result, class sizes had to be increased and 59 teachers and 150 other employees were laid off. He was only tripped up because he attempted to steal funds from the active insurance account and an employee noticed this. Otherwise, the embezzlement scheme, which involved the purchase of gemstones, would have gone on even longer.[460] (6/26/1993)

Oakland

Six school employees have been charged with theft and two others, the district's maintenance foreman and its director of state and federal funding, have been indicted on similar charges.[461] (9/13/1989)

The Attorney General charged the head of the Black Panthers with eight counts of felony embezzlement involving a $250,000 grant to fund a community-learning center for disadvantaged youths. He is also being investigated for allegedly using $50,000 worth of bonds he controlled for a charity to secure his bail on an illegal-weapons charge.[462] (5/29/1985)

Ravenswood City School District

The superintendent was tried on 19 felony conflict-of-interest charges. Prosecutors allege that she stood to gain when the school district gave loans to employees. Although she was found not guilty, charges and allegations continue.

The State Superintendent has asked the county superintendent to conduct an investigation based on articles printed by the Mercury News alleging, "extravagant spending for travel, inadequate documentation of the spending of millions in federal and state aid, and fraudulent claims submitted after a school fire."

In addition, two school aides claim that they were ordered to take tests for pupils in their special education class. The superintendent claims that the district found "no evidence other than the word of the instructional aides;" yet, a student confirmed that cheating had occurred.

A year later, a state takeover was being considered, and the County Superintendent issued a report with 91 recommendations including "a lack of checks and balances to prevent bogus employees from getting on the payroll."[463] (7/12/2001)

Sacramento

Computers worth over $150,000 were stolen from schools because "they are so easy to burglarize." Thefts of technological equipment are a growing concern.[464] (6/5/1996)

San Diego

Authorities are investigating an alleged six-year kickback scam in which one or more district employees, working with a computer company, swindled the schools out of thousands of dollars worth of computer equipment. School detectives are investigating everything from double billings to equipment not received and false sales. About $600,000 worth of merchandise may be missing, however, investigators have not confirmed this. Thus far no charges have been filed but one employee has been placed on paid leave.[465] (8/17/2002)

Interestingly, two years prior a similar problem was investigated and an investigation found: "Its accounting system was disorganized and susceptible to corruption."[466] (9/23/2002)

Again and again, warnings are not heeded. The only logical conclusion is that those in charge do not want to plug the financial loopholes that make FraSte possible.

San Francisco

School Scams[467] (10/17/2002)

A former school security director, an employee since 1984, was accused of using $200,000 of school funds to pay for trips to Hawaii, New Zealand and Puerto Rico, as well as, paying for computer, camera equipment and other luxury items. Part of the scam included false and inflated invoices. He also logged in the most overtime pay amounting to $55,000.

A $1,000 per day consultant who managed the district's facilities division was charged along with his wife, his brother-in-law, and a business partner to have conspired with a heating contractor to pocket $850,000.

The company involved has agreed to pay $500,000 to the district in restitution and $500,000 in fines for its role in an elaborate scheme that involved two former employees of the company and a former school district manager.

Energy Scam

The district attorney has charged a former facilities manager with 22 felonies in connection with a $30 million energy contract during the 1999-

2001 period. The company paid a kickback of $400,000 to the manager and a relative.[468] (10/9/2002)

Internet Scam

Six electronic firms were indicted on charges of defrauding a $2.25 billion-a-year federal program to give poor schools money to connect to the Internet.[469] (4/9/2005)

San Marino Unified School District

A former maintenance director was charged with embezzlement and fraud that took place over a 15-month period beginning in April 2000. He created false invoices and billed the district more than $50,000 in labor and materials that he collected.[470] (1/9/2002)

Walnut Creek

The former treasurer of an elementary PTA is being investigated in the embezzlement of $15,000 in club funds. Bank records indicated that money from the club's fund was transferred into the treasurer's personal bank account.[471] (10/3/2002)

Weed School District

The superintendent of 20 years was charged with five counts of embezzlement and four counts of grand theft involving potential misappropriation of a $30,000 grant, and secret bank accounts that could have been used to funnel the grant money from school accounts. Other possible abuses included credit card misuse, double dipping on per diem expenses, and misuse of school money to pay for tickets to baseball games outside the county.[472] (12/4/2001)

The superintendent pleaded guilty and must pay $40,000 in restitution.[473] (10/25/2002)

West Contra

A former teacher was forced to resign after uncovering misuse of funds at Helms Middle School. He has sued the school district and teachers union for fraud and breach of contract. The lawsuit claims that accounting irregularities were rampant during his employment in 2000-2001. When he complained to school officials, he became the subject of a disciplinary hearing and the union refused to provide counsel.[474] (1/8/2003)

West Fresno Elementary School District

Unbelievable

The superintendent was charged with embezzlement and theft of public funds. He was accused of double-billing the California Association of School Administrators for thousands of dollars in expenses, and of stealing several thousand dollars from the 1,000-pupil district between 1996-1998.[475] (11/1/2000)

The two-school district rests behind a goat field and junkyard, and 90 percent of the students are low income and half are learning to speak English.

At the time, there were no milk deliveries, teachers were not getting paid, and the district faced a $1.5 million dollar deficit out of an $8.5 million budget. The Fresno County superintendent, teachers and parents said a thirty-year party of extravagant spending and nepotism was translated into easy money for friends and relatives.

Bank and credit card statements showed that money was used to buy perfume, electronics, and questionable airplane trips for school board members and others.

It's hard to believe that in 30 years no one tried to put a stop to such corruption.

Over the last 18 months, there have been five superintendents including one who was hired despite a grand-theft conviction for filing false travel claims in another school district. Noteworthy is that the five board members have been in place for decades.

The board president stated: "We are not broke, and no judge and no county superintendent is going to take West Fresno away from us." Yet, the county superintendent was given the power a year ago to veto any expense or personnel decision in an attempt to get the district solvent, but the board ignored his orders and even refused to work with a court-appointed fiscal expert.

Allegations included medical benefits to people who didn't work for the district, hiring custodians who were then given higher job titles with $30,000 a year increases, and a state planning grant of $34,000 from which school board members wrote numerous checks totaling more than $10,000 to themselves, relatives and friends. School computers came in the front door and went out the back, and there are no records of how the district spent a $6.8 million federal technology grant.

Board members were fined $1,000 each for legal fees and warned they would be each fined $500 a day more if they don't produce a budget by November 24th.[476] (11/15/2002)

Willy Sutton, a famous bank robber of the 1930's, was wrong in responding to a question as to why he robbed from banks. He said: "That's where the money is." He obviously didn't know about the school treasure chests. They can be robbed, no gun or threat is needed, and there is little, if any, prison time to worry about.

Colorado

Aurora

The former maintenance director plotted with a supplier to steal $205,000 by billing for non-existent supplies.[477] (3/1/1990)

Denver

Audit Sleuths

The district has a staff of four internally auditing its books. What is unusual is that they report directly to board members. This can be an effective system so long as the board is not corrupt as was the case in the West Fresno district. It would be even more effective to have an independent auditing staff free of any school influence and have it report to town or state officials as well.

Amazing

A Denver high school shop teacher hid hundreds of items in a house built with secret passageways, closets with false bottoms, and an indoor firing range. The teacher was accused of taking thousands of items from the school.[478] (6/24/1994)

Laxity

A top Denver school official pointed to lax banking practices and unclear accountability that allowed a former East High School principal to embezzle money.[479] (6/14/1995)

Wife's Revenge

Authorities, on a tip from an angry wife, went to the home of a West High School's head custodian and found a stockpile of everything from toilet paper to computers that he allegedly stole from work.[480] (12/5/1996)

Elizabeth C-1 District

While the district was facing a budget shortfall of $2.5 million in 2002, requiring a $1.5 million state loan, the district had catered parties, freewheeling credit cards, and secret bonuses that administrators heaped on themselves. Six-year prison sentences were given to the superintendent and chief financial officer who were convicted on 27 counts of embezzlement, fraud and forgery.

Apparently, the board learned its lesson (it rarely happens) because two years later it was named the best managed financial system in Colorado.[481] (4/12/2005)

Jefferson County

A former business manager of 10 years was arrested and charged with embezzling more than $395,000 that he stole in small amounts over five years by submitting false invoices to purchase tools for maintenance workers servicing the district's 145 schools. He began by stealing small amounts from the petty cash fund. Interestingly, he said that he was never questioned about his frequent purchases from the petty cash fund that he used to buy jewelry, clothes, high-stakes gambling trips, hockey tickets, and nightclub rendezvous.

He gave a novel and honest answer as to why he did it: "It wasn't the money…it seemed like it was a way for me to be nice to myself."[482] (10/19/2002)

This is an excellent example to illustrate that much of the FraSte taking place is not due to greed, but rather a belief of being entitled to share in the proceeds of the school treasure chest.

Connecticut

Bridgeport

An investigation was conducted to determine whether a long-time school electrician collected more than three months' pay while working at another job (allegedly doing union work). However, he has not been accused of any wrongdoing, but he has failed to produce doctor's documentation covering his absences.[483] (3/31/2002)

Clinton

The former finance director was convicted and jailed on multiple counts of larceny and forgery for embezzling $80,000 "to fund his passion for Porsches, racing and the good life."[484](11/29/1994)

His passion for pleasures ended with an 18-month prison term and $135,482 in restitution.

Middletown

The ex-treasurer of the Lawrence School PTA was accused of embezzling $14,000 (missing was fund raiser start-up money and cash not deposited).[485] (11/3/2000)

Hartford

Six trash haulers agreed in June to pay $1.1 million to settle charges that they rigged bids and illegally allocated business among themselves in serving local school districts.[486] (9/22/1993)

A custodian was charged with stealing more than $20,000 from school lunch revenues.[487] (11/30/1998).

Portland

The Attorney General is suing three trustees of a scholarship fund established for town students claiming that nearly half of the $375,000 was spent on their own families' educations.[488] (6/13/2002)

At least they were considerate enough to spend it on children.

Vernon

A payroll clerk was sentenced to two years in prison for embezzling $153,000. She forged 43 checks from the employee retirement account in order to gamble.[489] (4/5/2004)

District Of Columbia

Theft

A former D.C. school board member was convicted of four counts of theft and tax violations for stealing more than $20,000 from a retired teacher.[490] (10/26/1993)

Embezzlement

A school employee resigned after admitting she stole almost $44,000 over a two-year period. The money was stolen from a fund for the district's neediest children.[491] (4/1/1994)

Private School Fraud

The founder of a school for emotionally disturbed children was charged with wire and bank fraud and gross mismanagement. He is accused of inflating the number of students enrolled in the bills he sent to the district, and used school money to pay for four luxury cars. The school received an $825,000 contract with the DC schools even though the founder had no prior experience in education and no college degree.[492] (9/3/1997)

Breakfasts Missing

The DC public schools paid $1.7 million for school breakfasts and lunches from one vendor, but had no proof the meals were ever delivered.[493] (9/4/1998)

Union Embezzlement

The president of the 5,000 member teachers' union, who served since 1993, resigned because of financial irregularities in the union's records. Two other union officials were also asked to resign. They are suspected of having embezzled or improperly used $5 million. The audit maintains she had directed about $2 million to finance her shopping habits since 1996."[494] (10/30/2002)

Share-the-Loot

The union's chauffeur, who earned $90,000 per year, was accused by federal prosecutors of participating in a scheme to divert more than $1 million to himself and others. The documents revealed that the former union official engaged in a conspiracy with the goal of stealing millions of dollars from the Washington Teachers Union.[495] (1/28/2003)

He pleaded guilty and acknowledged that he had cashed $1.2 million of union checks during a 5 year span.[496] ((2/6/2003)

At least the lavish spending culture in D.C. was maintained. Yet, with all of the corruption in the district, key positions in the 13-employee internal watchdog office that scrutinizes how it spends and manages an annual budget of more than $1 billion are vacant.[497] The priority is obviously not on preventing and uncovering corruption.

Delaware

Brandywine School District

A special audit of the district found that a former employee and current employee were using school cafeterias to prepare and store food for their personal catering business.[498] (9/28/2000)

Another audit was conducted over several allegations including the theft of computers and stolen cash. In 1999, the district spent $50,000 to implement an Asset Tracking System that would provide an inventory of all assets. It also provided for updating when new equipment was purchased, existing equipment was moved to a new location, or when equipment became obsolete or unusable. Due to problems with the software updates did not take place (it's always the same excuse). A physical inventory was conducted in two schools. In one school 15 desktop computers, 3 laptops, 12 monitors, 9 printers, 2 TV's, 7 overhead projectors, 1 camcorder and 10 audio cassette players could not be found. However, some similar items not on the asset list were found.

In the other school, the discrepancy between the physical inventory and the district records "were too numerous to detail." One of the audit conclusions was that the ATS inventory was unreliable and that employees failed to properly record the issuance and return of property loaned to district employees.[499] (1/15/2002)

Florida

The Office of Program Policy Analysis and Government Accountability (OPPAGA) and the Auditor General jointly examine school district operations to determine whether they are using best practices adopted by the state's Commissioner of Education to evaluate programs, assess operations and performance, identify cost savings, and link financial planning and budgeting to district priorities.

The 2001 Legislature also enacted the Sharpening the Pencil Act to improve school district management and use of resources and to identify cost savings. The act identifies those districts scheduled to undergo review each year of the five-year cycle. It also provides that the Commissioner of Education adopt the standards for these reviews and establishes "meeting the best practices" as the goal for all Florida school districts.

These reviews are to identify ways to save funds, improve management, and increase efficiency and effectiveness. Private consulting firms selected by OPPAGA conduct the district performance reviews.

This is how state departments of education should function to help local districts.

Bartow

An elementary school principal pleaded guilty to stealing more than $30,000 from the school system and its PTA. She must pay $30,000 in restitution or face up to a year in jail. She was also sentenced to 10 years probation, ordered to pay $1,100 for the investigation, and will lose her teaching certificate.[500] (9/26/2002)

Some punishment! She will likely go to another state and get a job.

Broward County School District

A former elementary school principal who served in the district for 22 years stole $3,000 raised at Mother's Day and Father's Day breakfasts, took a TV from her school, and spent $700 of the school's money to buy a ceiling fan for her home.

The teachers are upset over a district request that they repay $4,147 in aftercare funds that the principal allegedly misspent on a faculty luncheon.[501] (5/7/2002)

Miami

Coaches Charged

Five school coaches at Southwest High School were charged with grand theft for awarding high grades to athletes for non-existent classes, and receiving $25,000 for teaching the non-existent classes.[502] (9/8/2000)

Free Catering

A business manager for a technical school had culinary-art employees cater her wedding.[503] (11/3/2001)

Miami-Dade County

Bloody Blood Collection

A lucrative blood-collection contract was awarded to a non-profit agency that had a close working relationship with key school district staffers. The contract was worth over $2 million (resale of the blood to hospitals), and the district received $32,000 for college scholarships and $40,000 in plaques, T-shirts, and trophies. "Officials at South Florida Blood Banks contend that the selection process was wired from the start to favor its rival."[504] (9/3/2002)

This is what must be called "blood money."

Inspector General Appointed

As a result of criminal misconduct and questionable financial dealings in the district, the school board created an inspector general's position that will have full access to records, workspaces, and authority to investigate allegations of fraud, waste and abuse.

According to a forensic audit corruption and mismanagement amount to $100 million. Among the findings:

1. Failure to monitor warranties or perform rudimentary maintenance.
2. There are curious documentary links that demonstrate a possible common interest showing lease purchase site acquisition methods that provide a bonanza to the fee owner.
3. Pandemic malfeasance and potential fraud that began before 1998 involving a $980 million capital bond's largess continue unabated despite cries for reform.
4. Identified a number of employees whose actions/inactions appear unacceptable.
5. Capital funds rolled over year-to-year appear frequently used for non-capital purposes.
6. Politics dictate awarding of contracts.

"In all our prior experience, we have never seen such complete lack of organization, communication, professionalism and waste."

Their surprise simply indicates that the extent of school corruption is not well known.

New Smyrna Beach

A former middle school bookkeeper was sentenced to 15 years' probation and ordered to pay back $71,000 she embezzled from money submitted by teachers for deposit into the account for student clubs, the yearbook, and fund-raisers.[505] (5/23/2002)

Georgia

Brunswick

The former head of the local Parent Teacher Student Association embezzled more than $2,100. Interestingly, "she had a prior arrest for embezzlement in another state, used aliases, and altered personal identification information."[506] (10/9/2002)

Gwinnett Public Schools

A special education teacher at Lanier Middle School was arrested on charges of stealing Ritalin from the school's clinic.[507] (10/30/2002)

Ware County School System

A former bookkeeper was arrested for embezzling $168,320 from high school student activities funds. The money had been collected as admission to high school football games and other sporting events as well as from sales of student yearbooks.[508] (4/12/2002)

Savannah-Chatham County

An 18-count indictment charged that a former board member, owner of an insurance company, conducted a kickback scheme that netted $22,500. "He used his position to undermine and frustrate established bid procedures."[509] (2/14/2001)

Hawaii

A joint Senate/House Committee was established to determine whether special education money was reaching such children. They reported that the special-education program was burdened with a host of bureaucratic and financial problems, some of which could merit criminal charges. As an example, one private provider overcharged the state for services of a therapist who charged for 127 hours of work in one day (the provider was obviously taught modern math).

A ten-count indictment was issued against a therapeutic aide for medical assistance fraud. She was accused of billing the state for $1,800 in services that were not provided. Officials claimed that this was the just the "tip of the iceberg."[510] (5/16/2002)

Idaho

State School Superintendent

More than $336,000 in unnecessary spending for the budget year ending June 1999 occurred because employee's actual travel expenses were not reviewed. As a result, employees paid more than necessary for airline tickets because the most economical airline was not used, charged personal side trips in rental cares, and rented expensive full-size cars rather than less expensive mid-size cars.[511] (9/7/2000)

Boise Education Association

The former executive director for 12 years was given a 14-year prison term for embezzling an estimated $400,000 from the Association.[512] (11/13/1982)

Illinois

Aurora

A former principal at Holy Angels Parish Elementary School embezzled over $11,000. She deposited checks donated to the school and government milk subsidies in her credit union account and then spent the money for personal use.[513] (3/15/2001)

Chicago

Since 1995, Chicago schools has had an Office of Inspector General whose mission is to "ensure integrity in the operations of the Chicago public Schools by conducting meaningful, accurate and through investigations into allegations of waste, fraud and mismanagement as well as recommending legislative and efficiency initiatives." Units include: Contracts Investigations, Employee Integrity, and Support.

The following are just two samples of what such reports from the Office of Inspector General reveal, and they only include some of the corrupt activities uncovered:

Annual Report 1999

Lost Employees

Fifty-two employees who had not reported for work for more than 60 days were still listed in their positions. Twenty-seven of then received $80,000 in health benefits. The study identified a pervasive lack of management relative to personnel records.

Free Money

A supplier took advantage of a data entry error to cash checks payable to another vendor. The vendor had no legitimate business with the district, but he managed to cash more than $100,000 in checks.

No Background Checks

A privatized service provider failed to conduct criminal background checks before placing employees in schools (it even sought employment referrals from a non-profit specializing in the placement of ex-convicts).

Overcharged

A vendor overcharged the district of at least $900,000.

Duplicate Charges

Vendor payments included duplicate charges amounting to $21,000.

Grade Changes

Acting on a tip, the Employee Integrity Unit investigated allegations of massive grade charges at a high school.

Engineer Ingenuity

A school engineer was renting space at a school to an outside agency for three years. He deposited the rent checks in his own account amounting to $28,000.

Some corruption activities are certainly creative.

Annual Report 2000-2001

No Refund

A high school substitute teacher failed to refund trip fees after a field trip was cancelled.

Embezzlement

A control coder issued ten checks to herself totaling $1,370 for fraudulent reimbursement. Money contained in sealed deposit bags was less than the amount written on the deposit slips. Forty-five discrepancies were traced to a particular cashier who claimed she simply made mistakes while counting the money.

A school clerk submitted fraudulent transportation reimbursement requests for herself and seven others in the amount of $3,500. None of the individuals had children in the school.

Payroll Fraud

A business manager received overtime pay to which she was not entitled.

Theft

An assistant principal stole a pager, laptop computers, and other computers, and a high school teacher sold drafting equipment kits to students and did not deposit the money.

What the two audits illustrate is that when there is a system in place to look for FraSte, it will be found because, like it or not, it exists in all school districts to some degree.

Bus Bribery

A former auditor who worked undercover for two years helped to crack one of the largest public-corruption cases in the district. Her former supervisor, the administrator of management services, was charged with accepting

$200,000 in bribes from bus contractors. It all began when she was offered a bribe to overlook an inflated bill from a school-bus contractor. [514](3/8/1989)

Employees Disciplined

As part of an on-going effort to rid the schools of corruption, forty-four district employees were disciplined or fired including 14 teachers and four principals.[515]

Video Theft

A security team videotaped a statistician as he loaded $50,000 worth of modems, mouse and keyboards into his car from a district warehouse.[516] (6/5/1996)

Chapter I for Convict

In a rather bazaar case, officials at one high school used $1 million in Chapter I state poverty funds to bankroll fund-raisers trying to free a convicted Puerto Rican independence movement terrorist. There was even an attempt to take over the school council, control the hiring of the principal, and take over the Chapter I funds. A legislative report concluded: "Instead of spending money to educate children, the funds' recipients included...criminal defense attorneys, kidnappers and attempted assassins." [517] (3/4, 3/5, 11/23, 1999)

There are no limits to how the Robin Hood Hogs use school funds, and the extent they will go to have a power base.

Parents Charged

Eighteen parents were among the more than two-dozen defendants charged with fraudulently obtaining more than $2.6 million in student financial aid. They were aided in their scheme by a tax preparation service that provided false income tax returns. [518](3/28/2001)

It's really nice to see how so many people can work together to commit corrupt acts.

Seized Sick Pay

As a result of a transition audit, a retired principal of Locke Elementary School was investigated for writing out checks totaling $66,000 without submitting the proper paperwork. A further investigation by the inspector general's office obtained detailed gaming records showing that she had lost $170,000 gambling.

The sick pay she had due amounting to $85,000 has been seized pending a complete investigation.[519] (1/27, 2003)

Training Luxury

A teacher-training academy spent dollars on everything from physical fitness, stereo equipment and architectural boat tours. The auditor general's office questioned some $330,000 in state funds, as well as, putting $616,000 of interest earned money from a state grant to 'unrestricted' accounts."[520] (4/9/2003)

Cook County

The township school treasurer stole $390,000 from Calumet Park and Riverdale school districts, two of the state's poorest, over a two-year period. Although sentenced to seven years in prison, he will not have to make any restitution. To add "insult to injury," under state law the school districts had to pay the cost of the legal fees not only for him, but also for the two trustees (a relative and a neighbor) who were responsible for supervising him. The legal bill will add another $100,000 to the loss.[521] (8/2/2002)

Of course, it's the taxpayers who pay the "restitution." It's fascinating how taxpayer money can be spent so foolishly, yet, there is nothing illegal involved.

East St. Louis

A former high school athletic director admitted to embezzling $90,000 from school coffers and having sex with female students. As part of a plea bargain, he agreed to cooperate with the FBI in a larger investigation of corruption within the district.[522] (11/5/1997) It's always worse than it first appears to be.

Huntley

A former school nurse pleaded guilty to stealing prescription drugs, intended for pupils. Over 300 Ritalin and Adderall pills were taken from locked medicine cabinets at four different schools.[523] (11/9/2002)

Iowa

Perry

In the course of two years, the district went from having a $1 million reserve to a debt of $318,000 and projected to grow to $500,000. This was the result of expenditures exceeding revenues by about $700,000 each of the past two years. The business manager knew of the dwindling cash, but he didn't feel comfortable circumventing the superintendent. She (the superintendent) claimed no knowledge of any deficit. The auditing firm also claimed it did not know about the financial problem.[524] (4/23/2002)

So what was the auditing firm auditing, the blackboard?

Warren Community School District

A battle over which town will get the first new elementary school since 1923 led to voting fraud. People whose addresses were nothing more than cornfields or long bulldozed barns had somehow registered for absentee ballots.[525] (6/12/1991)

Kansas

Hayesville

An 18-year old elected to the board of education came equipped with forensic eyes. He found that the superintendent of schools had questionable credit card charges of $11,000 for a single month.[526] (7/2001)

Topeka

A former Topeka man was sentenced to more then six years in prison and ordered to make $22.6 million in restitution for schemes to defraud state high school associations and injured students. He had established a phony life insurance program for students who suffer catastrophic injuries during school-sponsored activities.[527] (3/16/1999)

Kentucky

Kentucky has an office of the Auditor of Public Accounts and one of its responsibilities is to help those who manage public resources identify and implement good business practices. In 1987, it issued a report to the Kentucky Department of Education that recommended it to improve monitoring and technical assistance efforts pertaining to cash management programs in local school districts. In 1997 it embarked on a training initiative to improve fiscal responsibility and accountability in state and local government.

This is another good example of what all states should be doing to help schools.

State Dept of Education

Money Shuffle

An auditor charged the Department with violating state laws by transferring unspent money to various schools districts rather than returning it to state coffers. This practice enabled a former deputy commissioner to embezzle more than $500,000 by billing an education cooperative for more than 50 fictitious consultant-contractors. In addition, it went against state purchasing regulations in paying $300,000 to the National Faculty, a teacher training company.[528] (5/3/2000)

Shame, Shame

A former finance chief pleaded guilty to embezzling more than $500,000 over a four-year period. She created fictitious employees and ordered the Kentucky Education. Development Corp. to issue checks to those names. She then endorsed the checks and cashed them.[529] (4/11/2000)

Jefferson County

Two former school officials, a deputy superintendent and the chairman of the school board, admitted that they had stolen $322,485 from an educational foundation between 1994 and 1997. They received nine-month jail sentences and are paying restitution.[530] (7/20/2000)

Meade County School District

A bookkeeper was posthumously indicted for embezzling $932,981 over a period of nine years.[531] (3/25/1998)

West Point School

A secretary who served the only school in a town of 1,200 for 20 years was charged with embezzling more than $90,000 over three years. She wrote more than 100 checks from student account funds to herself, her boyfriend, and the local bank. The bank was also being sued because they allowed her to cash checks that were not made out to her. It took the auditors over three years to finally notice bookkeeping discrepancies.[532] (7/20/2000)

It's incredible how such a large sum could be embezzled in such a small school without anyone noticing that something was wrong. This and other FraSte incidents certainly indicate that regular or superficial audits cannot be trusted.

The auditor made an extremely profound statement that every policymaker, school board member, and school administrator should heed: "Just about any system that can be devised can be circumvented." That's why an aggressive, consistent, and forensic system needs to be in place to guard every school treasure chest.

Louisiana

New Orleans

Potpourri[533] (2/25/1998)

- An investigation surrounding the contract buyout of the superintendent uncovered allegations of missing money from candy sales, athletic events, and other student fun-raisers.
- A principal faces trial on charges of stealing more than $7,000 in student activity funds.
- Four substitute teachers and custodians were indicated for submitting more than $5,000 in false time sheets,
- An inventory of school equipment came up $2 million short. It's hard to believe that such a corrupt school system had an inventory system in place that could actually detect such a loss.

Kind to Father

A janitor, the father of the superintendent, earned $85,144 in overtime in two-and-a-half years. The auditor claimed the pay was "questionable given the amount of hours paid per day, the length of time worked, and his admission he submitted inaccurate time sheets."[534] (6/12/2002)

Stolen Property

A newspaper investigation turned up over $669,000 in lost or stolen property during the 1996-97 school year. Among the missing items were three pianos, 10 air conditioners and two tubas.[535] (3/8/1998)

A newspaper can uncover missing equipment of no small amount; yet, the school district either didn't care or simply didn't know.

Unlicensed Contractor

A company that was awarded contracts to repair three schools assured school officials it had proper licenses and financial backing, and it boasted of renovating the Superdome roof. None of these claims proved to be true and the company was taken off the job. However, before it was fired, the company was paid $4 million for repairs that insurers say should have cost half as much. The board will end up paying over $3 million more to fix the schools which still haven't been fully repaired.[536] (8/11/2002)

Legalized Rip-off?

A newly established consulting company started by a Loyola University law school professor after the 2000 hail storm made millions of dollars in an "unusual array of contracts" to manage an $18.5 million hail damage insurance claim. Interestingly, the company had no experience in claims adjusting or construction management and had listed a dorm room as its office.

It's an interesting story of charges and counter-charges and legalized mumbo-jumbo. Whether the entire convoluted process was legal or not has not been resolved. What is evident is that few of the roofs damaged by the storm have been repaired, the head of the insurance department has resigned, and the state auditor is investigating the $70 million dollar school insurance department.[537] (9/22/2002)

Payroll Scam

Employees pleaded guilty to stealing more than $70,000 by issuing fraudulent checks. According to the State Auditor, employees have cashed an estimated $3 million in paychecks sent out either in error or with criminal intent.[538] (9/1/2004)

More Indictments

A federal grand jury indicted 11 more people in the widening corruption probe including teachers, secretaries, credit union employees and representatives of two insurance companies.[539] (1/5/2005)

The police superintendent made a profound statement concerning the corruption probe: "Corruption in the school system is like eating an elephant, we just took the first bite."

He probably should have indicated that there is more than one elephant in the system.

Maryland

Hampstead

The elementary school PTA treasurer, a banker, admitted to embezzling over $64,000; it is the largest such theft from a PTA fund. The thefts began only a few months after he became treasurer and involved 41 unexplained withdrawals that were deposited in his personal account. The money was raised for a new playground and wireless computers. Considering that the school has 600 students and the town only has a population of 5,000, the amount involved is staggering. He agreed to repay $56,000.[540] (1/30/2003)

Prince George's County

The chief of the accounts payable department pleaded guilty to embezzling more than $1.1 million between 1981-1993. He was sentenced to five years in prison.[541] (3/4/1994)

Massachusetts

MTA

A former director of the Massachusetts Teachers Association has been charged with stealing $802,000 from the union treasury. Union officials claimed that the alleged plot was so intricate that even standard auditing procedures could not uncover the theft.[542] (4/9/2003)

Here is another example why routine audits are not effective in uncovering FraSte. Forensic auditing should be required, if not yearly, at least every other year.

Everett

The superintendent tapped a $218,000 "slush fund" of special education money to pay for parades ($24,000) chamber of commerce breakfasts, newspaper ads ($53,000) and dinners for teachers. The superintendent is also awaiting trial on charges of receiving stolen school air conditioners.[543] (4/8/2005)

Lunenberg

The district attorney is investigating the disappearance of a substantial amount of money. The problem was discovered during a review of finances and it went back several years. "I hope the district will be able to explain this in a satisfactory way."[544] (1/30/2003)

New Bedford

A former William H. Taylor elementary school principal was indicted for stealing more than $40,000 between 1992-1996 from student fund-raisers (craft fairs, candy sales and other fund-raisers). She pleaded guilty to embezzling $20,000 in order to finance a gambling habit. What was interesting about this case is that parents complained to the Board of Education that something was wrong and an investigation by the school district found nothing wrong.[545] (1/13/2000)

Southern Regional School District

Travel Expenditures

Some employees are under investigation after a recent audit revealed questionable travel expenditures including lobster dinners, alcoholic beverages and even a Christmas tree. Additionally, five employees spent almost $3,000 each at a busing conference.[546] (9/29/2000)

Embezzlement

An assistant superintendent who managed the finances for the Bay Path Regional Vocational Technical School in Charlton was convicted of embezzling $5.5 million over seven years. He used the money to buy 40 thoroughbred racing horses.[547] (7/2001)

He probably planned to use the horses for pupil transportation.

Michigan

A rash of embezzlement cases and allegations has plagued school districts. What is most shocking is that regular audits and monitoring systems did not prevent the frauds. "Unscrupulous school employees have capitalized on loopholes and a lack of controls." To make matters worse, "while school boards play a major role in the oversight of schools, elected board members often lack the expertise to spot problems in audits and financial reports."

The article also made an important observation: "Sometimes it's not just the district personnel, sometimes it's the culture. It's a culture that does not put children first, a culture that's more concerned about power and control."[548] (10/2/2002)

Detroit

Embezzlement

- Audits of 30 schools covering 1996-1999 found up to $860,000 was missing.[549] (12/6/2000)
- A former senior accountant since 1982 was charged with 145 counts of uttering and publishing false documents involving a $1.28 million embezzlement scheme. He approved checks from an emergency-expenditure fund to two business owned by members of his family.[550] (4/8/1992)
- An elementary school principal was arraigned on charges that he embezzled money from the student activity funds totaling $7,381. School bookkeepers at three other schools also pleaded guilty to embezzlement.[551] (1/29/2002)

Embezzlements[552] (4/25/2001)

The following cases were uncovered by audits, the first in 12 years, and hundreds of thousands of dollars were found missing or misspent. There are still 200 schools to be audited.

- A high school principal reimbursed himself for $95,000 over a two-year period for personal items ranging from gasoline to a trip to Italy for his son.

- A former bookkeeper for Central High School was charged with embezzling. The warrant was based on an audit that found $27,278 missing.
- A former bookkeeper at Finney High School was found guilty of embezzlement and was ordered to repay $32,271 in restitution.
- A former bookkeeper at Redford High School pleaded guilty to forgery and embezzlement amounting to $16,400.
- A former bookkeeper at Kosciusko Elementary School was charged with forgery and embezzlement amounting to $20,000.
- Reimbursements to a former principal at Henry Ford High School were questioned amounting to $96,000 that included $10,000 for personal expenses and $3,700 for alcohol. No receipts were provided for $50,000 of reimbursement.

After 12 years, it should have come as no surprise that FraSte was alive and well. The lack of audits was clear evidence to potential corruptors that no one really cared about corruption.

Milk Price Fixing

What really "takes-the-cake" is the arrogance displayed by school officials when the district commits an illegal act and the cost is passed on directly to the taxpayers. Fifteen years ago, a milk supplier sued the school board for price fixing. A verdict granted the supplier an $11 million award. It was a former school board president and former contract officer who concocted the price fixing. As a result, a direct tax assessment was levied on the taxpayers to cover the cost of the judgment without any advance notice. State law allows school districts to pass the costs of legal judgments on to the taxpayers.

The poor taxpayers need to be pitied because a school official brazenly announced: "In the future, if we have more judgments, we'll levy." To make matters worse, audits of 50 schools found $1.5 million missing or misspent and two more school officials were convicted of criminal wrongdoing.[553] (7/20/2001)

Principal's Piggybank

A report also charged a principal with using the school's money to "boost his personal finances and furnish his home with electronics." There were also questionable expenses totaling over $92,000 paid to vendors who reportedly were his friends. The principal claimed he was following the direction of prior supervisors and didn't believe he did anything wrong. His attorney questioned whether "he had been appropriately trained."[554] (12/18/2001)

What the lawyer is saying is that no "appropriate training" is needed to commit FraSte, it's only required to be honest. It's doubtful if a jury would agree.

Payroll Fraud

A principal and five teachers each received $10,000 for fraudulent work hours in 1996-1997. "We were given that (the pay) to keep us quiet about what we were really embezzling—hundreds of thousands of dollars in state-aid money." However, The Attorney General's Office declined to press criminal charges because there were no findings of criminality.[555] (12/19/2001).

Is it any wonder why the culture of corruption exists in Education America?

Auditor Hired

A senior staff-level auditor general has been hired to oversee spending after a year-end financial review found irregularities in the use of purchasing cards. In addition, an outside accounting firm will conduct random audits of individual school buildings. Originally, audits were to have been conducted every two years, but they were not conducted "despite finding millions of dollars missing or misspent in the first reviews of high schools two years ago."[556] (12/5/2002)

The children are betrayed and the taxpayers be damned!

Lack of Controls

The purchasing cards of all but a few of the district's high-level administrators were revoked after a review found questionable expenditures and a lack of documentation. This action came after school officials moved to prosecute, fire or discipline several school-level administrators accused of misspending more than $2 million in district money.[557] (12/6/2002)

Tech Wreck[558] (11/15/2002)

- Five schools paid a vendor $36,300 for computer equipment and office furniture. The only problem was that the equipment was never delivered.
- A similar problem was found at an elementary school where $20,530 was paid for computer equipment, installation and training, but the auditor could not confirm delivery.

- An audit of a high school found $31,330 was fraudulently transferred from the checking account to pay cellular phone companies.

And on and on it goes and where it stops, nobody knows.

East Detroit

The district's assistant superintendent for business services was bribed to keep quiet about inflated bids on school construction projects. He was also charged with diverting $438,000 to his personal checking account. His attorney claimed: "He is a bit player in a years-long swindle of the district."[559] (9/14/2001)

Who are the rest of the players?

It Never Stops[560] (6/20/2002)

A contractor who oversaw the district's $28 million bond program and the former maintenance director were named as unindicted co-conspirators in the scheme. The money that was pilfered resulted in budget shortages that required teacher layoffs and other cuts in order to make up for the loss.

The corruption probe is still unfolding, but what is very interesting is that it was two board members who were responsible for uncovering the frauds; yet, they were criticized by other board members for being on a "witch hunt."

When other board members consider exposing corruption as a witch-hunt, it indicates that the culture of corruption is ingrained in the system and is considered acceptable and tolerable.

False Invoices

In a related development, a former Detroit businessman admitted to submitting as much as $150,000 in false, inflated invoices to repair the vehicles of district officials and others between 1996 and 1999. The former school board president also had his private car repaired at school expense.[561] (8/13/2001)

Bribed Board Member

A current and former member of the East Detroit school board pleaded guilty to accepting more than $69,000 in money and goods in exchange for steering business to a contractor overseeing a $28 million bond project.[562] (6/20/2002)

Ionia Intermediate School District

The former PTO treasurer of a Belding elementary school pleaded guilty to embezzlement amounting to over $13,000. She received a sentence of probation and house arrest.[563] (5/9/2001)

Wayne Westland School District

The PTO of Edison Elementary School was missing $22,000. This is the third time police have investigated allegations of embezzlement in the district.[564] (5/3/2001)

Pontiac School System

A former Central High School principal, her sister, and a teacher, who was also bookkeeper for the student activities fund, were charged with embezzling more than $50,000 from the activities fund.[565] (10/13/2001)

River Rouge School District

Four top administrators have been suspended for alleging bilking the system out of $1 million. Although the Michigan State Police and state treasury officials were notified five months ago of financial irregularities, they did not respond. According to an attorney hired by the board to investigate the irregularities, "We haven't seen any oversight from those offices."[566] (10/8/2002)

When investigative bodies do not follow through on alleged corruption, it becomes clear that the entire system is crippled by complacency.

Among the irregularities were hundreds of thousands of dollars in contracts awarded without competitive bidding or school board approval, the superintendent was paid about $110,000 more than the board authorized, 398 hockey sticks were bought but the coaches received only 50, and the superintendent's son was paid a full time salary for work done in the city at a time when he was away at college. Interestingly, auditors apparently did not check transactions to find out if they complied with district policies like competitive bidding requirements.[567] (10/9/2002).

If they didn't audit such obvious audible items, what were the auditors auditing—paper clips? Faulty and incompetent auditing seems to be rather common.

Minnesota

Minnesota has an Office of the State Auditor that among its responsibilities conducts special investigations.

St. Charles School District

A special investigation of the School Age Child Care Program operated by Independent School district #858 resulted in criminal charges against the SACC Coordinator. A minimum of $30,479 was misappropriated from SACC funds.[568] (11/17/1998)

MISSISSIPPI

The Investigative Division of the State Office of The State Auditor conducts audits of schools and some examples follow:

State Auditor Report (7/31/2000)

In 2000, it reported that it had issued 18 demands for over $1.2 million of which only $677,000 was recovered.

Meridian Public Schools

A middle school secretary was charged with embezzling $1,900 and the case was transmitted to the Attorney General.

Yazoo City Municipal Schools

The athletic director was charged with embezzling over $32,000 and the case was transmitted to the Attorney General on 5/3/2000. On July 7, he entered into a Pre-Trial Intervention Program and was required to repay the embezzled amount plus investigative costs of $10,000.

State Auditor Report (7/31/1999)

Columbus Municipal Schools

A bookkeeper embezzled over $90,000 and the case was transmitted to the Office of the Attorney General. She was sentenced in February 1999 to ten years to be suspended upon satisfactory completion of one year intensive supervised house arrest and to repay $50,000 plus a $10,000 fine.

Jefferson County School

A former accounts payable clerk embezzled over $2,000. This amount plus interest and investigative costs were repaid.

Noxubee County Schools

A principal embezzled over $7,000 and the case was transmitted to the Attorney General on 12/3/1998. He was sentenced to six years, but was recommended for Intensive Supervision House Arrest for one year and after successful completion to a post-release program for five years. He was also required to repay the embezzled amount plus a fine of $500.

State Auditor Report, 7/31/1998

Clinton Public Schools

A junior high school bookkeeper was charged with embezzling $28,852.33 and the case was transmitted to the Attorney General on 4/15/98. She was given a five year suspended sentence in June 1999 and required to repay the embezzled amount.

Tallahatchie County School District

A veteran superintendent was indicted on 81 counts of conspiracy and 35 counts of embezzlement amounting to $238,000.[569] (9/4/1998)

Missouri

Statewide

The Federal Trade Commission and the Missouri attorney general's office reached agreement with three school-transportation companies accused of forming a joint venture to avoid competition[570] (9/22/1993)

Independence

A bookkeeper with 22 years of service was charged with 24 counts of felony stealing and three counts of misdemeanor stealing involving $90,000 over a period of six years. She accomplished the embezzlement by creating fictitious invoices, issued checks to the false companies, and deposited the money into a family account. The scheme was uncovered when an employee found a computer generated invoice in a pile of documents printed on the office computer.571 (7/3/1998)

Kansas City

Three school bus companies agreed to dissolve a joint venture created to divide up the district they would service.572 (9/22/1993)

New Jersey

Statewide

Roofing Scams

An investigation of 23 districts revealed rip-offs of over $10 million in roofing contracts. One common abuse was for a consultant to design the specifications with high-cost materials available from only one contractor who would submit a highly inflated bill, and the consultant would then get a kickback. The state does not have adequate safeguards in place to prevent unscrupulous contractors from ripping off taxpayers. It's estimated that over $12 billion was involved in roof scams.573 (9/20/2000)

Special Education Corruption

Owners of six private special education schools were indicted on charges that they stole $3.66 million from taxpayers by giving eight of their relatives and friends high-paying jobs (up to $766,000) that did not require them to work. Fifty school districts contribute 100 percent of their budget by paying $30,000 per pupil.574 (8/30/2002)

Newark

A former mayor was charged with conspiracy, bribery, and fraud for bilking the Irvington, NY school district for work his company did not perform. Two Irvington school board members who were part of the scam received thousands of dollars in kickbacks.575 (8/2/2000)

Sussex County

A bus transportation contractor was accused of fatally shooting a rival bus contractor after luring him to Florida with bogus promises of a bus deal. He is charged with dumping the body from his speedboat into the Atlantic Ocean more than a dozen miles from shore.[576] (11/27/1996)

There is no limit to what the hogs will do, even murder, when it comes to FraSte.

Woodbridge Township School District

A former superintendent was charged with official misconduct, bribery in official matters, and compensation for past official behavior. He solicited a $3,000 bribe from a Philadelphia consulting company hired to find the best premiums and insurance for district workers. The superintendent, who had been an employee of the school district for nearly three decades, was suspended with pay after being arrested.[577] (5/15/2002)

Wyckoff

The Internal Revenue Service raided the school offices in this affluent town looking for money laundering, corruption and budget irregularities. Among the budget irregularities were false invoices and checks being issued to six fictitious companies. The former business manager pleaded guilty to helping embezzle $1.7 million.[578] (11/2000)

New Mexico

New Mexico has an Office of the State Auditor that performs special school audits.

Taos Municipal School District No. 1

The business manager misappropriated $11,236. Checks were made payable to him for which there was no documentation or other proof these monies were expended on the District's behalf. The audit only covered this particular incident. "Had an audit of the districts financial statements been made, other matters might have come to our attention that would have been reported to you."[579] (8/22/1996)

Why wasn't an audit made of the financial statements? It may have been too embarrassing.

Gasden

An elementary school employee was placed on leave after the principal discovered money missing from a school fundraiser. "Exactly how much money it is, we don't really know yet, but it's a substantial sum. The bookkeeping system there was in such disarray that we have to conduct the audit."[580] (3/18/2000)

Nevada

Lake Tahoe School District

A 12-year accounting employee pleaded guilty to embezzling $102,000 over a 3-year period. She embezzled the money to solve personal financial problems. "It was done very well, in a very clever manner...because she was basically on her own."[581] (4/28/1998)

Washoe County School District

A former employee was arrested for embezzling $75,000 from the Partners in Education Program that accepts cash and donations from private businesses. She admitted embezzling the funds by writing numerous checks to herself or to cash and forging the second required signature on each check. She embezzled about $500 per week to fund a gambling habit.[582] (8/24/2000)

Another employee was charged of bilking the district out of nearly $40,000 to purchase outdoor recreation equipment using false invoices.

A former high school bookkeeper is serving a 9-month jail sentence for embezzling $62,357 from student activity accounts.[583] (10/6/2000)

New York

New York City

New York City is one of a handful of cities that has its own investigative office to ferret out fraud and corruption. There are about 42 investigators and 9 lawyers assigned to the office that was created after a 1988 commission was established to look into charges of corruption in the school system. Sixteen months later, the panel charged that it found "serious corruption and impropriety almost wherever we looked."

The office uncovered some rather interesting situations:

- Thirty-eight employees in the division of school safety had been illegally collecting both a pension and a salary for 10 years or more at a cost of about $3 million.
- The division's deputy executive director was faulted for putting a dozen of his relatives on the payroll.
- A custodian was photographed lounging on his boat during his workday.
- Flight logs showed a custodian was working as a pilot on district time.
- Records of telephone calls revealed a custodian ran a law practice from his school office.
- A search of a school's basement turned up shot-up paper targets and hundreds of spent rounds of ammunition confirming suspicions that a custodian had set up a firing range.[584] (11/25/1992)

Officials claimed to have established controls in 1988 to stem abuses in the custodial system, obviously, the reforms failed. The problem is that the custodians function as "quasi-independent contractors" administering their own annual budget for supplies, equipment, and salaries. Unlike contractors, they have employment protection as both union members and board employees. Such a system violates every fundamental principle of accounting for managing government funds.

School Aid Fraud

A vice-president of a trade school earning $1.5 million from 1983 to 1987 pleaded guilty to creating false high school diplomas for students so that they could get federal grants and loans. The amount involved was $25 million.[585] (3/15/1989)

Asbestos Fraud

An investigation of the asbestos-management program revealed that asbestos was found in an area of a school certified as asbestos-free, Many false and inaccurate inspection reports have been discovered and allegations of fraud and conflict of interest are being investigated.[586] (9/29/1993)

Corruptors have no regard even for the safety of children and employees. Nothing counts except their greed.

Bribery

An investigation of the system's leasing and maintenance departments uncovered evidence of $4.6 million in fraud and $260,000 in bribes. Four former board of education employees and 14 others (lawyers and contractors) were charged with felonies. Among those arraigned was the former deputy counsel who received $150,000 in bribes. Ironically, the position was created largely to clean up fraud and corruption (he did clean it up for himself).

These charges come five years after a racketeering scandal led the state legislature to strip the district's school-facilities division of its power to build new schools, but the current charges relate to fraud before 1989.[587] (6/1/1994)

Sex Abuse

Edward Stancik, who directed the Special Investigations Office at the time, was surprised by the sheer number of sex-abuse complaints that poured into his office.[588] (9/29/1993)

Perhaps more interesting—in the light of the Catholic church child sex-abuse scandal in 2002—is that a 1994 investigation found that teachers were sometimes transferred to other schools after being disciplined for child sexual abuse, but their disciplinary files were not made available to their new principals. The report admitted that the practice "allowed known child abusers to continue within the system, moving from victim to victim."[589] (10/25/1995)

Apparently, the children are pawns to be used at the pleasure of child abusers and no one cares. It's sickening!

The numerous cases of sex abuse in schools have not been included in this book because it's a subject for another book.

Lion Hearted

Four school Construction Authority supervisors were charged with stealing lion statues worth $60,000. The bazaar nature of this case is that one of the supervisors put 2 of the statutes on his front lawn, but the others have not been found.

Three others were accused of squeezing contractors for $35,800 in bribes.[590] (4/3/2002)

CPR Credit Fraud

A physical education teacher was accused of selling CPR and first-aid certificates to high school coaches so that they would not have to take the two-day course. He received 293 checks and money orders totaling $17,361.[591] (5/21/1998)

Produce Bids Rigged

Officers of a Long Island food distribution company pleaded guilty to rigging bids on millions of dollars of produce contracts awarded by the City.[592] (3/15/2001)

Frozen Food Bids Rigged

Five executives and three food companies pleaded guilty to rigging bids on $126 million dollars of frozen food contracts from 1996-1999. The rigging schemes included bribes and kickbacks. The Department of Justice release indicated "The conspirators in these and related cases succeeded in eliminating all meaningful competition for frozen food contracts."

The conspirators held secret meetings where they agreed to carve up future bids to supply and deliver frozen food to the schools.

To date, the Department's investigation of bid rigging, bribery, fraud, and tax-related offenses in the food distribution industry has resulted in charging 30 individuals and 14 food companies with riggings bids for the supply and delivery of food to various public and private customers in the New York metropolitan area.[593] (5/2/2001)

It's rather astonishing to find how widespread FraSte extends its tentacles.

Cadillac Wash

Indictments were issued against a contractor and 18 custodians for allegedly rigging bids and accepting kickbacks for a window washing contracts. The custodians received $60,000 in bribes. There is nothing new about this type of rip-off that goes back to 1992. According to the attorney general, "everything here was ripe for fraud." The Chancellor also admitted the system is broke and vowed to make it foolproof.[594] (2/11/2002) The only "foolproof" system in New York City is rampant, persistent, blatant, and shameless corruption.

Personal Touch

The head of the Office of Parent and Community Partnerships, a top aid of the Chancellor, was fined $8,000 for forcing underlings to work for her pet charities and run her errands while on the job. They were even paid overtime for the projects. Yet, she was still working for the board earning $144,000 a year[595] (7/31/2002)

Bogus Stuff

School employees have been caught for allegedly stealing thousands of dollars by filing bogus invoices and time sheets. Others have been found who have had drug and criminal convictions."[596] (1/13/2003)

Computer Contract Ripoff

Five people, including a former school superintendent and a millionaire developer, pleaded guilty to fraud charges involving $6 million of contracts to install computer labs between 1996 and 1998. Those involved distributed $3 million in kickbacks. Falsifying documents and obtaining insider information accomplished the scam. By agreeing to pay restitution, all were spared jail time. The scam was uncovered when a legitimate low-bidder complained.[597] (10/9/2002)

Bridgehampton Union Free School District

A former school treasurer was charged with embezzling $80,000 and she pleaded guilty to grand larceny.[598] (12/18/1996)

Bronx Community School District

A report describes the district as a patronage mill in which jobs have been sold for cash or awarded for political favors. The Chancellor subsequently suspended the entire school board.[599] (9/29/1993)

Kickbacks

A former supervisor of an early childhood development program for an impoverished Bronx school district pleaded guilty to using a kickback scheme to embezzle thousands of dollars in school funds.[600] (3/4/1995)

Brooklyn PS 128

The Chancellor ordered the removal of the principal who was indicted for using school funds to build a gym for himself.[601] (4/11/1995)

Forgery

A custodian was charged with stealing $8,500 by forging 185 invoices and receipts for the purchase of supplies over a period of 3 years.[602] (1/13/2003)

Orchard School District

The superintendent was placed on paid leave amid allegations of misuse of credit cards and cell phone. Since September more than 30 calls to escort services and six chat lines were made. The board did not know he had a credit card.[603] (4/13/2005)

William Floyd School District

The superintendent was charged with stealing more than $750,000 by simply writing checks to himself.[604] (/9/1/2004)

Roslyn School District

The superintendent and senior administrator were charged with stealing more than $1 million. The senior administrator allegedly used the funds to purchase four homes, a Lexus and other luxury items. The superintendent, one of the highest paid on Long Island, used the money for luxury purchases, as well as, granting his roommate's company more than $800,000 in no-bid contracts. There are still $8 million of undocumented expenses to review.

The district has sued the auditing firm for $12 million claiming the firm failed to provide adequate safeguards.[605] (2/2/2005)

It always gets worse as the shovel unearths more. "Although an audit earlier this year found that $11.2 million allegedly had been pilfered between 1996-2004, the four charged are accused of stealing slightly less than $7 million."[606]

Can the taxpayers sue the school district for also failing to provide adequate safeguards?

North Carolina

Durham

The parent of a student was called by his English teacher informing her that her son had not completed all his work; yet, the parent had been told repeatedly that her son was doing fine. It seems that his failing grades were changed to keep him eligible for the school's football team. She warned other parents about "grade-tampering, grade-changing, grade-fixing, and an institutional conspiracy to cover up willful and malicious acts of unethical and immoral conduct."[607] (9/29/2000)

Rockwell Elementary School

A secretary who worked at the school for over four years was charged with stealing more than $20,000. Discrepancies in a deposit slip tipped off the bank officials who notified the school principal.[608] (11/5/1999).

She pleaded guilty and received suspended prison sentence and five years probation. In addition she was ordered to pay the school district $27,000.[609] (4/6/2000)

Ohio

Statewide

A state audit of a virtual charter school showed the it overcharged the state by $1.65 million for teaching hours it could not substantiate, and that $500,000 worth of computer equipment given to students who left the program was not recovered. A former principal was running the school.[610] (2/7/2002)

Cleveland

A voucher school had bilked the state out of more than $85,000 by reporting enrollments double the school's actual enrollment.[611] (March 2000)

Lebanon

A school principal in Clermont County lost his job after being sentenced on a theft charge for double billing; he claimed it was a bookkeeping error. This was the second incident for the principal who double-billed in a prior district.[612] (10/13/1999)

Twinsburg City Schools

The former superintendent was charged on 12 criminal counts alleging theft in office, insurance fraud, forgery and perjury. In order to avoid a possible 20-year prison term, he agreed to a plea deal that will cost $49,000 in restitution.[613] (8/2/2002)

Wayne Trace School District

A 14-year school board member who was chief executive officer of a bank was charged with embezzling at least $40 million; the amount included $1 million of school funds. Fortunately, the money was restored to the school district through the FDIC and state emergency funds.[614] (6/12/2002)

It's still taxpayer money that provided the bailout. The poor taxpayer always pays the FraSte bills.

Nardonia Hills School District

A school employee who was being investigated for using district credit cards to buy personal items resigned. The incidents occurred over four years during which time there were two other business managers.[615] (1/8/2003)

Oklahoma

Statewide

The Office of the State Auditor and Inspector does audits of school districts.

Oaks Mission School District

The former superintendent was indicted by a grand jury on two counts of embezzlement and one count of obtaining money by false pretense. He surrendered his certificate that the State Board revoked.[616] (4/10/1991)

Catoosa School District

The former finance director was alleged to have embezzled over $125,000 from March 1998 to March 2000. She resigned her post last July after auditors raised questions about checks deposited at the Tulsa Teachers Credit Union. On March 15, she was indicted on federal charges.[617] (2/22/2001)

Dahlonegah School District

Charges were filed against two members of the board including embezzlement, payment of false claims and multiple violations of the Open Meetings Act. Both were charged with authorizing over payment of some $12,214 in claims made against the school board members over a four-year period. According to the Assistant District Attorney, "I expect to file additional charges against other individuals in connection with wrongdoing."[618] (1/9/1998)

Geronimo Public School

Among a number of fund irregularities found in an investigatory audit was that interest from all activity fund accounts was deposited in a miscellaneous account rather than being disbursed to the appropriate sub-account from which the interest was derived. The interest money was used to pay for faculty dinners and flowers for individuals.[619] (7/1/1992-6/30/1997)

Lane Elementary School

One of several funding discrepancies found during a special audit was a technology grant that was written by the Superintendent's spouse who was also employed as a school librarian. It was claimed that the work was performed during non-working hours, but the audit noted that there were no withholding taxes paid nor did the school prepare an IRS Form 1099.

The audit also found that, although the board was previously alerted to internal control problems involving the Activity Fund and related accounts, the district continued to disregard State Rules and Regulations. It was found that several thousands of dollars of General Fund monies were transferred to the Activity Fund for petty cash expenditures during the fiscal year 1998-1999. State law prohibits schools from having in excess of two hundred dollars in petty cash accounts and limits the total expenditures to $2,000.[620] (7/1/1997-6/30/1999)

Boards expect employees to adhere to rules and regulations, but apparently they are exempt. Shame on them!

Mustang Public School

An investigatory audit of the high school cafeteria program involving collections and deposits revealed they did not always match. In examining a series of collections amounting to $155,465.00, only $119,060 was deposited leaving a shortfall of over $36,000. It was also found that other cash collections were not shown on deposit slips, but there was an increase of a like amount in the checks deposited. Further investigation revealed that checks for night school fees were substituted for the cash. A further review of 43 cash sheets did not agree with the totals listed on the deposit tickets. The report concluded: "The former treasurer embezzled $27,956."[621] (7/1/1996-3/31/1999)

Oregon

Coos Bay School District 9

An unknown perpetrator embezzled a Blossom Gulch Elementary school fund amounting to $10,000. The money had been raised over a period of three years for new playground equipment.[622] (10/17/2001)

Pennsylvania

Statewide

Fifty-five school districts have been defrauded of at least $71 million in a "Ponzi Scheme" perpetrated by a financial adviser who was entrusted with proceeds of municipal bond issues. The adviser once worked as a consultant to the state education department.[623] (11/12/1997)

A settlement was reached with four companies convicted of rigging bids to sell roofing to three school districts.[624] (9/22/1993)

Morrisville School District

Einstein Academy, started in 2001 as an independent virtual school, is being accused of misappropriation of public funds, reckless spending, extortion, failure to provide special education services, and blatant disregard for state regulations. The Academy could only account for 86 out of 1,232 computers sent to students who later left the school, and the parent company overcharged the school by $300,000.

According to the superintendent, "We told them what to do in order to survive and they just wouldn't do it." During the 2001-2002 school year, the state funded the Academy with $9 million of taxpayer dollars

There are a variety of legal suits and counter-suits, but the founders are not discouraged because they have started another Christian online school.[625] (8/26/2002)

After this fiasco, how could they possibly be considered for another charter school?

New Hope-Solebury School District

A California couple has pleaded guilty to using trickery and blackmail to defraud the district out of $2 million. They were blackmailing the former business manager into paying them money for pens that were never delivered.

They had tricked the official into improperly accepting a small gift in return for an order of pens and then threatening her with exposure unless she sent them money using bogus invoices.[626] (5/2/1990)

Philadelphia

The city received over $20 million in extra state funds by claiming 14,000 days of attendance for students that never attended school. School officials claim it was a matter of technical errors.[627] (March 2000)

Redbank Valley Area School District

The superintendent of schools was charged with theft of two school computers that were meant to replace equipment damaged in a flood. He had previously been accused of improper spending of district funds.[628] (1/24/1998)

Slippery Rock

A former middle school principal was charged with forgery and theft involving $6,632 from students' magazine sales to pay gambling debts and carry on an extramarital affair. He has agreed to repay the district.[629] (11/12/2002)

Rhode Island

Statewide

A Finance Analysis Model for Education, known as In$ite™, is a software program designed as an easy-to-understand information and finance reporting system for school district expenditures.

The State Legislature in collaboration with the Rhode Island Department of Education has established a more detailed and informative system of reporting education expenditures for all school districts.

In$ite™ includes all sources of funding (federal and state grants, town/city general revenue funds, state aid, and other specialized funds that each district may receive) to analyze each district's expenditures.

With the millions of dollars being spent to educate our young people, it makes sense that decision-making data be available to district leaders, school leaders, and state leaders regarding where our resource dollars are being spent. In$ite™ is a system tool that helps greatly in this effort, as it provides consistent ways to review expenditures for every school district and in the near future for every school.

With this type of software available, why aren't all boards using it to track their dollars?

Providence

The school department overpaid hundreds of thousands of dollars for a rigged building lease, a former mob haunt before it was rented to the city for $1.2 million. A school official, testifying in the trial of the Mayor being charged with racketeering, bribery, conspiracy, money laundering and mail fraud, stated that the department paid nearly twice as much for what he expected.[630] (5/7/2002)

South Carolina

Statewide

South Carolina is also using Coopers and Lybrand's Finance Analysis Model (In$ite), and is currently in its second year of gathering and reporting school-level data. This data program was strongly supported by the state Chamber of Commerce, the state School Board's Association, and the Chamber's Business Center for Excellence in Education. As a top-down education reform, however, it did not receive a warm welcome from school administrators.

At present the long-term prognosis for In$ite is unclear as it continues to serve as fiscal performance accountability measure that is largely ignored by taxpayers, parents, politicians, and practicing educators.

Clearly, accountability is not considered necessary or appropriate. Remember, there is no law against being incompetent or stupid.

Sumter

This case that was previously cited about the Assistant Superintendent who masterminded one of biggest cases of public corruption ever prosecuted in the state had some interesting twists to it.

The accountant charged in connection with the case is suing the district claiming that officials were negligent because they did not have better control over their finances, and gave too much control to the former assistant superintendent and finance director.[631] (6/9/2000)

What must be added is that "for many years auditors had given the school district favorable scores on their yearly review of its finances."[632] (6/25/1998)

How could the auditors have missed millions of dollars that were stolen? What this demonstrates is that auditors either are not interested in looking for fraud or do not know how to look for fraud.

Tennessee

Knoxville

The former treasurer of Vine Middle Magnet School PTA was charged with taking more than $6,000 raised by students for yearbooks. As a result, the yearbook could not be published.[633] (10/23/2002)

Embezzlement also occurred at the Carter Elementary School PTA. The presidents of the county and state PTA are concerned about what the theft of $10,000 will do to their organization's reputation.[634] (6/20, 2002)

Texas

Statewide

Rigged Bids

A food distributor and wholesale grocer agreed to pay $60,000 in civil penalties and legal fees to settle charges that it rigged bids in selling food to districts in Texas. Interestingly, last year it paid $100,000 to settle similar charges.[635] (9/22/1993)

Charter School Fraud

Three charter schools are under investigation for "various allegations of fraudulent activity related to their request for and receipt of state money."

Two of the schools, Heritage Academy in Dallas, and Renaissance Charter in Irving, were charged with over-reporting student attendance with Heritage owing $1.5 million and Renaissance $2.9 million. The same family members run both schools and they deny any wrongdoing.

The third school, Harrison Charter, was closed because of mismanagement. The school had received $850,000 and accumulated a deficit of $400,000.[636] (11/03/2002)

Twenty-four charter schools have been closed since the first charters were awarded in 1996.

Another charter, Alphonso Crutch's Life Support Center, is also facing revocation of its license because almost $500,000 of expenses was not fully documented. The Owner claims the calculations are flawed. He also employs more than a dozen relatives at the school. .

Some of the money was apparently used to buy women's lingerie at Victoria's Secret and an X-rated video. The owner claimed that the items were purchased with private funds and that the video was not shown to the students. Who was viewing the video and when was it being viewed?

The explanation for the lingerie would certainly be applauded for political correctness: "It was given to our students to meet their unmet needs and to build higher self-esteem."

This must be part of the sex-education curriculum, but there was no mention of any surveys to determine what the "unmet needs" were, nor was there any indication of how it would enhance self-esteem. If this is what education has come to mean, heaven help us!

It would probably make a good plot for a comedy series.

Other items included tires, tire rims, bar stools, dog food, videotapes and dinners.[637] (11/6/2002) However, "if the same standards applied to shut down charter schools were applied to Dallas and Austin districts, they would be shut down for criminal misconduct."[638] (3/2000)

Carroll Intermediate School District

Twenty-two current and former administrators spent $77,000 on their district credit cards for dinners, theater tickets and expensive gifts. Up to this time, district policy did not require individual receipts, expense reports or any explanations for charges. Board members claimed that they had no idea that so many credit cards had been issued and how they were being used. A review is underway to determine whether the expenses were related to legitimate school purposes.[639] (10/30/2002)

Would anyone really be surprised if the credit cards were misused?

Crosbyton School District

A former business manager and his wife, a former secretary to the school superintendent, were indicted for embezzling $120,000 between 1987 and 1994.[640] (1997)

Coppell School District

The former director of transportation and community services employed for 19 years was charged with felony theft for stealing $387,000 over a seven-year period from community group donations. He deposited hundreds of checks, rent funds for school facilities, into his own bank account. There was nothing in his background to cause suspicion; the board was shocked and distressed because "he was someone we trusted."[641] (5/6/1999)

It usually is the most trusted person who commits FraSte!

Dallas Independent School District

Retaliation

Seven Dallas school employees were suspended in an investigation including four are high-level administrators. Some of the suspended administrators are suspected of threatening subordinates who wanted to report corruption to the investigators.[642] (6/4/1997)

Overtime Fraud

Thirteen maintenance employees were indicted for collecting about $168,000 for overtime hours they never worked; they all pleaded guilty.[643] (8/6/1997)

Superintendent Misappropriation

A superintendent used $16,279 of school dollars to purchase bedroom furniture for her home. The irony is that the superintendent requested the FBI to investigate the district because "corruption was rampant and employees had illegally reaped millions of dollars in fraudulent pay." A 4-year investigation resulted in 15 convictions including four high level administrators. It was this probe that uncovered the superintendent's fraud resulting in a 15-month prison term.[644] (2/11/1998)

After her release from prison, the former superintendent went to work for a clothing factory. They better watch their buttons!

Activity Fund Theft

Five schools were investigated after more than $89,000 turned up missing from activity funds. A former athletic director, a clerk, a principal, and office manager each from different schools were involved.[645] (4/12/1998)

Imagine the planning and lying that has to take place to keep this type of scheme going.

Roofing Scam

A former contractor was found guilty of taking more than $383,000 involving unperformed roofing repairs. A school district inspector was also indicted for receiving kickbacks from the contractor of over $100,000.[646] (8/8/1998)

Embezzlement

A former employee was sentenced to eight years in prison for embezzling $25,000. A payroll clerk who assisted him faces charges of taking another $26,000 for herself.[647] (9/9/2000)

El Paso

The risk manager of the Socorro School District, one of the poorest in the state, embezzled $4.7 million. The money was used to pay a golfing buddy for worthless background checks at $3,500 each that were not needed; the district already had the criminal history for each employee. The manager was sentenced to 10 years in prison.[648] (8/6/2000)

Fort Worth

An investigation revealed that two construction companies, paid over $32 million since 1990, overcharged the district and used school employees for contracted work. In addition to this problem, the board is questioning the audit firm's timelines, fees and experience…one phase leads to another phase" with over $300,000 being paid to the firm so far.

The scandal ended in June with the Director of Maintenance and the contractors receiving 8-year prison terms for defrauding the district of an estimated $15.9 million.[649] (9/1/2004)

San Angelo Intermediate School District

Five indictments were obtained against the former superintendent. The indictments allege that the superintendent appropriated funds from the district without the consent of the district on eight different occasions between March 22 1999 and May 17, 2001. The thefts totaled more than $15,000.[650] (2/13/2002)

Wilmer-Hutchins School District

Federal agents from the FBI and IRS descended upon this district of 3,800 students to uncover evidence relating to a multimillion-dollar budget deficit, missing money and equipment. What is so tragic is that the school population is predominantly minority and they need every resource imaginable.[651] (6/12/1996)

There seems to be no shame on the part of those who indulge their glutton appetites in even the poorest and neediest districts. Eventually, there was a state takeover of the district lasting two-and-a-half years, but it doesn't negate the fact that the needy district had been plundered.[652] (3/20/2002)

This district has been troublesome for decades. It should have come as no surprise that the voters rejected a tax authorization that would have allowed the district to keep funding essentially flat from last year.

Incredible as it may sound, a decision was finally made to shut down the district's schools for the coming school year"[653] (6/28/2005). The issue that is unresolved is where do the students go for schooling, what district will take them, and what happens to the staffs?

Chalk up another success for corruption!

This is another example of the impact corruption has in Education America and, it's another perfect example of betrayal of the children and the public trust. The question is why did it take so long to take action? This is certainly the ultimate in the "educational rape" of children who are the neediest.

Vermont

State Department of Education

An independent audit is being conducted following the discovery that between $300,000 and $400,000 in federal funds is missing. The department has been unable to account for the whereabouts of the money.[654] (4/8/1992)

It's amazing how so much money cannot be accounted for. They must have been using invisible ink.

Virginia

State

The Attorney General filed suit against three dairies for price fixing for school milk contracts.[655] (9/4/1991)

Fairfax County

PTA Embezzlement

The PTA treasurer at White Oaks Elementary school was convicted of a misdemeanor embezzlement charge for stealing $8,000. She was not bonded and there was little oversight of her work.[656] (1/14/1993)

PTA groups never seem to learn how easy it is to steal from their treasuries. It's probably because they simply cannot believe that one of their own would be so corrupt.

Embezzlement

- The finance officer at JEB Stuart High School was charged with embezzling $44,000 of school money during a four-month period.[657] (7/15/1992)
- A Frost Intermediate School teacher was charged with embezzling funds from the PTA that she served as treasurer for three years.[658] (12/4/1992)
- The finance officer at the middle school was charged with embezzling about $27,000 from the school to pay credit card bills.[659] (2/16/1994)
- The finance officer at Langley High School was dismissed after a routine computer audit determined that as much as $50,000 was missing.[660] (4/9/1994)
- The former treasurer of the Thomas Jefferson High School Colonial Boosters Club was charged with writing 16 checks during 1998 payable to himself. Earlier during the year, the junior varsity girl's basketball coach was recorded by a surveillance video camera removing $200 of athletic events proceeds from a school office.[661] (6/6/2000)
- An educational assistant was charged with stealing from checking accounts at two schools.[662] (2/2/2002)
- An administrative assistant was charged with embezzling $5,000 by using a school credit card to pay personal expenses.[663] (2/12/2002)

Frederick County

A former treasurer of the Armel Elementary School PTO was indicted for embezzlement of more than $200 between 1999 and 2001.[664] (3/7/2002)

Leesburg

Payroll Fraud

A bookkeeper for the Loudoun Country public schools was charged with issuing more than $205,000 in paychecks over a three year period to former employees and then depositing the checks to her own bank account. What is interesting about this case is that the bookkeeper had pleaded guilty in 1991 to embezzling funds from a company where she previously worked.[665] (3/3/2002)

PTO Embezzlement

The president of the Balls Bluff Elementary School PTO and his wife admitted embezzling $13,000 raised by the group.[666] (7/22/1999)

Manassas

Theft

A shop teacher at Stonewall Jackson High School was charged with embezzlement for selling a car donated to his car repair class and keeping the money for himself.[667] (11/8/1997)

PTO Embezzlement

A former PTO president was charged with embezzling more than $6,400 earmarked for school purchases.[668] (6/25/1992)

The PTO treasurer of Yorkshire Elementary School embezzled $14,000 over a three-year period and used the money to cover her personal expenses.[669] (11/11/2001)

Martinsville

A high school choral director, a former Miss Virginia, was charged with embezzling $1,226 from a band boosters club.[670] (7/24/1996)

Prince William County

A sixth grade teacher was charged with embezzlement at Rippon Middle School.[671] (5/13/1998)

Roanoke

The assistant principal of Bassett High School and his wife, an elementary school teacher, were indicted on charges of embezzling nearly $97,000. However, the money was stolen from their church and not from school funds. Nevertheless, both were suspended from their jobs.[672] (6/21/2002)

Woodbridge

An assistant cafeteria manager at Hylton High School was charged with five counts of embezzling $16,000 in cash and checks from the cafeteria.[673] (1/22/2000)

Washington

The Washington State Auditor's Office publishes annual fraud reports including school districts. Examples from some are listed below:

Fraud Report 1996

Educational Service District #123

The superintendent falsified a variety of accounting records to cover unauthorized purchases for himself amounting to $25,340.

Fraud Report 1997

Bellevue School District #405

A snack bar employee accepted payments for food, but did not record the sales on the cash register. Funds were then removed from the unrecorded sales amounting to $6,469.

Bellingham School District #501

A high school athletic director falsified accounting records from dance proceeds.

Edmonds School District #15

A teacher took the proceeds from three student field trips. Parents were told to write checks to the teacher, who then handled the financial aspects of the trips through a personal checking account in violation of district policies.

A high school drill team advisor took proceeds from student activity funds. Collections from students and parents were deposited in the advisor's personal checking account in violation of district policies.

North Thurston School District #3

A high school attendance secretary took cash receipts from a variety of sources, primarily traffic safety fees. The employee did not deposit cash collections amounting to $17,178.

Toppenish School District #202

A teacher/assistant coach failed to turn in all proceeds from a fund-raising activity for a high school boy's basketball team. While all checks were turned in, there was no currency from the event.

Tumwater School District #33

A food service supervisor took cash from a high school food service operation by depositing less money in the bank than was collected. Daily cashier reports were altered and signatures of other employees were forged to conceal the irregularities.

Tumwater New Market Skills Center, District #33

The administrative assistant responsible for a checking account where all proceeds from the school's beverage vending machines were deposited wrote checks to herself, a credit union, or to "cash."

Fraud Report 1998

Lake Washington School District

The custodian of bank accounts for an advance travel fund issued checks made payable to her and then deposited them into her personal bank account. The intricate scheme involved transferring funds from other accounts and altering payee names. The embezzlement amounted to $188,000.

Fraud Report 1999

Shoreline School District

A computer repair technician removed computer equipment over a period of at least seven years and converted it to his own personal use. The total value was $34,550.

Fraud Report 2000

Deer Park School District

Revenue received from five fund-raising activities did not equal what was deposited—a shortage of $2,895.

Mead School District

The transportation department altered ridership counts on 15 school bus routes overstating the number of students who rode the buses causing the district to over-fund the account by $22,000.

Seattle School District

Associated Student Body Fund cash receipts from various fund-raising events were stolen between receipt of the funds and the deposit.

Food service cash receipts were stolen from a secretary's desk at an elementary school and 15 bank deposit receipts could not be found.

Tacoma School District

A guidance office assistant processed fictitious claims for reimbursement from the petty cash fund amounting to $3,000. The employee also forged the supervisor's signature.

Seattle

SPICE Program

For 3 years the school district attempted to hide an embezzlement fiasco "born of stupidity and incompetence" amounting to $430,000. The School Program Involving Community Elders (SPICE) that provided meals and community activities for senior citizens at the schools was ripped off by the secretary in the amount of $180,000. She was convicted on 68 counts of theft.

The story gets more intriguing because the district's legal counsel, logistics director and former human resources administrator all agreed to delay reporting the theft until after a school levy vote occurred in March 1996.

What better example of the fortress mentality and the public be damned syndrome?

It gets even more amazing because the executive director of SPICE who reported the theft was himself charged with using $54,000 to pay for cell phone bills, home security equipment, personal computers, parking tickets and airline ticket upgrades. He claimed it was all in the name of benefiting the program.

He also claimed ignorance of an additional $250,000 in meal revenue, and there was no accounting of what happened to the funds.

The question is "whether wisdom, efficiency or competence can prevail in government monopoly more interested in damage control than fiscal control."[674] (4/13/1999)

Administrator Resigns

A respected director of middle schools resigned over a series of fiscal improprieties and a breach of professional ethics. Because of her resignation, the investigation will not be continued.[675] (9/15/2002)

West Virginia

Ranson

A former elementary school secretary was charged with 125 felonies for allegedly embezzling nearly $40,000 by submitting forged overtime request forms and purchase orders. She was in charge of fund-raisers and the money was taken from cookie sales, field trips and a school dance.[676] (6/6/2002)

Wisconsin

Beloit School District

A high school secretary faces tentative charges on 54 counts of fraud for allegedly writing checks to herself totaling $6,800 from the athletic fund.[677] (3/19/1999)

Phelps School District

A former bookkeeper in this district of only 200 students was sentenced to seven months in jails and four years probation for stealing an estimated $44,000 between 1997 and 1998, but the district lost another $93,000 in penalties and interest for failing to make timely payments. Despite the loss, the school district did not request jail time.[678] (4/13/2000)

Port Washington

A woman who embezzled more than $12,000 from an elementary school PTA was sentenced to 30 days in jail and five years probation. Her husband paid the money back as soon as he found out about the embezzlement.[679] (6/19/2000).

Wisconsin Dells School District

A former Dells High School secretary was charged with embezzling thousands of dollars from a variety of school accounts.[680] (4/20/1995)

Preview of Scandal to Come

The scandal on the horizon (it may even be taking place right now) is the free tutoring available to students under the NCLB Act. The school system is required to pay for the tutoring. The numbers involved are really unknown at this time, but there will be millions. About 300,000 students qualify just in the Los Angeles school district, and parents can select their top two choices from 40 private, state approved providers.[681] The sums of money involved cannot even be estimated at this time, but it will be in the millions.

The lesson to be learned is ever so clear. Where there is money there will be corruption, and it is as simple as that. In spite of this obvious and known fact, no one seems to consider potential corruption until it happens.

Summary

What is rather puzzling and difficult to understand is that the steps required to prevent FraSte from happening are neither costly nor complicated. Most simply involve sound financial policies, effective procedural practices, education, and training. (See Appendix I and II)

Why is it that basic and simple procedures are not taken to prevent the devastation and humiliation caused by FraSte? It's easy to say that it is ineptness or ignorance, but there is really only one conclusion: Those individuals responsible for managing and monitoring school dollars effectively, efficiently and honestly, seem to care more about their image than they care about the children entrusted to their care. The result is that the children and the public are betrayed each and every day.

In the end, it's the taxpayers who pay again and again because they have no choice, and that's what keeps FraSte marching ever so successfully on its relentless path.

CHAPTER EIGHT

Corrupt U.S. Department of Education (DOE)

"The lust of government is the greatest lust." James Harrington

Although the Constitution does not provide any role for the federal government in public education, its legislative and financial tentacles have been infused into every fabric of school life. With the passage of the No Child Left Behind Act signed into law in January 2002, its role is now hammered into a suit of armor around every public school in the nation. Yet, its financial contribution to public schools is only around 7 percent, but it certainly gets a big bang for its taxpayer-provided bucks. The dollars may be small, but they are responsible for controlling and influencing practically every aspect of school policy and budgetary decisions.

What must be added to the federal legislative and executive powers over schools is the judicial role as well. Critical school issues have been decided by a jaundiced judicial system, and the direct and indirect influence on school policies and practices have been dramatic and serious. Mandated school busing and the use of school vouchers at religious schools are just two examples.

The arm of government that entangles its tentacles around every school is the U.S. Department of Education responsible for dispensing the bulk of federal education dollars. As part of this responsibility, it also audits the states and school districts to ensure that the money is spent according to laws and regulations. Therefore, it is important to understand how this office has grown over the years and how it attempts to function in carrying out its mandate. The Department's influence over schools is powerful; yet, this was not what it was originally created to do.

History

The DOE was created in 1867 to collect information about schools and teaching that would be useful to states and districts. While the agency's name and location have changed over the past 135 years, this early emphasis on getting information on what works in education to teachers and education policymakers continues down to the present day; but this responsibility is now a small part of its bureaucratic and controlling structure.

World War II began a significant expansion of Federal support for education. The Lanham Act in 1941 and the Impact Aid laws of 1950 eased the burden on communities affected by the presence of military and other Federal installations by making payments to school districts. And in 1944, the "GI Bill" authorized postsecondary education assistance that would ultimately send nearly 8 million World War II veterans to college.

The Cold War stimulated the first example of comprehensive Federal education legislation, when in 1958 Congress passed the National Defense Education Act (NDEA) in response to the Soviet launch of Sputnik. The focus of NDEA was to ensure that highly trained individuals would be available to help America compete with the Soviet Union in scientific and technical fields. The NDEA included the improvement of science, mathematics, and foreign language instruction in elementary and secondary schools and vocational-technical training.

The anti-poverty and civil rights laws of the 1960s and 1970s brought about a dramatic emergence of the Department's equal access mission. The passage of laws such as Title VI of the Civil Rights Act of 1964, Title IX of the Education Amendments of 1972, and Section 504 of the Rehabilitation Act of 1973 which prohibited discrimination based on race, sex, and disability, respectively made civil rights enforcement a fundamental and long-lasting focus of the Department of Education.

In 1965, the Elementary and Secondary Education Act (ESEA) launched a comprehensive set of programs, including the Title I program of Federal aid to disadvantaged children to address the problems of poor urban and rural areas. However, the core mission of ESEA is to help disadvantaged students improve academically. This mission has been a substantial failure after 40 years of efforts.

In 1980, Congress established the Department of Education (DOE) as a Cabinet level agency. Today, DOE operates programs that touch on every area and level of education. The Department's elementary and secondary programs annually serve about 15,000 school districts and more than 50 million students attending roughly 92,000 public schools and 27,000 private schools. It has grown from a $14 billion agency in 1980 to over $50 billion. Since then, a number of amendments have been added.

The latest effort, and one of the most significant, is NCLB. Its 1,000 pages of verbiage, yet to be fully interpreted and fully implemented, will have consequences on educational policies and procedures beyond what anyone can imagine. In time, the bureaucrats and the courts will interpret the provisions of the Act far beyond what was intended; this has been true of all federal legislation involving federal aid to schools.

Resistance to NCLB is certainly mounting with schools and unions in at least 10 states joining lawsuits seeking more education funding. At least 18 sates have introduced bills that would protest or waive some of the law's requirements that are more stringent.[682]

The resistance should come as no surprise because schools do not want to adhere to real and comparable standards. Even though much of the criticism is over lack of funding, it is a façade. No amount of funding will ever be enough because there would then be other excuses for failures.

The DOE's official mission now is all-powerful and all encompassing, e.g. to ensure equal access to education, promote educational excellence, and leave no child behind. This is a classic example of how a small and well-defined governmental mission designed to provide information grew into an Octopus that engulfs and controls just about every aspect of public education.

<u>Waste and Mismanagement</u>

According to the DOE, "While programs and responsibilities have grown substantially over the years, the Department itself has not. In fact, its staff of 4700 is nearly 40 percent below the 7,528 employees who administered Federal education programs in several different agencies in 1980 when the Department was created. These staff reductions, along with a wide range of management improvements, have helped limit administrative costs to less than 3 percent of the Department's budget. This means that it delivers more than 97 cents on the dollar in education assistance to states, school districts, postsecondary institutions, and students."

At least this is what the department spin-masters claim. However, the undeniable fact is that waste, mismanagement, fraud and corruption have been epidemic in the DOE since its role changed in 1965. The Inspector General reports made on a regular basis to Congress read like a carbon copy of previous reports listing gross mismanagement and wasteful practices that defy correction.

The fact is that it is a pork-barrel department for the politicians and entrenched bureaucrats, and this is why changes of administration have never resulted in any significant improvement or reforms other than more and more dollars added to the pork barrel. An article entitled it as "The Department of Embezzlement."[683]

Harsh and damaging words, perhaps, but the facts are also harsh in revealing gross mismanagement, waste and theft of federal education dollars. Therefore, it is important to take a closer look at this agency that is responsible for dispensing billions of dollars and auditing the states and school districts to ensure that the dollars are spent according to laws and regulations.

As indicated previously, the DOE has its own Inspector General (IG). The IG's office is an independent, 272-person unit that watches out for fraud, waste, and mismanagement among the department's programs and contractors. It conducts audits of programs paid for by federal grants and contracts, oversees collection of student loans, investigates suspected cases of fraud, and monitors the department's internal management and operations. A congressional subcommittee and the General Accounting Office also have responsibility for monitoring the DOE.

The findings that follow demonstrate that no matter how many times the DOE is cited for mismanagement, and no matter how often theft is uncovered, the same practices continue year after year. The DOE response to just about every audit is that "they are full of inaccuracies and changes to correct the problems have been made since the audit report." As will be seen from the history, nothing really changes.

In addition, Congress passed legislation requiring all major agencies to install accounting systems that would produce statements that could be audited. As of October 2002, only the National Science Foundation has such a system. Legislation is meaningless without accountability.

Funds Owed to DOE

A report by the IG claims that states, students, school systems and contractors owe the Department more than $160 million. The department is currently examining a total of 3,367 cases in which federal auditors question the way recipients spent federal funds.[684]

Inspector General Report

The IG report indicated that payments made to Student Loan lenders were overpaid by more than $51 million in fiscal 1982 that also resulted in interest costs to the government of about $1.2 million.[685]

Task Force Report

A task force composed of business executives reported that the Education Department could save taxpayers $2.83 billion over the next three years by adopting 60 cost-cutting measures. The department could save $1.19 billion over the next three years simply by consolidating its major student-loan programs into a single unit.

According to the Office of Management and Budget, one of the problems was the department's emphasis on "the prompt delivery of funds at the expense of accurate accounting procedures." This focus resulted in repeated citations for excessive waste, fraud, abuse, and errors.[686]

General Accounting Office Audit (1985-1986)

"Flawed financial-management methods are exposing billions of dollars in federal funds to the potential for waste and fraud."[687] Among the findings:

1. The overall department accounting system is not adequately backed up by more detailed data, and is often incompatible with accounting systems for individual programs or functions.
2. The department does not adequately keep track of government property in its domain, particularly that held by contractors and grantees.
3. The department's system for keeping track of the grants and contracts it awards contains inaccurate data, and is incapable of providing timely information on topics such as the number of grants awarded for projects in a particular subject area.

The Department response was that the findings were inaccurate and that most of the problems identified had been addressed. This is the typical response.

Idle Money

According to a report by the Inspector General, the department carries on its books more than $665 million, the residue of an estimated 17,000 grants awarded over the past 16 years to education institutions and contractors.

Some of many examples include: The Detroit Board of Education received $190,147 in 1984 for its <u>Follow Through</u> program, but used only $23,932; a Mississippi school district used only $332,096 from two grants totaling $572,746; and a special school district in Arkansas was awarded $463,774 for a bilingual program but only spent $226,732. Interestingly, the district officials said they did not use the whole amount because the department gave them twice as much as they were entitled to receive.

However, these examples also reveal a more pathetic problem. Schools that cry for more money don't spend what they have available from grants. Why? It takes too much work. Yes, it's really that simple and that tragic.

Now get this! Slightly more than 500 of the unused awards worth $70 million cannot be recovered if funds were spent for programs other than that spelled out in the grants.

The IG also concluded: "The department needs to resolve its longstanding weakness of failing to systematically close out grants in accordance with prescribed timeframes."[688]

Student Loan Program "High Risk"

Despite the DOE's effort to combat fraud and abuse in student-loan programs, substantial problems remain and it continues on the "high risk" list compiled by the General Accounting Office and the Office of Management and Budget. The report found "material weaknesses in internal controls for determining program costs, monitoring payments and insuring accurate financial reporting."

According to testimony by the Deputy Secretary, "To totally fix these programs, which have suffered from managerial neglect for many years, will take time." [689]

New Policy[690]

Grant recipients can be barred from receiving any federal grants or contracts. This new regulation is to ensure that wrongdoers barred by one agency cannot obtain federal money from another agency.

Critical Audit[691]

All audits of the DOE have been critical, and the 1998 audit is an example. Using the audit, the House Subcommittee on Oversight and Investigations concluded:

"The agency keeps shoddy records and mismanaged billions of dollars. The agency can't account for $6 billion in spending for unidentified programs, authorized an $800 million loan to one student, and issued $127 million in duplicate payments."

The department was one of six federal agencies that received incomplete designations for fiscal 1998 audits meaning that audits were unable to verify whether financial statements were reliable. As usual, the department officials claimed, "the accusations stemmed from reporting mistakes."

Persistent Financial Mismanagement

A General Accounting Report to the Task Force on Education, Committee on the Budget, House of Representatives, indicated, "the DOE has experienced persistent financial management weaknesses beginning with its first agency-wide financial audit effort in fiscal year 1995. Auditors have reported largely the same serious internal control weaknesses, which have affected the ability to provide reliable financial information to decision makers both inside and outside the agency."[692]

Student Loan Fiasco

Student loans amounting to over $77 million were forgiven for falsely claimed deaths or disabilities.[693]

Theft

The IG reported to a Congressional committee that it "couldn't say for sure just how much money the agency has lost to waste, fraud or abuse." Also, she could not give details on how $1.9 million of Impact Aid money for schoolchildren who live on South Dakota Indian reservations got diverted to two Maryland bank accounts. The money was used to purchase a $46,900 Cadillac, a $50,000 Lincoln Navigator and a $135,000 building in a suburb of Washington. The rest of the money was diverted to other bank accounts.[694]

Mismanagement

The department hired a contractor that sent notification letters to 39 students informing them that they had each won a Jacob Javits graduate-fellowship award worth up to $100,000. It turned out that they had been selected as alternates, not winners. [695]

There was no indication whether anyone asked why a contractor was hired to send out 39 notices. Could it be that all the secretarial personnel were too busy?

Title I

A congressional audit reported that most states could not say how much improvement the $8 billion program helped low-income children.[696]

What this would indicate is that once the awards are made, the DOE walks away from any monitoring to ensure compliance or to get money back that is not spent.

Come Clean[697]

The DOE has been unable to achieve a clean financial audit for the past two years. The agency admitted that department employees and contractors stole more than $300,000 in electronic equipment, collected $600,000 overtime pay, and several individuals stole nearly $2 million in impact aid funding.

Again, the typical excuse: "The problem was due to kinks in the computer system."

Financial Mismanagement

According to the Inspector General, at least $450 million was misused through improper payments, fraud, and other instances of financial mismanagement in the past three years alone. Although the Department identified eight instances of duplicate payments to grantees and vendors totaling $198 million between May 1998 and September 2000, she found 13 more instances totaling an additional $55 million. She stated to a House subcommittee: "The Department has many serious financial-management challenges."

The House subcommittee was focusing on why the department failed—for the third year in a row—to earn a "clean" audit of its financial records. According to one member of the committee, "We've got a department that manages about $80 to $100 billion per year and they're doing it with a Third World accounting system."[698]

Audit Problems

A department employee blew the whistle on financial waste in the agency and his reward was to be escorted from the agency by armed federal security guards for exposing the mismanagement and corruption involved. He claimed that there was no security over the system to prevent embezzlement, and no audit trail to find out where the money was going. His claim was supported by a report issued by the Senate Committee on Governmental Affairs.

Riddled With Fraud

Twenty-one employees were authorized to write checks of up to $20,000 without supervision, and from May 1998 to September 2000, 19,000 such checks were written totaling $23 million.

Over 200 employees had credit cards in their names with most allowed to charge up to $10,000 per month, an additional 36 employees were authorized to charge up to $25,000 per month, and two others up to $300,000 per month.

Of 676 credit card statements reviewed, 141 statements with purchases valued at nearly $1 million were not signed by a supervisor. Several purchases included items that could be used for personal purposes including computers even though department policy states that computers cannot be purchased on credit cards.[699]

Since the revelations of the credit card debacle, more than 30 government credit cards have been confiscated and those remaining have had spending limits cut by up to (notice the words "up to") 90 percent.[700]

Grants Disbursement

An allegation by an employee whistleblower, John Gard, in the Office of the Chief Financial Officer (OCFO) claims the fundamental problem in the department is that its computer system for disbursing grant money that was implemented in 1997 and known as the Grants Administration and Payment System "does not contain proper internal and external security controls, audit trails, or accounting functions." As a result, DOE has been unable to fully account for grant monies, audit its accounts, or produce financial statements necessary for year-end reconciliation's.

The Office of Special Counsel investigated the charge and it determined that "a substantial likelihood that violations of law, gross mismanagement, a gross waste of funds and an abuse of authority had occurred."

Another report by the General Accounting Office was critical of the "agency's financial management system and manual internal controls over grant-back activity and related funds control…and confirmed that financial management system deficiencies, inadequate systems of funds control, and manual internal control weaknesses continued to exist."

Again, the response from the DOE was classic bureaucratic gobbledygook: "Although the investigation did identify violations of federal financial management laws, the allegations did not rise to the level of gross mismanagement."[701]

Probably no amount of mismanagement and waste in the department would ever rise to the level of "gross mismanagement."

Office of Inspector General

The IG responded to a joint request by the House and Senate to update them on its audit, investigation, and inspection efforts on the most significant challenges facing the DOE for the October 2, 2000 to March 31, 2001 period. These challenges include the following: [702]

- Improving financial management and the management information technology
- Strengthening systems security
- Designing and implementing effective internal systems controls for preventing fraud, waste, and abuse
- Ensuring that correct measures are selected to place appropriate focus on program performance and that data sources for measures are of sufficient quality
- Developing and implementing the Student Financial Assistance systems Modernization Blueprint
- Moving the DOE to a paperless environment
- Balancing compliance monitoring and technical assistance to meet accountability and flexibility needs
- Obtaining income verification from the IRS to prevent fraud

In other words, years of the same charges of mismanagement and waste have been fruitless. It is incredible to think that no one, including Congress and the executive branch, have not had any success or power in fixing this incredibly inept and mismanaged department.

Because the corruption problem is so massive the previous Secretary of Education, Rod Paige, was forced to hold a press conference on April 20, 2001 specifically on the issue of fraud and mismanagement. He outlined a new strategy to examine and correct long-standing problems with financial mismanagement and abuse. "Every dollar we waste on fraud or mismanagement is a dollar that could be used for teaching our children, and this department cannot and will not continue wasting those precious resources."[703]

A team to oversee this new strategy will address 343 audit recommendations that had not yet been acted upon. Not that it matters since whatever they claim to correct remains a problem.

Interestingly, John Gard who knows where the problems are was not included with the original team to help with the new strategy (he has since been appointed to a management improvement team). He suspected that "senior management officials in the department were setting up the Agency to rip it off during the conversion to the Grants Administration and Payment System in 1997". According to Gard, "A super-user identification and password were released to about two dozen top employees and contractors, allowing them to conduct, modify and delete financial transactions without any trace."

He also informed the IG about refund checks available to be cashed for personal use by department employees. Acting on his information, the IG raided the office of Chief Financial Officer and found $2 million in refund checks lying unsecured on an employee's desk.

Gard also charged that money was funneled to hundreds of accounts called "pseudo recipient" including a bank in Puerto Rico that received $4 million. These accounts were conceived for the purpose of diverting taxpayer money.

His reward for exposing the corruption was to be assigned a clerical job that took less than 4 hours a week to complete.

If this is how an honest employee is treated, it puts into question the Secretary's resolve to solve the financial problems that have plagued the agency for years.

There can only be one conclusion that can be drawn from such a history of flagrant and open mismanagement and fraud: This is how the politicians and bureaucrats want the department to function so that the rip-offs and payoffs can continue. All the testimony, reports and audits are great rhetoric that produce no significant reforms, and there is no reason to believe that attempts at new strategies will be any different.

In July 2001, Rod Paige again addressed the lack of fiscal responsibility in the Department: "We cannot expect our schools to be accountable if we aren't accountable…This department owes it to the American people to do a better job of managing their money than has been done in the past. I'm here to get that done, and there will be no excuses." He has called for a "culture of accountability."[704] Tell this to John Gard who risked his career to expose the corruption and mismanagement.

Perhaps the only words that ring true are those of the Deputy Secretary Bill Hansen: "It's going to be a steep mountain to climb."

The important question here is why wasn't this done sooner rather than waiting for years when it was generally known how corrupt the agency was? However, as can be seen with the rest of the examples, nothing really changes.

Embezzlement

A telecommunications specialist pleaded guilty on two criminal counts in a scheme to defraud the Department of more than $1 million dollars. Six other employees resigned as a result of the investigation.

In 1999, the specialist illegally purchased 10 computers, 15 printers, 9 laptops, 4 CD drives, a 62-inch TV, eight digital cameras and 75 cordless phones for herself and family members (charges for the telephone calls were billed to the government totaling over $300,000). The scam included falsely reporting regular pay and overtime pays amounting to $700,000. Six family members also pleaded guilty.

Her scheme did not just include purchasing electronic equipment. In addition, she used technicians from two telecommunication companies to perform personal services for her and her family such as driving her daughter to doctors' appointments, and buying crab cakes.[705]

Pell Grants Plundered

The most sophisticated and brazen scam involved members of a Hasidic community in Rockland County, NY. A bogus seminary financed by Pell grants was awarded to nonexistent students between 1987-1992. "The school administrators falsified resumes, fabricated board-meeting minutes, and cooked up student progress reviews to keep the federal aid flowing.[706]

General Accounting Office (March 2002)

Significant internal control weaknesses in payment processes and poor physical control over its computer assets made the department vulnerable to and in some cases resulted in fraud, improper payments and lost assets. "We identified several instance of fraud in the grant and loan areas and pervasive control breakdowns and improper payments in other areas, particularly involving purchase cards."

Although several changes were made to policies and procedures over disbursements to improve internal controls and program integrity, they have not been effectively implemented.

Summary

The question that must be addressed is how this department can lead the nation's effort to improve educational performance, and to monitor and manage programs involving billions of dollars, when it cannot manage and reform itself.

Just as it is immune to any real reforms, the public school bureaucracy has also been immune from any meaningful reform.

The pervasive corruption in the U.S. Department of Education is but another example of how children and the public trust are betrayed by those who are entrusted with the treasures of opportunities that were designed to aid every school district. Furthermore, it is a classic example of "the taxpayers be damned" mentality that pervades governmental entities and institutions.

It is incredible to believe that with all the powers of Congress and the executive branch meaningful accountability cannot be brought to bear on this mismanaged department.

CHAPTER NINE

School Failures: State And City Takeovers

"It is as fatal as it is cowardly to blink facts because they are not to our taste."
John Tyndall

In recent years, there have been many takeovers of school districts by states and others by mayors because they were dysfunctional and mismanaged academically, fiscally and/or administratively. This practice, unheard of until the first takeover in 1989, demonstrates the deplorable condition of many school districts most of which are urban. It is important to note that most school boards remain elected and among the country's 25 largest districts, only six have turned to appointed panels. However, if poor performance and mismanagement are used as the criteria, many more boards should be replaced or some other independent form of responsible monitoring needs to be implemented.

Twenty-nine states have passed laws that permit state officials to exert authority over a district in the case of academic bankruptcy or woefully low-performing schools. The takeovers do not follow any particular model, but typically, they often stop short of tossing out all of the leading players and the school board in particular. According to the Education Commission of the States, "States have been real hesitant to take on the urban beast....urban districts are all about money and power."[707]

A major reason for the reluctance to takeover efforts is that too often it has resulted in costly lawsuits and bitter community reactions. Such problems slow down the effort to improve the management system, drains resources and time, and reinforces community resentments.

There are, of course, other forces at work that make takeovers very difficult. But the bottom line issue is probably best stated by David Rogers in his 1968 book, 110 Livingston Street, about the New York City school system: "The Boards greatest expertise was in promoting a politics of futility. Likening the million-pupil system, awash in money and failure, to a punching bag...hit in one place and it simply returns to an old equilibrium."[708] The years that have passed since the book was published have shown that nothing changes no matter what is done in money, reforms, or restructuring.

However, the NCLB legislation has added a new impetus for reforming schools because it requires states and districts to identify and restructure chronically low performing schools. This is another reason why there is growing opposition to the legislation.

An article, "School Takeovers and Enhanced Answerability," that examined this issue concluded: "State takeovers are detrimental because they do not address the systemic problems that impede quality education."[709]

Every district that has been a takeover target had a school board, and every district had years of problems brought on by ineptness, ignorance, apathy or just plain, pathetic politics. With these factors in play, it is no wonder why the boards were not able to correct the gross mismanagement of their districts. In fact, in most cases, the school boards helped to contribute to the decay. In plain, unadulterated English, they betrayed the children and the taxpayers they were responsible and obligated to serve. Why is it that so many boards are so arrogant, apathetic, powerless and inept? Is it that they prefer the chaos and confusion of mismanagement in order to acquire and maintain power and influence?

As will be seen in the takeover cases, even when warnings were given and opportunity given to correct the obvious problems, boards did nothing to really prevent some takeovers. Apparently, too many of them felt that they have an entitlement to run the district without oversight, without accountability, and without regard to the children they are there to serve.

What must also be kept in mind is that takeovers of one kind or another are a last act of desperation, but the reality is that there should be state interventions in hundreds of other districts. The fact is that over 8,500 schools do not meet the standards of the NCLB Act and many others will follow.

It is a deplorable and shameful situation and no matter how much money is spent to solve the problems, it is never enough. No amount of money will ever be enough when the problem is mismanagement, apathy, ineptness, politics and corruption.

One of the major problems in takeovers is that eventually the district will be turned back to the local political machine whose power was never taken away. In other words, there is nothing to prevent the district from sliding back to its corrupt ways.

To make matters worse, there is little research to draw on for guidance about what works and what does not work. Even with more research, no magic formula for success is likely because of the diverse conditions prevailing in such dysfunctional school districts that vary in size and different governing structures.

Therefore, it is important to know where takeovers have occurred, why they were necessary, and if they worked.

Alabama[710]

Barbour County School District

In 1996, the State took over the district due to financial problems. In 1997, control was given back to the district, but in 1999, the State again took control back because of financial problems.

Macon County School District

In 1996, the State took control of the district due to financial problems, but gave control back in 1997.

Wilcox County School District

In 1996, the State took control of the district because of financial problems; but control was returned in 1997.

Gadsden High School

In 1999, the State declared the takeover of the high school because of lagging student performance. However, it really involved just sending in an intervention team to get the school back on track.

Jefferson County School District

The State took control over the district due to financial problems.

Litchfield High School

In 1999, the State assumed control of the school because of academic problems.

Other Takeovers

In 2000, the State assumed control of the follow schools and districts because of academic problems:

- Lowndes County Middle School
- Cloverdale Junior High School
- Russell County High School
- Cobb Elementary School
- Jess Lanier High School

Arizona

State

The State will be taking over daily operations of 11 failing schools. It includes the removal of five principals, replacing teachers, and possibly combining campuses. The takeovers were due to poor test results.[711]

Scottsdale Unified School District

The district was sued in 1998 for rigging bids and misspending $11.7 million in public funds. A report by the Auditor General accused employees of splitting bids to avoid purchasing laws and taking kickbacks of free Phoenix Open box seats and deep-sea fishing trips to San Diego. As a result, it has been under a settlement that orders it to follow the law or face a $150,000 fine for each offense if it breaks the law again.[712]

A new superintendent hired in 2000 was instrumental in turning the district around and state scrutiny ended in August 2002.[713] Obviously, the right leadership is one of the critical components of successful schools.

Arkansas

State

Under a new law passed in 1996, the Department of Education targeted 25 school districts for possible takeover unless they improved their financial and academic problems. As a result, 13 of the districts were been declared in "academic distress," 7 in "financial distress" and the remaining districts received warnings.

The legislation gives districts three years to raise student performance and improve finances. If there is no improvement after one year, the State assembles a team of educators to recommend further changes. If that fails, the State decides whether to dismiss the school board or local superintendent. The final option is to consolidate a troubled district with a neighbor.[714]

Altheimer School District

In 2002, the State intervened in the district because of low student performance on state tests that had not improved in six years.

Elaine School District

In 2002, the State intervened in the district because of low student performance on state tests had not improved in six years.

California

Coachella Unified School District

In 1992, the State took control of the district due to financial problems and hired an administrator to run the district until 1996. A trustee was also appointed to monitor the school finances.[715]

Compton School District

In 1993, a state administrator was assigned to run the 30,000-pupil district because of financial bankruptcy and low student achievement, and the school board was stripped of its powers. Although the local board was retained, all of its decisions were subject to review and veto by a state-appointed superintendent. Although this is considered an extreme action, the reaction can also be extreme. Someone fired a gun at the appointee, and, as a result, guards are now provided for every new superintendent.[716]

Since the takeover, test scores have improved, the dropout rate dipped slightly, attendance rates have improved and campus crime dropped 59 percent. However, board meetings "are as ugly as ever."

In 2002, the district was returned to local control because it met its goals in five areas: community relations, personnel, facilities, finance, and student achievement. It also finished repaying a $20 million dollar state loan. A new superintendent was hired, but a state trustee continued to monitor the district.[717]

Emery Unified School District

In 2001, the district, with only 900 students, was put under state control because of a financial management crisis. The control included district decisions regarding leases, contracts, labor negotiations, curriculum, and operations.

The district has ten-years to repay a $2.3 million state loan which is 20% of their budget. It was put into debt by the former superintendent who was fired in 1992 from the Compton school district that was also taken over by the state because of financial mismanagement. The superintendent has since pleaded guilty to two felony counts of misusing public funds.[718]

Oakland School District

In 1989, an emergency loan package was provided by the State. However, the district was required by legislative action to accept a state appointed trustee with veto power over expenditures. The reason for the takeover was its near insolvency condition, and an unfolding theft-and-patronage scandal that "brought the system's serious financial and administrative problems into stark relief."[719]

Despite Proposition 13, the property-tax-reduction and limitation legislation, the school board failed to cut costs, protected staff members from layoffs, and borrowed from funds intended for desegregation efforts and cafeteria expenses.[720]

Voters then approved a city charter amendment enlarging the school board from 7 to 10 members, and allowing the mayor to appoint 3 members.

In 2002, a state financial expert was appointed to oversee the budget after accounting discrepancies revealed missing millions and a budget deficit of over $100 million.[721]

Richmond School District (West Contra Unified School District)[722]

In 1991, the State took control of the 31,000-pupil district, an action never taken previously, because of a budget problem that was "the most severe ever faced by a California district." In order to avoid a district bankruptcy, state loans in the amount of $25 million were needed. To balance the budget, the district needed to cut $25 million from its budget. Hundreds of employees were cut and the collective bargaining agreement was changed.

In spite of the fact that the budget problems were becoming more pronounced, local officials insisted that state and federal grants, and other actions, would enable them to balance the budget. State auditors found serious flaws in the way the district routinely managed its money.

Yet, a grand jury investigating the bankruptcy did not bring any charges against the school board or superintendent because there is no law against mismanagement no matter how damaging the consequences.

This statement should be branded into the hides of every taxpayer when they are asked to pay more taxes to support the schools. It's a green light for mismanagement to continue unabated and unashamedly with nothing illegal involved.

What contributed to the problem was that the district embarked on a bold program to rapidly transform the schools by creating special programs in every building and allowing parents to send their children to any school.

However, the Governor refused to agree to the $29 million loan package and the district then filed for bankruptcy protection under Chapter 9 and threatened to close the schools. Because of a suit by parents, a superior court judge ordered the state to keep the schools open. The state superintendent then appointed an administrator to oversee the district's finances.

In response, the district threatened to renege on its debts; in order to prevent a panic in the municipal bond market, lawmakers passed a law restructuring the debt. The legislation also renamed the district and it is now known as the West Contra Costa Unified School District.

Who or what was responsible for this financial fiasco? According to the superintendent, "most of the blame belongs to the state legislature because of its failure to provide adequate funding." An interesting remark considering that the district's budget had increased 49% between 1986 and 1990, while its expenditures rose 76 percent. It's also interesting to note that the superintendent had a past history of financial mismanagement.

It's absolutely incredible to imagine that such gross mismanagement and obvious accounting finagling and manipulation, part of which was declared unconstitutional under state law, did not result in anyone being punished except, of course, the taxpayers and students.

This case is certainly another classic example of "the public trust be damned."

West Fresno Elementary District

This financially troubled district previously refused all help to correct its financial problems, so it was approved for a takeover by the Legislature; however, the governor vetoed the bill. He said: "It would set a risky precedent for the state to wrest control from school boards before their districts became insolvent."

The governor finally relented after the teachers didn't get paid. A second takeover bill amounting to $2.5 million was passed, and the school board was stripped of its voting power. In addition, a state-appointed administrator was appointed to run the district.

The problems are far from over because the district is faced with over 20 lawsuits and several hundreds of thousands of dollars have already been paid out in some settlements. "This district is a lawyer's dream come true."[723]

Connecticut[724]

Bridgeport

In 1988, the State took control of the school district because of financial problems. In 1996, the state relinquished its control over the schools.

Hartford

In 1997, the state legislature enacted a law to abolish the locally elected school board and empowered the governor to appoint a board of trustees for the 24,000-pupil district.

In 2001, the law was amended and four members of the school board were elected. The remaining members were appointed by the mayor in consultation with state lawmakers and officials with the appointments requiring approval by the city council.[725]

Waterbury

In 2001, the State took control of the district due to financial problems. Control was returned in 2003.

West Haven

In 1992, the State took control over the town and school district due to financial problems. Control was returned in 1995.

District Of Columbia[726]

In 1995, the U.S. Congress created a financial control board to operate the 77,000-pupil district. The board appointed a new superintendent, a retired Army general, and created a board of trustees to oversee the district. Several schools were closed and some principals were fired.

In 1999, voters approved the reduction of the school board from 11 to 9 members with four members appointed by the mayor and the other five elected.

In 2001, the financial control board returned the school system back to the local board.

Florida

Some Florida schools are ripe for takeover by private companies. Four firms are interested in managing failed schools in Miami-Dade County and possibly Broward County. Schools rated as "F" for two or more years are potential candidates for takeover.

Interestingly, Edison Schools, one of the private firms involved, had most of its stock purchased by the public-employee pension fund.[727]

What seems obvious is that they expect to make a profit from this investment, but it would seem that there is a conflict of interest involved with this stock purchase.

Illinois

Chicago[728]

The problems and governance of the schools has been a perennial problem. In the late 1980's, a token takeover took some control from the district's school board and central office. Control was put it in the hands of parents in the form of local school councils.

However, achievement levels did not improve, parental involvement did not increase, and there were scandals with some school councils. This should not come as any surprise because the school councils were as inept as the boards. Obviously, giving power to the people was not the answer

In 1995, the state legislature at the request of the mayor granted him the power to reorganize the district administration into a corporate model, regulate the local councils, and appoint a smaller school board.

The mayor appointed a non-educator as the district's CEO who streamlined the administration and privatized some non-instructional services. He also began to root out waste discovering, for example, $1 million in spoiled food and $250,000 in unused furniture and supplies.

A new Office of Accountability that was given the power to intervene in poorly performing schools diminished the power of the local councils. More than a hundred schools were put on academic probation and some principals fired.

In 1997, seven failing high schools were "reconstituted (next chapter), forcing all teachers to reapply for their jobs." In 1998, the legislature again attempted to fix the state's 500,000 pupil school system, the largest in the state, by setting up an authority with power to hire and fire principals and allowing newly created, elective local councils to approve school budgets

By 1999, these and other actions resulted in improved test scores that leveled off in 2000. Political rivalries then resurfaced, and the CEO departed.

The lesson seems to be that "getting tough" only results in limited improvements, and then new strategies are needed.[729]

According to a report by a Chicago business group, "neither increased funding or administrative changes will produce significant gains in student achievement…the schools are structured for failure."[730]

This is probably one of the most profound and truthful statements about too many urban schools; yet, money keeps pouring in, but nothing really changes.

East St. Louis School District[731]

In 1995, state officials appointed a three-member panel to "clean up" the financial and academic problems within the 13,000-pupil district. "Students are suffering under unacceptable conditions because of financial mismanagement" over the past six years. Two independent audits reported that administrative procedures were totally inadequate.

In addition, board members had bypassed a number of state directives, including instructions to solicit bids for contracts and consolidate district bank accounts. Remedial plans submitted since 1988 to correct the problems have been consistently ignored.

Ignoring state directives can only occur when there are no lasting consequences to such actions.

In a last ditch effort to avoid the takeover, the board presented a plan to hire 50 more teachers with $200,000 coming from the city and a $150,000 donation from the owners of a local river gambling boat. The state rejected the plan.[732]

In four years, a $2.6 million budget deficit was turned into a $5.9 million surplus.

Round Lake School District

The state appointed a finance authority to manage the district's budget and squeeze enough revenue out of the tax base to pay for educating a growing student population. Without this action, the district with 6,000 students would have gone bankrupt.[733]

Iowa

Hendrick School District

In 1990, the state seized control of the 200-pupil district for not being in compliance with state academic standards passed in 1987. Its governance was handed over to a regional education agency. School officials were told in 1989 that they were not in compliance because instructors were teaching subject areas in which they were not licensed and required courses were not being offered. The district was again warned in 1990 of the deficiencies.

The district response was that the standards were too difficult or expensive for a rural school. The critics of the action charged that it's the first step to consolidate districts and "kill off rural schools."[734]

Kentucky

State

In 1984, the state was the first to pass a law allowing state intervention in local districts deemed to be failing academically. The law is rather unique and quite specific in implementing a four-stage process. All schools are considered in Phase I; either a district is deemed to have no deficiencies or it must have a state-approved improvement plan. If a district fails to comply or adhere to the timelines established in its plan, it is declared "educationally deficient" and enters Phase II. During this phase, the state department provides monitoring and technical assistance. If the district continues to fall below the minimum requirements, it is then moved to Phase III, state intervention. A state team can then assume a direct role in the hiring of personnel, the expenditure of funds, the revision of curricula, and the direction of programs. If the superintendent and school board fail to abide by recommendations for making improvements, the district enters Phase IV, the removal of the superintendent and school board.

Pike County School District[735]

In 1988, the state superintendent of education, with the approval of the state board of education, took control of the district due to "educational deficiencies." Nepotism and lax financial management were also cited for reasons to assume control of its financial affairs. Under the provisions of the takeover law, the board could not make purchases or hire employees without the written approval of the state superintendent.

In 1999, the State released the district from the "declaration of emergency."

Floyd County School District[736]

In 1998, the state superintendent of education appointed three board members to the existing school board that then voted to accept a takeover by the state because of "educational malpractice" within the district.

Factors contributing to the intervention of the 9,400 pupil district included the attendance rate which was below the state required minimum of 93.5 percent, and failure to improve attendance by 2 percentage points each year as required by law. In addition, achievement skill levels in reading, math, writing, and spelling were not mastered by 80 percent of the students at each grade level as the regulations required nor was a 2.5 percent improvement level achieved.

A curriculum audit by the state showed severe management problems and severe shortcomings.

The state also assumed control of the district's finances. In two of the past five years, its budget of $23 million had been overspent by $340,000.

Whitley County School District[737]

In 1998, the state intervened because of "educational deficiencies." The attendance rate was below the state minimum and improved less than 2 percent in the previous two years, the dropout rate was above the minimum of 5.5 percent, and achievement levels showed deficiencies in subjects at many grade levels.

The district does have a rather insurmountable socioeconomic problem. More than 80 percent of the 4,100 students are eligible for free or reduced price lunches, and it covers an area of 420 square miles of mountainous country. To make matters worse, the area's incorporated towns have independent school districts, leaving only rural, residential property as a tax base for the county district.

Lechter County School District[738]

In 1994, state officials assumed control of the 4,400-pupil district. Although the local board was retained, the state superintendent had veto power and could initiate actions if the board failed to fulfill its obligations. It did and, as a result, the state education commissioner removed all five school board members and the board's lawyer the following year.

The reasons included lack of oversight in areas such as transportation, food services, and purchasing, as well as, loose administration of special education programs.

The abuses had arisen in an effort by officials to reduce dropout statistics, dodge high special-education costs, continue receiving added state funds, free certain teachers for extra duty and pay, and make up for a lack of alternative programs. The district liberally applied the rules of homebound instruction with 10 percent of students involved for such reasons as claustrophobia, hyperactivity, and school phobia.

The Commissioner of Education also brought charges against the superintendent charging incompetence, nonfeasance, and neglect of duty.

The district was returned to local control in 1997.

Harlan County School District[739]

In 1992, the State took control of the district because of financial and management problems, but in 1996 it was returned to local control.

Louisiana

New Orleans

Although this city has not been subject to a takeover, a Local Education Governance and Administration Task Force was convened in September 2002 to consider strategies for improving the school system. A decision was made to eliminate all options and to leave the district's school board in place and to look for reforms the district itself could attempt. However, the decision is not final and the task force will break into four groups to consider options from within such as decentralization, outsourcing or privatization. Interestingly, the State has no interest to take over the district, and the mayor has no interest in running the district either.[740]

The superintendent who was hired only two years ago has resigned. During his tenure, the system lost millions of dollars and the feds are investigating allegations of corruption. Test scores remained among the poorest in the State.

Of course, financial problems existed prior to his tenure with the system facing a $31 million deficit and corruption was rampant.[741]

Maryland

Baltimore[742]

In 1988, the mayor was given the power to appoint the school board, select the superintendent, and place district finances under the city council. Despite a decade of effort, progress was "only incremental and only at some schools."

In the early 1990's, the district hired Education Alternatives Inc. to run several schools but dropped the firm after three years because of lackluster student performance and funding disputes.

Under the states academic bankruptcy law, schools with a history of low achievement can be identified as in need of "reconstitution." Fifty of the 180 schools were so identified.

The State Board of Education ruled out a takeover as an option and instead, in 1997, the state legislature entered into a partnership with the 96,000 pupil school system to run the schools. From this partnership, a new, nine-member board of school commissioners was created, with members jointly appointed by the governor and the mayor (four must be business executives from the private sector).

The mayor agreed to the partnership plan despite strong opposition from the minority community because he realized the system was "unresponsive" to his leadership and that there were aspects of management he could not get at. The mayor believed that solving certain problems such as class size would improve the situation, but he came to realize that "the entire system needed to be reformed."

Under the State's takeover plan, each school would be free of local board control and a private contractor brought in to manage the schools. Principals and teachers would likely, though not necessarily, be fired and replaced. The new staffs would have no ties to the district or teachers union.

This is the first time that individual schools have been taken away from board control.

In 2000, the state contracted with Edison Inc. to operate three of the state's poorest performers academically.

The intention of the takeover plan was to return the schools to local control after five years.

Prince George's County School District

In 2002, the State enacted legislation that abolished the locally elected board and created a nine-member board appointed by the governor and the county executive. The reason for the takeover was "a crisis in management of the public schools." The governor stated: "It is critical that we act now before the destructive pattern that currently exists causes permanent damage to the education of our children."[743]

Massachusetts

Boston

In 1991, the legislature enacted a law that abolished the elected Boston School Committee of the 63,000 pupil district and gave the mayor the right to appoint a seven member school committee. In 1996, Boston voted to maintain the appointed school committee.

Ten years after the new board took charge, scores are up, dropout rates are down and the superintendent has been running the 63,000-student system longer than anyone in 30 years.

Chelsea[744]

In 1989, the legislature enacted a law that allowed Boston University to run the 5,300-student school district under a 10-year management contract. The city has struggled with poverty, emigration, and new immigration.

Under the plan, the university and the district designed annual individualized learning plans for all students, a K-12 ethics-and-character curriculum, and home-based, high-tech preschools. It also addressed the high truancy and dropout rates, low-test scores, and low levels of parent involvement.

"If the resources of a leading university cannot make a difference in working with an urban school district, then questions must be raised about whether more drastic measures must be taken to improve urban schools or whether it is even possible to improve them."

The university model is rather simple: It will lead, seek advice before making key decisions, adjust thinking, and make decisions and allow others to do the same."

Lawrence[745]

In 1998, the Commonwealth entered into a joint selection process with the 12,000 pupil district for a new superintendent, an opened an office in the district to oversee daily operations and provide technical assistance to school administrators. It is the first time that the State School Board has used its authority to intervene in local schools under the 1993 reform law.

The prior superintendent was fired after the high school lost its accreditation and a state audit revealed management and financial irregularities and chronic low performance. Only 16 percent of the 11th graders read at or above grade level, and 55 per cent showed reading skills more than two years below grade level.

The audit report also asked the Attorney General to review findings that uncovered evidence of possible criminal violations involving purchasing procedures, oversight of consultants, and unreported employee fringe benefits.

Nashoba Regional School District

The finances of the debt-ridden 3,000-pupil district amounting to $3.4 million were placed under state control and a financial advisory board responsible for approving the entire district's spending. Interestingly, a $1.3 million shortfall was discovered in August and it is now three times larger.

An independent auditor said he found inappropriate transfers of money among school accounts going back several years. The Worcester district attorney and the state police are now investigating the problem.[746]

Michigan

Detroit[747]

In 1999, a state law replaced the city's locally elected board governing the 180,000-pupil district with an appointed seven-member board with the mayor selecting six members and the governor one member.

Inkster Public School District[748]

In 2000, the district hired Edison Inc. to pay off its deficit and manage the district. However, it set up barriers to the company and then reneged on paying Edison. In the following year, it avoided a takeover threat by promising to stop micromanaging, but the interference continued.

In 2002, citing that the "foolishness has to stop," the state superintendent invoked the state's fiscal responsibility act for the first time, and it became the second Michigan district to be taken over by the state. The reason for the takeover was based on a special commission finding of serious financial problems.

A financial manager was appointed who had the power to do anything from turning the district back over to the board, or dissolving the district and sending its students to adjacent districts.

Highland Park School District[749]

In 2002, the state targeted the 900-pupil district for state intervention because of city financial problems, but not a takeover. There is no state law permitting a state takeover. The city has a fiscal crisis because of rising debt and spending $3 million more per year than it takes in.

What is being proposed is that a state appointed CEO will be authorized to deal with all contractual issues facing the city and schools, a citizen advisory council will be formed to assist the CEO, and the school board will continue to function in an advisory capacity.

Not to be overlooked is that there are 21 schools that face penalties because of poor test results, but no takeovers are anticipated.

Minnesota

Minneapolis[750]

In 1993, the 44,000-pupil district hired Public Strategies Inc. to head the district's central management and take over the duties of the superintendent. However, the partnership was ended in 1997 because of disappointing student test scores and doubts concerning the private firm's ability to implement its plans.

Mississippi

North Panola School District[751]

In 1996, the 2200 pupil district became a state takeover because of the district's financial problems. Their $10 million budget fell short by $1.2 million and the prior year there was an $800,000 deficit.

In each of the prior three years, an independent accounting firm reported: "The books were in such bad shape that it could not issue an opinion." Under state laws, school districts are not allowed to operate with a deficit. In 1998, control was returned to the district.

Oktibbeha County School[752]

In 1997, the State assumed control of the district because of poor academic performance and other problems.

Tunica County School District[753]

In 1997, the State assumed control of the district because of poor academic performance.

Missouri

Kansas City

State lawmakers were considering a bill that would allow for the immediate takeover of the school district because it is riddled with so many problems particularly dismal test scores. It also needs an inspector general to trim waste and abuse, and improve the performance of principals and teachers. During the last mayoral campaign, five of the six candidates said they wouldn't hesitate to push for a takeover if the city's schools lose their accreditation. The eventual winner warned that although he doesn't want to implement a takeover, "if partnership and cooperation don't work, he won't be afraid to take drastic action."

The district did lose their accreditation in October of 1999, but it was granted provisional accreditation in April 2002 based on the academic progress it made over a period of two years. This removed the threat of a possible state takeover of the district.[754]

A fascinating, disturbing, and shameful history involving its desegregation experiment in 1985 can be found in the Chapter 12.[755]

The district plans to hire a private group or company to act as an interim superintendent. Only a handful of districts have resorted to such an unusual move.[756]

Niangua School District

The State Education Department stripped the accreditation of the district that has 332 students in one elementary and one high school. The reason was that the students failed all five standardized testing criteria used in the state accreditation. It has two years to improve or face a potential state takeover.

Currently, the State has 31 school districts with provisional accreditation.[757]

New Jersey

Camden

In June 2002, the Governor proposed to give the state unprecedented control over the city's troubled public schools that has a budget of $276 million and is the largest district in South Jersey (18,000 students and 4,000 employees). The proposal would have given the Governor veto power over board actions and would represent the first time the state has proposed such a change. The board would then have been reconstituted by having the governor and mayor appoint three members each to the nine-member board, and the voters would elect the remaining three members.[758]

However, a court overturned the legislation declaring it unconstitutional.[759]

Currently, it is under a more limited form of state oversight with a state task force overseeing the district's finances and operation because of mismanagement, poor test scores, and the highest dropout rate in the state.

Technically, it would not be a full-fledged state takeover, but the reality is that a governor's veto over any school board decision certainly represents a "quasi" takeover.

Jersey City School District

In 1989, the Jersey City 31,000 pupil school district became the first in the United States to be taken over by the State Board of Education. The district, the second largest in New Jersey, was charged with patronage in hiring, violation of state contract-bidding laws, political interference in the schools and general mismanagement that affected students and their abilities to learn.

The Administrative Law Judge stated: "Ample proofs establish that the children attending public school in the district are not receiving the thorough and efficient education to which they are entitled, that political interference originating in earlier school administrations has continued, that public money allotted to education in the district is being misspent, and that district problems chronicled in so many state reports are deep-rooted and endemic."

This was the conclusion after 103 days of hearings and sifting through 2,000 pages of testimony. The hearings revealed "case after case of unqualified people getting jobs because they had performed political favors for various mayors or their underlings...and landing a principalship depended on whom you knew." Textbooks were 30 years out of date and the curriculum had not been revised in 18 years.[760]

Within four years, the state appointed superintendent achieved results in the same school district that was paralyzed by corruption and mismanagement.

- Central office positions were reduced by 117.
- Sixty-seven teachers had pay raises withheld, 13 lost their jobs, 20 other resigned and 90 non-instructional staff were fired
- All the principals were evaluated and some were demoted and replaced.
- Curriculum was revised and new textbooks were purchased.
- All school were painted and repaired; a high school swimming pool that was filled with garbage was cleaned and made operable.
- Pre-kindergarten programs were expanded, and all-day kindergarten enrollments tripled.
- Advanced placement courses were established in all of the high schools.

What did not show improvement were test scores, but this should come as no surprise. Changing the culture of 82 schools where administrators indulged in expensive restaurant meals while school buildings crumbled is a formidable task. What must be understood is that years of gross mismanagement and a culture of apathy cannot be corrected easily, quickly, or painlessly.

Interestingly, the superintendent at the time of the takeover won a place on the school board, and he has indicated his desire to continue running the district when it is returned to local control.[761]

In 2000, the state board approved returning control of the district's budget and finances to the local board.

Newark

In 1995, the 41,000-pupil district was taken over by the state management team because it had failed to give its students a minimum education for decades. In addition, buildings were crumbling, bathrooms lacked basic supplies, and the lunch program was so overstaffed it was described as a "jobs program." However, the district's top administrators had expense accounts in 32 restaurants and attended conferences in Hawaii. As a result, the State cut nearly 700 administrative and non-teaching jobs that freed up $26 million for instruction. Since then, it has made only modest gains academically.

The city took the state-run system to court alleging financial mismanagement and that it should be held accountable for a $73 million funding gap that prompted the district's 1999 financial crisis. Furthermore, they want to prove that the state takeover has been a complete failure because of bad management. This is probably the first time that a takeover city has challenged how the state has managed a system.

However, state officials found that the district couldn't produce monthly financial statements, and one audit found that $25 million could not be accounted for.[762]

Paterson

In 1991, after years of performing poorly on assessments and reviews, the 25,000-pupil district was taken over by state officials. According to an audit conducted three years later, substantial progress had been made but many serious problems remained. Standardized test scores remain too low (only 59 percent of the 11th graders passed the reading portion of the high school proficiency test) and many of the buildings are deteriorating. An estimate was provided indicating that $70 million would be needed for capital improvements over the next three to five years.

The audit does report: "By many measures, the schools are qualitatively and quantitatively better today than they were four years ago."

Interestingly, the State Education Commissioner called for changes in the takeover law that would return control of Jersey City, Newark and Paterson back to local control. He called the 14-year-old law "ill-conceived and poorly executed."

The state takeovers have been called "the state's equivalent of the Vietnam War, a long-running, intractable effort with little hope of resolution."[763]

A report claimed that "State control since 1991 has failed to turn the schools around. Yet, it spends $12,000 per pupil—10 percent above the state average. It goes on to recommend that school choice, vouchers or scholarships be considered at much less cost…it would enable many Paterson students to attend private/parochial schools where achievement levels are far higher."[764]

New Mexico [765]

Santa Rosa Consolidated School District

In 1998, the state education department assumed financial control after the district ended the school year with a $100,000 deficit.

Santa Fe Independent School District

In 1999, state officials assumed control over the financial decisions because of financial problems within the school district.

New York

New York City

Mayoral Board

In 2002, state legislation gave the mayor power over the school systems 1.1 million students. The mayor will pick a new chancellor and seven members of a newly established 13-member board. The remaining members will be chosen by each of the five borough presidents. Thirty-two community school boards will be abolished, and local school superintendents will be selected directly by the chancellor.

The new board will be part-time and have no say in the daily management of the school system, but it will vote on the capital and expense budgets and on certain policy matters.

It should be obvious from the examples of fraud and mismanagement why such a takeover was required. Mayors sought this change over the past 25 years. It's interesting what one board member said at their last and final meeting: "The problem wasn't the fault of the individuals who sat on the board, it was the fault of the structure."

Mayor Bloomberg said that, "Today we are making history. This reform of school governance will fundamentally change the way in which we manage the education of our children. It will give the school system the one thing it fundamentally needs, accountability. We will no longer have to tolerate an incapable bureaucracy that does not respond to the needs of the students. We are replacing it with a governance structure that will give us the opportunity to fix our broken schools, provide our children with the tools they need to succeed in society, and finally give parents the ability to voice their opinions and concerns."[766]

The rhetoric is always inspiring; however, the New York Times delivered a dismaying report of the schools two years after the mayor made his promise. "The Bloomberg approach, featuring a new system of governance, elimination of the old Board of Education, and an end to social promotions, hasn't worked...The plan appears to be a dud...Nothing has changed."[767]

This sorry result despite the fact that he brought in hundreds of new principals, installed new leadership, reorganized the 32 districts into 10 regions, hired a parent coordinator for every school, and raised about $200 million in private money to supplement the education budget. However, 42 percent of the fifth graders in Harlem's District 5 have been told they are in danger of being left behind. For third-graders, it's 52 percent. Too bad, but he did try.

Roosevelt School District

In 1996, the State Legislature approved the takeover of the Roosevelt School District with one high school and five elementary schools. Students have chronically performed poorly on standardized state tests in this predominantly black school district, but there have been other problems. In the spring of 2001, classes were canceled for two days after a rash of fights and bomb threats. A three-member state management team was appointed to supervise an executive administrator who is responsible for working with the local superintendent to implement the states corrective-action plan.[768]

The takeover is beginning to show some results with better discipline, better maintenance, more security, dress conduct codes, and a stronger curriculum.[769]

Two board members promptly sued the state for $8 million claiming that the district was singled out because it was primarily all black and that residents were denied their voting rights by the board's removal from any decision-making authority.

Since then the state strategy has changed and now it places troubled schools on a list of "Schools Under Registration Review" and allows three years for them to shape up or be closed. Six schools have been closed down and about 100 are on the list, most of them in New York City.

Ohio

Cleveland [770]

In 1995, a U.S. federal court charged the state with running the 75,000 student school district through a state-appointed superintendent who was given the powers to levy taxes and close schools. What the superintendent found was a system with "horrible facilities, heavy debt, a graduation rate of 33 percent, and a senior passing rate on proficiency tests of only 3 percent.

As the new superintendent took over the "disaster called a school system," he also had to deal with a third federal judge to rule on the school systems desegregation plan. Unfortunately, the plaintiffs in the case play a big role in whatever actions are taken and hinder the needed changes required to turn the school system around.

He has become cynical about the intent of interest groups who make it almost impossible to get agreement on actions. "Urban districts are all about money and power." For example, trying to get rid of busing involves $60 million in desegregation money.

In spite of these problems, the first bond issue in 20 years was approved, all day kindergarten classes were restored, new textbooks were ordered, and long-overdue building repairs were started.

A state representative, Mike Fox, identified several issues in dealing with urban district problems. They include: reallocation of resources, decisions about what allocations will produce the best results, how to make sure that expectations for students are just as high as for students in suburban or rural districts, how to establish customer-centered market-driven structures, how to assure and fund safe school environments, and how to provide high-quality professional development.

In 1997, the state legislature shifted control of the schools to the mayor and charged him with appointing the school board and the chief executive officer.

Youngstown School District[771]

In 1996, the State took control of the district because of financial problems.

Oklahoma

Alluwe

In July 1993, the school was annexed to four nearby school districts. The mandatory annexation was caused in part by dwindling enrollment and financial problems.

Pennsylvania

Statewide[772]

Several school systems are being targeted for state takeover under the Education Empowerment Act that gives the education department vast new powers to intervene in low performing districts.

The law does allow for district innovations such as privatizing troubled schools, creating charter schools, reassigning staff, and even waiving state regulations as part of any improvement plan.

The following low-performing districts received new financial aid, increased regulatory flexibility, and greater state oversight:

- Clairton City School District, 1,000 enrollment
- Duquesne City School District, 1,000 enrollment
- Sto-Rox School District, 1,700 enrollment
- Wilkinsburg Borough School district, 2,000 enrollment
- Aliquippa School District, 1,600 enrollment
- Steelton-Highspire, 1,400 enrollment
- Lancaster School District, 10,800 enrollment
- York City School district, 7,500 enrollment

Assistance teams picked by the state from local colleges, businesses, or other professions will aid the districts. However, while some distressed districts are working closely with state assistance teams, others are ignoring them.

Philadelphia[773]

In 2001, the state took control of the sixth largest school district in the country for being "financially and academically troubled." The state education secretary remarked: "It probably is one of the worst performing school districts in America." The school board was replaced with a five member State Reform Commission. The district with 264 schools and 200,000 students has a $1.7 billion budget, but is $216 million in the red. .

Philly has been a very troubled district. In 1993, the legislators froze the state's school aid formula. What happened since was that the population of poor and immigrant students increased and now represent 80 percent of the student population while the tax base stayed stagnant.

Part of the agreement will infuse $120 million in new money annually to buy a million new books, improve curricula, provide bonuses for principals, training for teachers, and extra pay for 1,200 more mentor teachers. In addition, the teaching force is expected to be cut by as many as 500 positions.

Seventy low performing schools, picked solely on the basis of standardized test scores, will serve as models involving privatization, charters, independent operation and reconstitution. Forty-two schools will be privately run: 28 by for-profit school managers, six by nonprofits, and eight by universities. The remaining schools will be reconstituted, chartered or become independent.

A key factor in the privatization model is to allow the managers to hire staff, but it does not appear that this will be the case in any of the schools.

There is an interesting story about the takeover concerning an education reporter who decided to become a teacher in the school system. As a new teacher, she received no direction or even textbooks. She learned that "what or even whether she taught was of secondary concern to her superiors." She reported that dozens of students roamed the hallways, picking fights, setting fires and threatening other students and school staff with scissors. Although these students should have been transferred to discipline schools, the paper work process discouraged teachers from even bothering.

Special education classes had no permanent teachers, and when substitutes did not show up, the students were on their own to roam the hallways unsupervised.

She now believes that school administrators, union officials, and school board members are painfully far removed from the reality of urban schools. As a reporter, she covered a prolonged school board debate about ending social promotion. What she found as a teacher was that her principal could change student grades at will. After failing two of her own students, the principal raised their grades despite the fact that social promotion had been banned.

What is clear from this reporter's insights is that laws, rules, regulations and policies are not always implemented and worse, in too many cases, there is no punishment for the violators. It also demonstrates vividly and candidly that "no one is watching the ship."[774]

So it's not surprising to learn that academic experts question whether the plan will work because of the assortment of private companies and universities taking over the school and because parents need to be more involved.

It's rather astonishing that there doesn't seem to be an answer for improving urban education. Even more incredible is that educational and academic bankruptcy goes on for years before any serious attempt is made to correct it; in the meantime, the children suffer and their advocates remain silent and immobilized.

<u>Chester-Upland</u>

Since 1994, a state board has overseen the 6,700-pupil district's finances; but in 2000, a panel named by the Secretary of Education took over all operations. However, finances were not the only problems since 40% of its students drop out before graduation and 68 percent failed the math and reading portions of the state's exam.

In a move borne out by desperation, the panel hired three for-profit companies in 2000 to run 11 of the 14 schools in this district of 7,500 students. What this approach has done is to change the role of the school board from operating the schools to becoming a general contractor.[775]

Interestingly, a report that studied this districts takeover concluded: "It is an example of how not to restructure."[776]

> "There is a crisis in Chester-Upland—a fiscal crisis, a leadership crisis, an accounting crisis. In spite of the fact that the state has run the district for 11 years through a local board and 5 years under state direction, it is still in crisis."

It owes $10 million to vendors including $4.2 million to Edison, it has a total debt of $70 million, and it has lost its ability to borrow more. Millions of dollars have been lost in federal aid as well. Over $12,000 per pupil is spent for the 5,000 students that is above the state average of $9,300.

Duquesne School District[777]

In October 2000, the district was targeted for improvement because 70 percent of its students scored in the bottom group statewide, and then it was also declared, "fiscally distressed" by the state because it faced a $2.5 million deficit in and $11 million budget.

Harrisburg School District[778]

In 2000, the mayor was directed to pick a new school board to run the 8,800-pupil school district. However, the school board filed a lawsuit alleging that a new law granting state officials' permission to take over the district is unconstitutional. The board claimed that the Educational Empowerment Act singles out the 8,800-student district for takeover in a manner that violates the State constitution.

The measure gave nine other districts three years to improve before they would face takeovers, but directed the mayor to appoint a new school board for the state's capital city by July 1. The district is one of the few Pennsylvania districts whose scores on state tests have declined in recent years, and the State contends its problems are grave enough to require immediate intervention. The board attorney said the legislation was passed without consulting local officials.

"It was stealth legislation, sneak legislation. When you single out one district with different treatment, our constitution says that is not permitted."

A court decision rejected the board's claim, and the mayor appointed a new five-member board of control.

Rhode Island

Central Falls School District[779]

In 1991, this 2,700-pupil district requested a state takeover because it was "on the brink of financial ruin." The problem is that they simply have no room for growth in their tax base, whereas their expenses keep increasing. Currently, it has the highest tax rate in the state. The takeover will enable the district to get $1.8 million in state loans and grants. A special administrator will assume control of the district and report directly to the state education commissioner.

South Carolina

Allendale County[780]

In August 1999, the poor and racially segregated school district was taken over by the State because it consistently had the worst test scores in the state and little was being done to improve the situation.

Tennessee

The State placed 63 schools on probation. This was the third year in which state education officials have named the most troubled schools and given them extra support in an effort to boost achievement test scores.[781]

Texas

Somerset School District[782]

In 1995, the district was taken over because of poor student performance and mismanagement. In 1997, control was returned to the local district.

Wilmer-Hutchins School District[783]

In 1996, the State appointed a management team to run the 3,800-pupil school district. Local control of the district was returned in 1998.

However, the state was put back in charge in November 2004 because the Board consistently resisted cost cutting measures the State deemed critical. A state management team now has the legal authority to overrule nearly any board decision.

The district woes seem ingrained in a system of mismanagement and corruption even with state oversight and control.

Westminster Independent School District[784]

In 1998, the state board revoked the 176-pupil district's accreditation citing a lax curriculum, neglect of facilities, failure to complete paperwork and other factors. The district had been warned repeatedly since the 1950's that its accreditation status was in jeopardy.

West Virginia[785]

Logan County

In 1992, state officials took over the Appalachian district of 7,200 pupils after many years of poor management and personnel practices and low student achievement records. At the time of the takeover, 71 percent of elementary schools and 55 percent of secondary schools scored below the 50th percentile on state standardized tests.

There was also rampant cronyism on the part of school board members and the administration. People were hired and given the best jobs without much concern for the quality of their skills.

In spite of such mismanagement, the local board was not replaced. The presence of a state appointed superintendent, who was put in charge of the district, was criticized by the local newspaper and even teachers were skeptical.

Yet, four years later, the district rebounded from years of academic failure and financial mismanagement. The struggling local economy did not change nor was there any state bailout money. It simply took a yearly focus on several problems at a time and "taking the things we had and make them better." In 1998, the district was returned to local control.

This case is in sharp contrast to other takeovers, and it demonstrates that more money is not always the answer. Commitment and focus can do wonders.

McDowell County Schools

The state took control of the 4,600-pupil district in 2001 after a 144 page state audit. However, the district leadership requested this takeover because they could no longer handle the job.

One of the districts many problems was a 64 percent drop in student population over the past 20 years.[786]

The state board stripped the board of authority in financial matters, personnel, curriculum and the school calendar. It also removed the interim superintendent.

Mingo County School District

In 1998, the district was taken over by the state because "extraordinary circumstances" existed due to continuing budget deficits, low student achievement and a lack of leadership.

Lincoln County Schools

In 2000, the state took control of the district because of many problems including management, financing, facilities and academics.

Canada Does It Too

What is interesting to note is that takeover strategies are not unique to the United States. In Canada, school boards in Ottawa, Toronto and Hamilton have been taken over by the province for failing to obey a law demanding they balance their budgets. Toronto has a $90 million budget deficit and Ottawa has an $18 million deficit.

Supervisors will be in charge of trying to make cuts amounting to $130 million from the three districts, but the paid trustees will still be paid and be required to hold meetings and deal with parent concerns.

The problem manifested itself because the trustees of the three districts, contrary to law, refused to make the cuts necessary to balance the books.[787]

Summary

Clearly, takeovers have had a difficult history and the results are certainly mixed, but basically student academic failure has not been stopped. There are two very critical issues that surface concerning the school takeover problem.

The first is that the takeovers occur mostly in districts with predominantly minority enrollments. For example, in Jersey City, almost 75 per cent of the student population is African-American and Latino. Why wasn't there more of an outcry and demonstrations by the minority leaders both local and national in Jersey City? Why are minority leaders relatively silent on demanding more accountable schools in the urban districts?

The fact is that any outcry tends to occur only when a district is a takeover target in spite of the fact that it is an attempt to correct rather horrendous and long-lasting problems. In at least eight such districts, there have been lawsuits and accusations asserting that the takeovers singled out predominantly minority districts and violated the rights of voters to choose their local boards. Such an action was highlighted in a Texas takeover with charges that it violated the federal Voting Rights Act of 1965. The state did amend its law to expressly prohibit state interventions from interfering with local elections, but the Justice Department still insists it must approve any takeovers.

A U.S. Court of Appeals for the District of Columbia Circuit ruled that the D.C. takeover in 1995 did not have authority to fire the superintendent and transferred power from the elected board to an appointed board of trustees.

The Cleveland takeover also resulted in lawsuits by the Cleveland Teachers' Union and the local chapter of the NAACP claiming that mayoral control violated voting rights

According to the Rev. Michael DeBose, a former school board candidate who opposed the takeover of the Cleveland schools, "When you've got black people in charge and a majority-black district, people think they don't know what they are doing."

What seems to be forgotten or ignored is that takeovers only occur when there is clear evidence of poor student achievement, financial disarray, gross mismanagement, and only after years of inaction or incompetence by the local board. This has nothing to do with racial issues; it has to do with being responsible. How can it be a racial issue when the purpose of a takeover is to provide a thorough and efficient education for children who are being denied this fundamental right?

In 1997, the Education Commission of the States held a conference about state takeovers and identified other issues:

1. Teacher union positions
2. Politics on the basis of race
3. How to rearrange power
4. Lack of progress on student achievement

Participants at the conference agreed: "State and local actions to date have not produced the kind of transformation in urban districts and the student outcomes that everyone wants."[788]

Why haven't teacher unions, the NAACP and other organizations prepared lawsuits to force academic and financial improvement? They only seem to act when an attempt is made to improve the education of children that is one of the goals of any takeover attempt.

The real issue is why minority leaders, teacher groups, and parent groups in such communities did not demand state intervention to get their school districts to perform more effectively. They certainly are not powerless as evidenced by outcries and demonstrations for other issues affecting minorities. Why doesn't "thorough and efficient" education rank high on the list of rights that they are entitled too?

The second issue is why does it take so long for interventions to take place? Why don't the states intervene much sooner? If the local boards have been so inept, certainly a finger must be pointed at the state officials who allowed such corruption and mismanagement to exist for years. Perhaps, they too, should have been replaced. After all, education is a function of the state and the state has the power and right to intervene when local boards do not do their job.

However, what seems rather evident in school takeovers is that it's much easier to get a grip on school finances and management practices than it is to make significant gains in student performance.

A study released in 2000 concluded: "If you flip through the ledgers of state-run schools, fiscal management is typically restored but many still suffer from academic bankruptcy." Some common reform characteristics are to be found such as expanded flexibility and increased accountability. Chicago is cited for its effort to privatize ancillary services to improve performance, utilizing charter schools extensively, ending social promotions and terminating incompetent administrators.

"Successful intervention efforts recognize how important local knowledge is in the reform process and holding decision makers accountable…they frequently outpace the standard practice of throwing more money at a problem and transferring control from one bureaucracy to another."[789]

Another study concluded: "Concerning effectiveness of takeovers, research is lagging behind the pace of policy and practice…and there is a scarcity of research on the effects of state takeovers."[790]

Takeovers, when viewed in totality, are really an indictment against poor and inept state oversight; yet, this issue has not been addressed and it should be. There is absolutely no reason why it should take years of corruption and incompetence to prevail in any school district before there is some form of intervention.

A 1998 study of the takeovers in New Jersey City, Compton, and Logan County concluded that some lessons were learned:[791]

1. Align the local curriculum with state standards and tests.
2. Involve teachers from the outset.
3. Work to prevent turnover in key administrative positions.
4. Pick a realistic number of problems to address each year.
5. Open line of communication with the community.
6. Work to maintain consistency on the board.
7. Seek formal board training.
8. Seek help, don't get defensive

Of course, there is the issue of local control, but local control should not be a license to corrupt education that again is a function and responsibility of the state. However, another lesson that has been learned is that "Ill Will Comes With Territory in Takeovers," and "elbowing out local officials comes at the heavy cost of lawsuits, bitter media battles, and confused and angry teachers and parents."[792]

The Education Commission of the States reports that there is an important lesson to be learned from the takeovers: "States that don't give their managers broad and unequivocal authority are asking for trouble."

Furthermore, local control is really a fallacy because whether anyone likes it or not state controls have increased and federal control now overshadows both state and local board control.

The fact is that under NCLB state takeovers are mandated of so-called low-performing school districts. In New York State, the governor unveiled plans to give control of the state's five largest school districts—New York City, Yonkers, Syracuse, Rochester and Buffalo—to the mayors.

Another interesting issue is that results seem to be different when mayors take control of the local schools than when the state takes control. Mayoral control, perhaps because it remains local, tends to run a bit more smoothly and get somewhat better results. What needs to be recalled, however, is that at the turn of the 20th century school reformers argued the City Hall was too corrupt and too bloated with patronage appointments to be in charge of children's education.

What makes this strategy of mayoral takeovers hard to evaluate is that there is no common plan or approach and each is somewhat unique. In Chicago and Boston, the mayor exerted strong control over the schools; and in other districts, such as Sacramento, the mayor simply endorsed a slate of candidates for the school board.

A study by Michael W. Kirst concludes: "If you look at it in terms of 'are you better off now than you were before,' the answer would be yes."[793]

Another study concluded: "Mayoral takeovers appear to be more productive in terms of academic improvement."[794]

The reality is that takeovers yield very mixed results. Generally, state intervention strategies return fiscal soundness to districts typically in three to five years, but student achievement often lags behind because "student learning is more dynamic in nature and, therefore, not easily rectified by a single, standardized approach."[795]

The difficulty with takeovers is compounded by the fact that politicians set unreasonable expectations, enough time hasn't passed to give the changes a change to bear fruit, and partly because core problems are intertwined with social ills that are unaffected by a change in school leadership. Among the problems are poverty, lack of parental involvement, entrenched unions, bureaucracy on a gargantuan scale, aging buildings, and budgets so large that average board members and school administrators are unprepared to manage them.[796]

Another critical fact that needs to be addressed is that the traditional school governance of a locally elected (or appointed) board and a superintendent who manages the daily operations hasn't worked and doesn't work in far too many districts. Local control breeds indebtedness to politicians, patronage, unions, contractors, and other special interests. That's why outside intervention is necessary because the changes to reform the system are usually not popular.

The real overriding issue is one of responsibility and fulfilling the public trust and the law that "thorough and efficient" education is provided to all students. The reality is that the states have not been thorough and efficient in carrying out their responsibilities either and that's why the federal government is getting increasingly intrusive. It is their lack of thorough and efficient oversight that allows school boards to be corrupt and to mismanage school districts to the detriment of the children.

For example, the vast majority of local school board members receive no education or training in fulfilling a very complex, time consuming, and emotionally draining job, and they receive no training in how to manage multimillion dollar budgets. Such training is desperately needed and it should be the responsibility of the states to provide thorough and efficient education and training to all board members.

This issue has not been addressed by any studies nor has it been included as a strategy in any takeovers. The question is whether a thorough and efficient program of education and training for board members make them more effective and produce better results for a school district? It would certainly help those board members who are willing and eager to do their job responsibly and honestly.

A governance option that has not been considered is to have school superintendents hired by the State and assigned to local school districts. Yes, there could be some input by the local boards, but this would take away the "indebtedness" that local control breeds and allow the state to implement consistent state policies, practices, and standards.

There is much shame that has to be heaped on state boards and departments of education, teacher unions, parent groups, and other advocates for education. Why? They have not been forceful and aggressive enough in a timely manner in demanding that titanic action be taken when there is academic, financial, and administrative bankruptcy in local school districts.

The reality to all of these takeovers is that in every case there had been waste and mismanagement (WaMi) and, in most cases, fraud and stealing (FraSte) on a scale that is very hard to fathom. Until these problems are addressed aggressively and decisively, takeovers will continue unabated and with questionable results.

CHAPTER TEN

Reconstitution: Recycling Failed Schools

"The art of progress is to preserve order amid change and to preserve change amid disorder." Alfred North Whitehead

Thousands of low performing schools have already been identified and many more will be added under the No Child Left Behind Act. In the urban districts, two-thirds of the students fail to meet even minimum standards of achievement. It's a national and shameful disgrace. More money has done absolutely nothing to solve this perplexing and gnawing critical problem.

This is reiterated by Susan Neuman of the U.S. Office of Elementary and Secondary Education who said that the low academic achievement of the country's poorest children couldn't be raised by "pouring more money and more money into the system...Poverty should not be an excuse for academic failure...being poor is not a recipe for low performance."

Perhaps not, but it is an extremely strong contributor to low performing schools; and, unless ways are found to deal with this socio-economic factor more effectively than has been the case, the recipe for low performance will prevail.

State takeovers have been one way to deal with the problem; however, takeovers usually involve entire districts, not individual schools. Mayoral takeovers have been another strategy to take control of schools and it has been somewhat more successful.

The NCLB Act provides another option and allows students to leave a low performing school (after certain conditions have been met) and go elsewhere. Unfortunately, it is easier said than done. Where will they go and how will they get there? Schools that are already overcrowded or concerned with keeping class sizes down are not going to accept students who want to transfer from a low-performing school, and transportation problems add still another obstacle. The fact is that some districts are already limiting such an option. Even when it is available, some parents will not opt to remove their child from a failing school.

What is not understood and accepted is that a low performing school district or a low performing school meets the definition of "corruption" because it is a betrayal of the public trust. The public provided the tax dollars to support a "thorough and efficient" education for the children and the district failed to deliver. In essence, what happens is that too often the poorly performing schools are spending the money they have "poorly," and wasting and mismanaging other resources. This is corruption pure and simple.

However, it's even much worse because there are many strategies to turn around low-performing schools. Failure to attempt a turn-around effort is professional and moral corruption as well. What is even more corrupt is that the responsibility for a turn-around does not rest just with a low-performing school. Central office, the school board, and state departments of education are also responsible for monitoring school performance. How is it that thousands of schools have been low performing for years without being identified as such? No one really knew the extent of these failing schools until NCLB was implemented.

Obviously, there has been a colossal failure by too many superintendents, school boards, and state departments of education to take their monitoring responsibilities seriously. Failure to take timely and appropriate action to bring low performing schools up to at least adequate academic levels is corruption. There is certainly ample evidence that such schools can be salvaged with aggressive and intelligent administration along with a detailed plan of action.

It is absolutely mind-boggling that any school can continue to be low performing year after year in spite of the fact that a number of states have instituted procedures to identify such schools and to institute transformation strategies to make positive changes.

Is it that too many policymakers and administrators really don't believe that low-performing schools can be turned around successfully?

Another factor is that low performing schools may have little capacity to turn themselves around. Needless to say, if they did have the capacity to do so, they would not be low performing. If this is true, and it probably is in many situations, what are the obstacles that prevent the school from having the needed capacity? Why is it so difficult to assess what the problems are when there are common problems that can be counted on the fingers of one hand? Obviously, the answer has to be poor leadership at all levels and a complacent staff. This is why some such schools need to be changed from the inside out.

Reconstitution

The reform strategy used in many such circumstances is "reconstitution." It was an idea that began in San Francisco in the 1980's. Under this strategy a school's faculty and administration is disbanded, and a new staff, structure, and curriculum are put into place. This is a radical and controversial step, particularly with teacher unions, but it is usually preceded by time and resources to make improvements with the existing staff. During reconstitution, displaced staff is given the option to reapply for their old positions, but the problem from the union perspective is the impact it has on teachers who are not rehired. This is one of the issues that causes so much rife with unions and reconstitution. Of course, jobs come first and children are somewhere down on the list of priorities.

In essence, the purpose behind reconstitution is to transform an academically, financially, and administratively "bankrupt" school by bringing in a fresh, new, committed administration and staff. A Harvard education professor, Gary Orfield, describes the process as "trying to rebuild a rapidly deteriorating train as you're running down the tracks."[797]

Just imagine a school atmosphere that is described as "so poisonous the teachers couldn't teach and the pupils couldn't learn." This is how Rusk Elementary School in Houston, Texas was described. The school was reconstituted and within just one year, observers were lauding the improvement. It was the same school, the same students, but with new staff and commitment.[798]

One of the critical issues involved in this strategy is developing the criteria to be used in determining what is a low-performing school. Some determinants are dropout rates, student absences, unqualified teachers, teacher turnover, gross mismanagement and, of course, the key determinant of standardized tests. In other words, it's important to establish the criteria to be used, and then it needs to be very well articulated and communicated to staff students, parents, and community. Once this is accomplished, a plan of action must be developed and supported by everyone involved. Finally, the school is given a deadline for achieving the necessary improvements. Only when corrective efforts fail is reconstitution considered.

What is rather dumbfounding is that a survey by the National Education Association of schools involved with reconstitution found: "More than a quarter were unaware their schools had been pinpointed as low-performing, and 22 percent said their school shake-up came as a complete shock." Teachers in such schools characterized the process as "arbitrary, chaotic, and irrational."[799]

As an example, a surprise reconstitution happened at the John Adams Elementary School in Colorado Springs, Colorado in 1997. The staff had just returned from a productive daylong writing workshop when they were informed that all staff, from the crossing guards to the principal, had to reapply for their jobs. Only three of the 30 staff members returned to the school and most did not even apply for their old positions.[800]

However, it's difficult for any rationale person to believe that the staff of a low performing school doesn't know the school and students are doing poorly and have been under performing for years. An abundance of public information is readily available and presented to school staff and the community. Test results and school profiles are just two examples. The only logical conclusion that can be drawn from this example is that low performance is considered normal and acceptable. How bad does it have to get?

Like state/city takeovers, there are numerous problems and issues involved with reconstitution: political conflict, lowered teacher morale, inexperienced staff, inadequate resources, poor planning, and time factors. For example, in 1997, the superintendent in Prince George's County, MD, took a radical step to improve achievement at six low performing schools in the district of 125,000 students. He told the staff of each school that everyone from teachers to custodians had to resign and reapply for their jobs. New principals were brought in, and the schools were essentially reconstituted.[801]

A critical reason for his decision is probably common to all such schools and it should be engraved on every school board table: "We were getting so comfortable with mediocrity that we were in a 'feel-good' situation that wasn't getting any results."[802]

This is refreshing honesty to hear, and it certainly would be nice if more schools admitted this reality.

Stoddert Middle School was one of the schools designated for reconstitution because only 18.9 percent of the students met the state standard on a 1996 composite score of six testing areas. Maryland set a goal of 70 percent passing rate. The new principal rehired 27 teachers and 23 new ones. He ended up with a predominantly young and inexperienced staff with about 40 percent lacking certification to take on the challenge of teaching disadvantaged minority students.

Testing after one year proved very disappointing because three of the reconstituted schools, including Stoddert, performed more poorly.

But there were other school factors that contributed to Stoddert's failure. Nearly 60 percent of the students qualified free or reduced-price lunch, 99.8 percent were African-American and came from a neighborhood with a high crime and poverty rate. Even though the reconstituted staff at Stoddert spent hundreds of hours preparing the students for the state test, it made no difference because there was a failure to involve the parents and the greater community surrounding Stoddert.

In 2001, the Maryland State Board of Education voted to place the Westport School in Baltimore City under state reconstitution. In addition, it identified 12 low performing schools in Baltimore City and Prince George's Counties for local reconstitution. This is a probationary status in which the State provides additional resources and technical assistance and monitors progress in student performance. Currently, there are 102 schools under local reconstitution. Such schools need to submit management plans in accordance with state regulations and timelines, and state appointed experts are assigned to aid each school.[803] This is a far more common-sense approach.

Simply stated, schools cannot implement reforms or reconstitution in isolation from the home and community. The superintendent readily admitted that his plan didn't work out as he had hoped and realized it was an ill-conceived plan. He put it in place too hastily, just 45 days before the end of the 1996-1997 school year, and without enough input from school staff. What he was trying to do was to replicate without success what had occurred in San Francisco. His problem was he did not study the details of the San Francisco model.

San Francisco was the first school district to use reconstitution as a means to improve achievement in schools with a predominantly minority enrollment. It is one of the oldest and most aggressive practitioners of reconstitution, having restaffed eight schools since 1994 and eight others during the 1980's. What was different about the San Francisco effort was that the teachers and teachers' union were part of the process. This is an extremely critical factor if success is to be realized.[804]

A study headed by a Harvard professor in 1992 concluded that the dozen schools that were reconstituted and infused with new funds had shown more progress than schools in a later group that were simply given more money.[805]

This is an important piece of information because it demonstrates that giving more money to schools without any comprehensive action plan for improvement and intended results is foolhardy. Yet, it's done all the time, again, and again, and again. Educators and policymakers simply do not learn their lessons very well—they essentially failed "sandbox 101."

One of the reconstituted schools, Visitacion Valley Middle School, received national publicity for their test score gains. However, Kent Mitchell, president of the United Educators of San Francisco and a strong opponent of reconstitution, contended that it mostly failed. Professor Luis Fraga who was studying the history of reconstitution for several months said he had yet to determine whether it was successful.[806]

It is interesting to note that the new principal established a written list of 15 expectations for staff along with an explicit statement:

"If you have reservations about team teaching or thematic instruction; if you prefer to teach your subject separately, to set your own rules and procedures which differ from building agreements, to set standards for class groups rather than expectations for individuals, to focus on teacher directed activities rather than to facilitate student-oriented, hands-on lessons; if you prefer the status quo to continuous growth and improvement; if you are looking for a teaching position with little or no expectation for your commitment outside of the school day, you may want to look for a position elsewhere."[807]

The frank statement identifies many of the problems found in low-performing schools. Of course, there were consequences felt by the disposed Visitacion staff. They felt the process was so demeaning that they refused to go out on interviews to other schools. The principals from other schools "saw us as damaged goods from a damaged school."[808]

A recent reaction to the San Francisco model is that it has been a total failure. Why? "There is no disputing the fact that a disproportionate number of African American and Latino public-school students are victims of a widening academic opportunity gap, which is relegating them to dead-end, low paying jobs, and far too many to the juvenile-justice system."[809]

Interestingly, reconstitution was halted after the "reconstitution" superintendent left. Of course, a new superintendent begins a new reign of reform, and now there will be dream schools, a new program for redesigning schools. It still requires staff at selected schools to reapply for the jobs they previously held, but the superintendent claims that it's not reconstitution. However, if it looks like reconstitution, it acts like reconstitution, and if the talk is like reconstitution, it just might be reconstitution renamed to make it seem more palatable. There is resistance to the "dream school" model because teachers must reapply for their previous jobs.[810]

Another issue is that a particular school may not be conducive to being saved. Even the American Federation of Teachers Association acknowledges that some schools aren't worth saving. Therefore, rather than trying to reconstitute them, they should be closed and the students sent to other schools or be given other options such as vouchers. In Florida vouchers are being used to provide an option for students in low performing schools to attend private schools.

One of the more interesting options for staff is to give them monetary awards for improving the school and raising student achievement. It's a rather mindless and even insulting approach because it infers very directly that the staff has the skills and knowledge to do a better job but won't do so because they want more money. This approach did backfire in Cincinnati even with union support because the teachers defeated such a contract change, but it has been tried in other districts.

What seems to be a more productive model for improving a school is the Kentucky process. It focuses on building the capacity for success among teachers, students, and administrators, and the state allocates millions of dollars to make the process work. The schools get at least two years of full-time assistance and as much as $100,000, and all teachers and administrators must undergo extensive evaluation.

Steve Moats, a veteran teacher and member of the Kentucky Education Association, has worked as a "distinguished educator" trained to help schools in crisis put themselves back on the road to success. He Stated: "No one has ever lost their job because of their evaluation." The NEA approach is to focus on resources and programs to keep low-performing schools from sinking to the point of total reconstitution.[811]

However, it's very difficult to believe that the staff of a school that has been identified as a low-performer can be given extensive evaluations, yet no one is found who can't, won't or is incompetent to teach. If everyone was fully able to perform, how did the school become low performing? It sounds like the NEA is somewhat biased and prejudiced about its approach, but this certainly should come as no surprise.

In fact, there are critical and key elements in the entire process that seem to have been overlooked in all of the literature and examples on reconstitution. There are district and community obstacles that are beyond the control of a single school to change.[812]

- The school is located in impoverished areas where family distress, crime and violence are prevalent.
- State and district policies often provide limited financial, human, and programmatic resources to schools that do not have the capacity to support high-quality teaching and learning.
- Low achievement is usually accompanied by high rates of student absenteeism, dropping out, and delinquency. Over time, these factors in combination with chronic low achievement can cause stress and disorganization.

One of the problems that must be identified early on is to identify the existing district/community obstacles that must be removed or ameliorated that contribute to low performance. Typically, this is not done because the entire focus of the reconstitution effort is on the building, not the political, social and educational environment in which it exists. This is probably a major reason why a number of reconstitution efforts have failed, and it is a major reason why there are low-performing schools.

Another problem are the parents and their reaction to reconstitution. In one school that was being reconstituted, "the parents were angry...because their favorite teachers were being taken away." Unfortunately, parents too often support "favorite" teachers who are ineffective, but that are nice to their children.

There was such a reaction when two Cleveland schools were reconstituted. The announcement to reconstitute the Paul Revere Elementary School came three weeks before the start of the school year (the leadership making the decision never passed "sandbox 101" either). The rather abrupt decision was made because there was a glitch in scoring state tests and this delayed the announcement for six weeks. Obviously, there was no advance planning and preparation. Needless to say the parents were very upset, but they blamed the principal for the problems and questioned why she wasn't removed and not the teachers (only 10 of the 25 teachers were asked to stay)[813].

The problems at Paul Revere were of long standing and a complete overhaul was probably the correct solution, but wouldn't it have been better to spend a year planning and preparing in order to get the support of the parents and perhaps the union?

Denver, Colorado, followed a somewhat different approach by giving the superintendent the power to transfer teachers and administrators, impose a longer school year, longer school days, or add extra staff members. An entire school can also be turned into a charter school or turned over to a for-profit school operation. At least any school identified as low-performing based on a dozen criteria has a year to improve. However, the teachers, who had been excluded from the development process, were certainly upset because "it's singling us out as if we are the only ones responsible for kids' learning...we cannot control crucial influences over children's learning such as poverty and parental involvement."[814] True enough, but the staff of a school can certainly be influential.

Even when reconstitution brings extra assistance, professional development, and more dollars, it provides no assurance that improved results will follow. A survey revealed that only 46 percent of the schools that were given such assistance saw improvement in achievement and getting parents involved.

Boston, where there is an appointed board, is a good example. The mayor challenged Boston to "judge me harshly if schools did not improve." He chose the Jeremiah E. Burke High School as the one needing the greatest transformation. The high school budget was doubled, and more teachers and counselors were hired. As a result of these efforts, the school regained its accreditation in 1998. It sounds like a success story. But once Burke became "transformed" budget cuts eliminated the money that had lowered class sizes, paid for teacher training, and hired counselors. The school lost 37 staff members since 2001. What has been the result? "Students now curse at teachers, listen to music, and talk on the phone in class, or they roam the halls" (if they are in school at all).[815]

This is one reason why reconstitution is dimming as an important option. Chicago thought that this strategy was the way to go in the late 1990's, but it is now slowing the effort down and "seeking less extreme measures to inspire success at what they consider their worst schools." An important problem that surfaced was recruiting experienced teachers to a reconstituted school. Without enough of such teachers, success is hard to achieve. Under a new contract signed in 1998, the teachers are given a voice in repairing under-performing schools through a new process called "re-engineering"—a step between probation and reconstitution.[816]

What is incomprehensible to understand is why data indicating low performance is so hard to believe and accept? It's probably because failure is hard to admit, and this is why it takes so long for a school to make an effort to improve itself.

Success Stories

There are success stories of low performing schools being salvaged from failure and promoted to success.

Middlesex Elementary School in Baltimore County, Maryland, once ranked among the 10 worst schools in its district. Facing the threat of a state takeover, the school community pulled together to develop a comprehensive school improvement plan. It rose from the bottom to being ranked 35th among more than 100 elementary schools in the district.[817]

Why did it take a threat of "takeover" before the school decided that improvement was needed?

Amundsen High School, Chicago, Illinois, was placed on probation because only 11 percent of its students read on grade level. Through concentrated efforts by the whole school staff to coordinate instruction and intense professional development aimed at instruction, in one year it doubled the percentage of students reading on grade level.[818]

The real question that should have been vigorously addressed is how did so many students reach high school without being able to read on grade level? Prevention is much less expensive than remediation years later.

Biscayne Gardens Elementary School, Miami-Dade County, Florida was identified as a low performing school. With the support of the districts program for low-performing schools, student performance increased for three consecutive years in both reading and mathematics.[819]

Since the "cure" and support is at hand, why are there still many schools in the district that remain low performing?

Hillcrest Middle School, Ysleta, Texas, was given the states lowest rating because only 15 percent of students passed the state test of academic skills. The school, located in a high poverty area, had high faculty turnover, low parent involvement, and low expectations. A school wide program that was instituted to focus all efforts on improving learning resulted in 80 percent of the students passing all portions of the state test.[820]

So with the same staff and apparently no significant increase in resources the school turned itself around. One of the ingredients for success was simply a focus on learning rather than politically correct gibberish.

What is important about such stories is not simply the fact that a failing school succeeded in turning itself around. The important question that needs to be addressed is that since the "cause and cure" are known, why are there still thousands of failing schools and hundreds of thousands of students being failed by the system because of inaction and complacency? Betrayal of trust is corruption and failing schools should be identified not as failing, but rather as "corrupt" schools.

There is another issue that is essential to address, e.g. to identify the corrupt practices that enabled the school to become "dysfunctional" and to ensure that they are literally exterminated. Simply reconstituting staff, without exterminating the infestation of corrupt practices, procedures and even attitudes, will not achieve success, and it is probably why all many reconstitution efforts have failed.

Summary

There is enough experience with turning around low-performing schools successfully even before a school is reconstituted. There are enough examples to provide guidance as to what works for success and what contributes to failure. The fact that "reconstitution" seems to be losing steam would suggest that it is too difficult because it requires a lot of work and effort, it's painful, and constant focus is required.

Of course, there is another option and it is being exercised in some states and districts. In Florida, the solution is rather simple: Grant low performing schools a reprieve. The state has made a deal with the federal government to prevent nearly two-thirds of the state's public schools from being labeled as failures. The deal granted 825 schools "provisional" status for meeting federal reading, writing and math standards. This means that parents in those schools will not have the option provided under NCLB to transfer their children to higher-performing public schools or have them tutored at government expense.[821]

This is a copout, pure and simple, and it is another betrayal of children and the public trust. However, admittedly, it is a very simple solution.

What the research and examples have not highlighted at all is that keeping the focus on any change effort is hard to do. With time, the educational, societal and economic factors change resulting in priorities to emerge that force changes in maintaining a single focus. Administrators only have so much time in a day, a week, and a year. Many are shorthanded just to keep on top of the daily practical duties and responsibilities. For example, student mobility and turnover in a school can itself become an overwhelming priority because of the challenges it brings to a school.

This is why a school cannot do the job alone. It must have a school-community alliance group, trained and educated, whose only responsibility would be to keep the focus on improving the school. This is a no-cost strategy that is seldom used, but it can be extremely effective.

However, when all else fails, is there any other choice except to reconstitute a school by removing those in charge and starting fresh? Probably not!

Yes, focusing on continuous improvement takes courage, reallocation of resources, persistence, and patience. It also requires detailed planning and intensive research to determine the reasons for the successes and failures of others.

The point is that other schools have done it, so it proves that it can be done! The tragedy is that usually schools must first become a "basket-case" before serious action is taken rather than having a school effort focusing on constant improvement.

Why isn't this done much more often? One of the major problems is inept school governance (next chapter).

CHAPTER ELEVEN

Inept School Governance

"The right structure does not guarantee results, but the wrong structure aborts results and smothers even the best-directed efforts." Peter Drucker

The purpose of school governance, whether at the state, district or school level, is to ensure that a thorough and efficient education is provided for all students; but there is one very critical caveat—it should be done efficiently and effectively. Unfortunately, it is not happening! Instead, corruption (CheDe, WaMi and FraSte) breeds at all levels of bureaucratic school governance and it's getting worse. What is interesting to note is that the system of bureaucracy, invented by Napoleon, was deliberately designed to inhibit change.

An interesting article put a little different spin on it. "School bureaucracy has one purpose and one purpose only: to institutionalize the suspension of judgment (delay is the deadliest form of denial)."[822]

Pretty harsh words! However, it would certainly help to explain why all school reform efforts have failed to date. In other words, if the current system of governance doesn't change and become more effective and responsible, reform efforts will continue to languish.

A study provides another perspective about the problem of governance: "Current school governance structures impede focused system efforts to implement reform objectives, pulls schools in contradictory directions, and promotes bureaucratic responses to change." As a result, a National Commission on Governing America's Schools was established to determine "How states and communities can be organized to educate their young people more effectively." They should have also added "efficiently." The study was released in 1999 and it has been instrumental in propelling the governance debate, but debate alone doesn't necessarily mean constructive changes take place.[823]

"Schools are so egregiously mismanaged (WaMi) that the wonder is not that they accomplish so little, but that they accomplish so much under the circumstances. What little they manage to accomplish is the result of heroic efforts by dedicated professionals against insuperable obstacles." The author goes on to say: "Precious energies and resources are squandered on ill-fated ventures whose doom was foreordained (as was seen in previous chapters). School reform has become an industry where the product is the process itself with little accounting for or requirement to produce measurable results." In essence, he said, "Schools are not organized to do what is asked of them."[824] This is certainly a profound statement that may identify a fundamental problem of school governance.

Consider the results achieved thus far with the current system of governance. During the past 30 years, there has been a 17% constant dollar increase in education expenditures and it has produced virtually no improvements in test scores. The increase in spending did meet a goal of reducing pupil/teacher ratios. Currently, twenty-three states have pupil/teacher ratios between 10-15, twenty-five have rations of 16-20, and only two have ratios over 20. Lower the pupil teacher ratio has been a constant drumbeat to improve achievement, but the effort has produced no significant improvement.

According to the U.S. Department of Education, the pupil/teacher ratio in public schools fell from 22.3 in 1970 to 14.1 in 1999, a decrease of 27.4 percent. Elementary and secondary schools experienced similar decreases over the same period, from 24.3 to 17.6 for elementary schools and from 19.8 to 14.1 for secondary schools. The overall pupil/staff ratio fell from 13.6 in 1970 to 8.6 in 1998, a decrease of 36.8 percent.

What this really means is that education has become significantly less productive than it was three decades ago. In 1999, public schools required half as many more staff in total (up 58.1 percent) including a third more teachers (up 37.6 percent) to educate the same number of children to the same level of quality as they did in 1970.

Of course, the response from advocates of lower teacher/pupil ratios and lower class sizes will be that the ratios have not been lowered enough.

The graduation rate isn't much better either with only 74% for the class of 1998, but even this figure is probably much lower because much CheDe takes place in reporting the numbers. "Sadly, dishonest reporting about graduation rates turns out to be widespread."[825]

There is another more damaging yardstick to demonstrate how poorly U.S. students achieve and that is to compare them to international counterparts. A UNICEF study compared 14 and 15 year olds on the results of five different tests to determine their abilities in reading, math and science. What's new in the study is that it averages the results to give "the most comprehensive picture to date of how well each nation's education system is functioning as a whole."[826]

It concluded that South Korea has the most effective education system in the world's richest countries, with Japan in second place and the United States and Germany near the bottom. Even in adult literacy, the U.S. finished low. The study does not attempt to explain why the U.S. fared so badly, "that's for them to pick up and run with."

An interesting result of the study dispels the myth that countries with a high proportion of immigrant children are likely to fall lower down the comparative scale. The report shows that the share of non-native and first generation children living in each country does not affect the overall national rankings.

There is yet another measurement to demonstrate the unyielding stagnation and decline of educational output or results. The National Assessment of Educational Progress (NAEP), the nation's report card, measures student achievement in reading, mathematics, and science. In all three-subject areas, the test scores for 17 year olds show virtually no change from the 1969-73 period until 1999.[827]

So, by just about every performance criteria that can be measured regarding academic achievement and school outcomes, education can be considered academically bankrupt.

This is not to say that changes have not and are not taking place because all kinds of changes have been made, however, no significant improvements can be documented.

The biggest change is that the federal government (the ultimate and most formidable bureaucracy) has become more involved in education even though it has no constitutional role; yet, it provides only 7% of the education dollars. Of course, with each dollar come regulations, controls and political posturing that impacts all school systems and each dollar takes away more local control.

States too have become increasingly involved in issues that were previously left to local districts. For example, 49 states have established standards in a least some subject areas, 50 states test how well their students are doing, but only 24 states hold schools accountable for results. States have also intervened in low-performing schools and school districts, as well as, districts with corrupt governance, crumbling infrastructure, inept administration, and financial mismanagement.

This would not be happening if local school districts were all doing what they are entrusted to do—honestly represent all taxpayers and promote quality student learning. Michael Kirst, a professor of education at Stanford University and a member of a task force studying school governance, stated: "If you trusted the school board and superintendent to set high curriculum standards and testing, you wouldn't need state laws." So easy to say, but locally it can also be political suicide because too many schools and students would become identified as failures.

So it's important to examine this institution that has been described by an educational researcher as "an aberration, an anachronism, and education sinkhole...put this dysfunctional arrangement out of its misery."[828]

School Boards

Mark Twain said: "In the first place God made idiots. This was for practice. Then he made School Boards."

He must have had this board in mind: "A school superintendent awaiting trial on charges that he had school-bought air conditioners installed at is home has been given a 2 percent pay raise...yet, a Middlesex grand jury indicted him along with five corporations and 10 other people in March 2004 on charges related to alleged bid-rigging schemes in the Everett Public Schools (Massachusetts). A recent audit found sweeping management problems, including questionable bidding and hiring practices. Inadequate oversight of maintenance costs resulted in $520,250 in suspect spending including 30 bids that were questionable or not authentic. But a school board member defended the raise at a public meeting saying his record of educating kids was A plus."[829]

Twain's rather nasty quote suggests that boards have been under fire for many years, and with the example above and many others like it, he must have had some real prophetic insight.

However, what must be appreciated is that boards today, more than ever before, have awesome responsibilities. Consider the fact that in the early 1930's there were over 125,000 school boards with each usually managing a single school. Since then boards have been reduced to about 16,000, and now manage school districts of all sizes.

Because of the long history of board governance, they have become woven into the very fabric of every single community. Nevertheless, the question is whether or not local boards have outlived their usefulness.

What should not be forgotten is that this institution, with 100,000 school board members, mostly unsalaried and elected, has endured for over 200 years. The growth of public education under its governance can only be described as awesome.

School boards have nurtured an educational system that in 1776 had an average school year of 82 days, an average of five years of schooling in 1900, an average high school completion rate of 50 percent in 1950; it is now responsible for managing the education of 53 million children (20 percent of the population) who attend school for 180 days in over 16,000 school districts averaging a high school completion rate of around 75percent.

The reality today is that it's an institution under siege and under fire. A few of the reasons include: budgetary problems, chronic low performance in too many schools, unruly student behavior, dilapidated school buildings, voucher initiatives, a growing home school movement, state/city takeovers of school districts, the need to reconstitute some schools, and an intolerable achievement gap between whites and minorities.

One of the problems with boards was identified in a rather scorching article: "Too many school boards have become havens for political junkies, launching pads for mayoral wannabes, bastions of ideological discontent and sources of easy paychecks and poorly-monitored expense accounts."[830]

True enough in many situations, but it should not be forgotten that there are far more board members who want to improve schools; at least they start with this intention. The problem is that they don't know how to do what is required of them. Others become inoculated with the fortress mentality of protecting the system at all costs, while still others develop a "groupthink" mentality (members of the group believe with the majority believes even though they really don't agree).

Another complicating issue is that federal and state bureaucracies are basically immune from parental and local influence, yet they control 53% of the education money. Compare this to the "good old days" when 83% of the revenue was controlled by local school districts. And to complicate matters even more, such control provides an arena for unions, social do-gooders, politicians, and personal agenda advocates to promote their particular and narrow interests.

A dramatic example of today's problems, not atypical of urban school districts, is St. Louis, Miss. It has a per-pupil expenditure of $10,000 per year, one of the highest in the nation; yet, tragically only 42 percent of the students graduate. Certainly, this is not the outcome desired by board members, but they seem powerless, incapable, unwilling and/or too "politicized" to reform the system.

Therefore, it's no surprise that there are lively and heated discussions taking place concerning school governance by boards of education because the current system is not working the way it should. This is such an important issue that the Education Commission of the States established a center for school governance. The center has already assisted Kansas City and Florida to revamp its school governance structure.

As long as school boards are the governance structure, they are the key to unlocking the door of failing schools and failing education; they have the power to do so, district by district and school by school, and it is the only way that educating children to higher standards can occur. There should be absolutely no mistake about this.

In essence, they should and can be the reform leaders because they have the power to do what is needed to improve school results. If they fail in their responsibility to achieve much better school outcomes, they can expect the chorus of those who seek to change the current board structure to grow, increase in intensity, and succeed in changing school board governance.

As a result of the drumbeat of criticism and the increasing burden of their responsibilities, school board work is driving many people away from the job—the number of people running for school board seats is declining and members stay in the job for shorter periods. In addition, "More and more school board members run as single-issue candidates." According to Michael Kirst, co-author of <u>Governing Public Schools</u>, it has become an impossible job and "school boards are so splintered by their attempts to represent special interests or board members' individual political needs that they cannot govern."[831]

There is no doubt that the public is increasingly dissatisfied with school performance and school boards. A 1992 study of school boards by the Institute for Educational Leadership supports the publics' belief:[832]

- We are not providing far-reaching or politically risk-taking leadership for education reforms.
- Had become another level of administration, often micromanaging the school district.
- Were so splintered by their attempts to represent special interests or board members' individual political needs that they could not govern.
- Were not exercising sufficient policy oversight or adequately communicating about schools and the school system to the public
- Exhibited little capacity to develop positive and productive lasting relationships with their superintendents.

Nothing has changed! Reports and surveys since then have reiterated the same problems over and over again and things have gotten worse.

The 1992 survey also confirmed "boards spend too little time on major concerns and too much time dealing with administrative trivia." More specifically, board members rated themselves least effective in governing responsibilities involving leadership, planning, goal setting, board operations, board management, and policy oversight.[833]

If this is what board members really believe, why don't they change? After all, they do have the power to improve what they do and how they do it; but unfortunately, they either lack the ability or the will to change.

The single most important issue concerning school boards that has not received any serious attention is that they have not been given training and education before and during the time they are board members. A yearly conference is not the answer.

Probably the main reason why boards are failing thousands of schools and thousands of children particularly in the urban districts is that "political feasibility, rather than educational optimization, becomes the driving force in policy adoption." In other words, too many boards simply see themselves as maintaining the status quo.

There really is another honest issue to address. The dilemma facing boards that are sincere in their efforts to improve school outcomes can best be described as a two-sided coin. On one side is their desire and sense of responsibility to advocate for children and what they believe the school system needs to provide for their success. On the other side of the coin is their concern about keeping school budgets constrained to maintain community support. No one is saying being a school board member is an easy job.

The National School Board Association convention in 1994 did issue a report calling for reform in school governance because policy makers were asking a very serious question: "Is the local school board a failed institution?" Its executive director acknowledged: "School boards have misplaced priorities and fail to delegate enough management tasks."

Another problem is that because of more and more state and federal regulations and mandates, local control is being eroded and school board influence is weakening. In fact, a state school board conference in Ohio had as its theme, "Take Back Our Schools." It is true that polls still show that the public trusts school board members to make decisions about how to manage the schools, but the trust is certainly on the decline.

One of the more serious problems is that "there is a profound disconnect between how well the public rates its local schools and how well board members think the schools are doing."[834]

- Preparing students for college—72 percent of urban board members say the public schools are doing a "good" to "excellent" job, compared to only 37 percent of the urban adults.
- Teaching reading, writing, and math—49 percent of adults give a good to excellent rating versus 69 percent for board members.
- Maintaining high academic standards—58 percent of board members agree compared to only 39 percent of adults.

- Involving parents in schools—51 percent of board members believe they are doing a good to excellent job, but only 39 percent of parents agree.
- Hiring and keeping good teachers—68 percent of board members gave themselves a high rating, compared to 42 percent of the adults.

The most shocking disparity is that 82 percent of urban board members say their districts are doing a good to excellent job keeping violence and drugs out of schools, but only 33 percent of adults agree. A similar gap is found in how well schools are maintaining discipline, with 72 percent of board members rating performance as good to excellent, compared to only 32 percent of the adults.

A somewhat different disparity is shed upon the issues from a survey of 2000 school boards. "A majority of board members are typical citizens who describe themselves as professionals, politically moderate, and serve an average of six years…and that a significant majority have no further political aspirations."[835]

It also found that the largest school districts are more political, pay more attention to interest groups, and have more contested and costly campaigns than smaller districts.

Such disparities are rather incredible considering the abundance of evidence that is publicized in reports, surveys and statistics. To have such significantly different perceptions about reality on the part of board members is an indication that they are terribly ill-informed or that they do not want to face reality. In either case, it helps to explain why boards are becoming less influential and effective, and it is a further indication that school boards have probably become obsolete.

The report concludes: "They (school boards) must acknowledge the urgency of the situation…if they are to be effective in their primary task of raising academic achievement." The present and widening gap of achievement between white and minority students is an indication that urban boards are "stuck in neutral" in dealing with the problem and either don't or can't shift into high gear.

What is also suggested in the report is that the compositions of boards in urban districts do not represent the racial make-up of the community. True enough! However, changing the composition of the board in terms of racial mix will not change the results. Minority superintendents have been hired in urban districts, and they have not had any more success than other superintendents. Concentrating on such racial issues will be unproductive in terms of closing the achievement gap.

According to a five-state study by the New England School Development Council (NESDEC), boards that are in constant conflict, who have members who meddle in minutiae and don't communicate well with each other, have districts with lower test scores, fewer kids going to college and more dropouts.[836]

A 1999 report by the Education Commission of the States outlined some options. The most radical option would be the creation of an Education Development Board, a quasi-governmental planning agency to replace the local school board. It would be responsible for "raising money from federal, state, community, and private sources, allocate resources, manage a portfolio of independent schools and programs, foster partnerships, and help schools coordinate other community services."[837]

Two other options are also suggested. One would be somewhat similar to the current system except that individual schools would create their own budgets, hire and fire teachers, and allocate resources as they see fit (site-based management). Such a system would soon turn into "site based madness." The other would have the school district contract with private entities to manage the schools as "charter" schools; and, of course, this is beginning to happen.

In response to this report, the president of the National School Boards Association stated: "The report was irresponsible and that it takes a huge step backward by eliminating virtually all public accountability." Where is the accountability now?

Another suggested change would be to allocate the bulk of authority to the state; it would control "mission, money, measurement, leadership, infrastructure development, and district accountability." What would be unique in this model is that states would select local district superintendents, who would serve at the pleasure of the chief state school officer.

Of all the suggestions, this is certainly one that is worthy of exploration because local politics would be neutralized, at least to some extent.

There are, of course, many recommendations being made to improve school governance. Another suggestion is to replace school boards with "education policy boards" which would only focus on standards and school performance. Still another is to adopt the system in Hawaii where, believe it or not, there are no school boards, education is all state controlled. Obviously, this is a working example demonstrating that school boards aren't necessarily required. An interesting suggestion is to simply have the local city-town governing board (selectman, common council, etc.) be responsible for managing the schools and have the superintendent included.

Another report by the New England School Development Council[838] "advocates changing state laws to limit school board work to policymaking and long-term planning and to mandate professional development for board members."

Other policymakers believe that stronger efforts should be made to improve the effectiveness of school boards before they become irrelevant. Kansas City was forced to look at its governance structure because of a threatened takeover by the state. A task force report, "Steer Not Row" was an effort to strengthen local boards. Its recommendations are really applicable to all boards. In essence, it encourages boards to "drop the oars and steer, not row."

An interesting report makes the case that state education departments, rather than governors or legislatures, should lead the effort to improve schools in their respective states.[839] Of course, to do so would require legislation to change the local governance structure and district responsibilities.

However, all of the discussions and reports about school board governance changes miss the most important challenge and responsibility they have—forensic analysis of resource allocation (financial and human) and usage. Their failure in this regard helps to explain why there is so much corruption, stealing, waste and mismanagement, and thousands of low performing schools.

There is another issue that reports, studies, and discussions have failed to address. Boards must be possessed with a passion of will to improve school outcomes. The fact is that too many boards do not have such a commitment and the graveyard of thousands of schools that have been identified as failing, with many thousands more to come, provides ample evidence of ineptness and inability.

Tom Glass, a University of Memphis scholar who has spent his career studying the changing nature of leadership in our nation's school systems, "advocates for school board members to be selected by mayors, governors or blue-ribbon commissions." This change (mayoral control) has, of course, already occurred in some urban districts.

The reason for eliminating elected boards is that they "are not accountable to the public, seemingly possess modest skills, are very conflict prone, politicized and demonstrate they often cannot work successfully in tandem with superintendents...and the electoral process is not proving to be an adequate evaluator for urban boards."[840] Of course, the same can be said about many non-urban boards. Obviously his approach has appealed to some urban districts where the mayors have taken control of the school board.

Glass goes on to say: "The root problem appears to be highly politicized boards continually crossing the line between policy and management and in the process creating almost certain conflict with superintendents."

Alison Gendar puts it in more coarse terms and hit the nail on the head when she stated that the New York Board of Education is actually a "criminal conspiracy involved in the larceny of futures that belong to the city's children."[841] This can be said of many boards across the nation; if it were not so, the numerous examples of CheDe, FraSte and WaMi would not have been possible.

There is really no end to the recommendations being made to end the reign of school boards as they currently exist; nor is there any likelihood that there will be any end to the debates taking place concerning what governance changes would produce the most effective results.

Clearly, school governance issues are very contentious, complicated and confusing. However, what must be understood is that changes in governance presuppose improved school outcomes. "Unfortunately, there is very little research specific to public education on how or to what extent governance affects organizational outcomes, especially student achievement." But then, many of the changes that have been suggested have not even been tried.[842]

There is another rather insidious problem that is contaminating the public school landscape and that is the intrusion of courts and lawyers in just about every aspect of school life from special education to sports.

In a survey of 523 school principals, the American Tort Reform Association found that schools are eliminating or changing programs and activities because of litigation fears. In fact, 65 percent of the principals reported a difference in the kinds of school-related programs offered because of liability concerns and cost. Amazingly, 25 percent of them reported lawsuits or out-of-court settlements in the last two years. Almost 2/3 agreed that there would be more and more litigation in just about every area of school discipline and program. It's not surprising that 63 percent said: "More legislative reform is needed, most often citing more legal protection for teachers, staff, and administrators, a clarification of special education laws, protection from frivolous lawsuits, and limits on punitive damages."[843]

What needs to be emphasized in the strongest possible terms is that states must bear a great deal of responsibility for the problems of local school boards. The states, through legislation and departments of education, can do much more to help boards be more effective.

Mandatory training and education would be helpful to board members who want to do a good job but don't understand their role, and don't have the skills required to effectively monitor the schools. In addition, there must be civil and criminal consequences for malfeasance in office of school board members who want to enrich themselves financially and politically. What board members need the most are skills in budget management and analysis.

There is also an extremely important change that boards should make to help stem the tide of corruption. Boards must institute a policy that mandates the finance officer to report directly to the board on a monthly basis. For example, in preparing monthly financial reports and making financial predictions, the board and the superintendent would receive the financial statements at the same time. In addition, the policy should be explicit that the finance officer can only be fired with board approval.

This would help to provide a much better "check and balance" process for financial management so that the finance officer cannot be intimidated by the superintendent to fudge or alter figures.

A policy also needs to be instituted that would require the annual budget preparation process to include, as back up documents, original budget requests from the various departments and schools and that they be signed by the person who prepared the original requests.

In the final analysis, what boards need to understand and accept is that their first responsibility above all else is to accept the fact that they have a sacred covenant with all of the taxpayers to ensure that school dollars are safeguarded from any fraud, waste and mismanagement. It is up to the administration to advocate for children and to present the case for school needs, not the board. Unless boards face up to this reality, they will continue to fail not only the taxpayers but the children as well.

No doubt, there will be those who say in spite of all the negative results achieved under current governance systems, "the glass is half-full." However, considering the enormous resources that have been poured into the glass, the only rational conclusion is that the glass is more than half-empty.

Any doubts that the present governance systems have not been effective should be resolved by action taken by recent legislation in California to move responsibility for policy decisions to the governor's office and away from the elected superintendent of public instruction

To put it all into perspective consider this: "For more than an hundred years much complaint has been made of the unmethodical way in which schools are conducted, but it is only within the last 30 that any serious attempt has been made to find a remedy for this state of things, and with what results? Schools remain exactly as they were."

Who spoke these prophetic words? Comenius in 1632! The more things change, the more they stay the same until there is an apocalypse event—a virtual revolution

Until Education America faces the harsh reality that the present governance systems have failed far too many of the nation's children, and that it has been an embarrassment in terms of performance when compared to the industrialized nations of the world, will there be serious debate about changing the governance systems as they now exist.

Superintendency

Among the major problems, particularly in urban districts, is that boards and superintendents are not working in harmony. For example, a study of 30 large urban districts found that there were 137 superintendents from 1990 to 2001 or an average of 2.6 years of survival per superintendent.[844]

What happens too often is that the superintendent is pinned with the responsibility when district test performance is poor or on the decline (it may be true in some cases), but boards don't take any responsibility for poor results.

But the superintendency is also in a revolutionary phase. There is an emerging trend, particularly in large school districts, to hire superintendents with no education background. For example, the superintendent of schools in Los Angeles is the former governor of Colorado and several other urban districts have followed suit—New York City, Jacksonville and Okaloosa County, FL, Cobb County, GA, Kansas City, MO, Chicago, IL, Greenville County, SC, Oklahoma City, OK, San Diego, CA, Seattle, WA, and Philadelphia, PA.

Employing non-traditional superintendents has not resulted in any real change because it simply substitutes a different type of "bureaucrat" and the system bureaucracy remains basically intact. For example, the non-traditional superintendent in Seattle had a municipal finance background; yet, the district has a $30 million deficit. The players may change, but nothing really changes because the system and structure are still intact.

There are other types of governance options that are being added to the mix of efforts to do something different, not necessarily more effective.

Charter Schools

The Chester-Upland School district in Pennsylvania solved its governance problem in a very interesting and novel way by simply turning over the district to private vendors—a Pontius Pilate approach. As a result, all the schools were converted to charters. Certainly, it's an admission that the school governance structure was unable, incompetent, or unwilling to make the hard decisions required to educate its children. It's also an admission that money is not the problem because charter schools don't get more money, but they tend to manage resources more effectively.

The outcome of the experiment has been a disaster with Edison, the largest vendor with 8 of the 9 schools, pulling out because it has not gotten paid about $4 million. "During the past tumultuous year there were book shortages, teacher shortages, and a riot at the high school that led to 28 arrests." But part of the problem was that the district controlled the finances and hid the fact that it was facing a $35 million budget deficit.[845]

The reality is that the reason charter schools are being supported nationwide is to eliminate the bureaucratic structure above the school building level; obviously, recognition by policymakers that perhaps the current structure for school governance is a virus infecting efforts to reform and improve education and educational outcomes.

Although its relatively early (they are so new on the educational scene) to tell whether this "governance" reform" will improve student achievement, things don't look very good. In Arizona, a state that started early to fund charters and probably has the most charters, a study by Arizona State University concluded: "Charter schools have failed in their promise to reform the public school system and improve student academic achievement...The failure becomes even harder to understand given the advantages that charters enjoy in their freedom from the rules, regulations and contracts that are said to bureaucratically burden the public schools."[846]

It would seem that this study might knock the wind out of charter proponents who believe that giving unbridled freedom to charter operators will improve results.

Another reality is that charters are now easy targets for FraSte to take place because of extremely poor regulations and monitoring. The fact is that more and more charters have been identified with fraudulent activities, all at the taxpayers' expense, and many of these were given as examples in the WaMi and FraSte chapters.

Vouchers (school choice)

Providing money vouchers to parents that can be used to pay tuition to other public or private-parochial schools is yet another attempt at changing governance. With vouchers, parents indicate with their feet (sending their child to another school) that they are dissatisfied with the school they are in. It is called "school choice."

So how is this approach working? The school system that has the longest and most extensive experience is Milwaukee, WI. School choice has been going on for fifteen years and involves 115 schools, 14,000 children with 70% of them attending religious schools, at a cost of $83 million. Interestingly, no one really knows what is happening with this program, so two reporters decided to find out by visiting 106 of the schools. They made some interesting observations.[847]

The voucher schools feel, and look, surprisingly like other schools in the district—they are all struggling in the same battle to educate low-income, minority students, and there are at least as many excellent schools as alarming ones. In other words, parental choice does not assure quality.

"Indeed...much of the political debate over vouchers is divorced from what's going on in classrooms. With the exception of the element of religion, it's the same story that's being played out in urban classrooms across America—a story of poverty, limited resources, poor leadership and broken families."

Nothing is really different! There are bad voucher schools and excellent voucher schools just as there are excellent public schools and poor public schools. What is on the positive side is that parents are given choices so that they can't claim they are held captive by a public school system.

Site Based Management (SBM)

Another way the governance issue is trying to be addressed is site-based management (SBM). The purpose of SBM is to decentralize the traditional "command and control" school bureaucracy. It's designed to increase school building autonomy and to share decision-making with teachers, parents, students, and community members. This governance reform is based on the assumption that "reducing bureaucratic controls will prompt teachers and principals to exert greater initiative and to tailor instruction to the needs of students." As a result, there is an expectation for higher student achievement, more equitable and efficient use of resources, improved accountability, more involvement, and greater satisfaction on the part of staff, parents and the community.

Thousands of school districts have implemented SBM (including those in other countries). However, many schools were required by state legislation (Arkansas, California, Colorado, Florida, Hawaii, Kentucky, North Carolina, Texas, and Utah) to adopt some form of SBM; therefore, it tends to be more of a "political hype" rather than "educational hope."

So it should come as no surprise that "few of the key personnel directly involved in public education really support it." The reason for this is that control and authority must be shared. In addition, the transition to SBM, if done correctly, requires large-scale system changes; and change is threatening.

A critical responsibility that must be delegated is building and program budget flexibility because it is the key factor that determines if SBM is really being practiced. After all, the budget provides the power to implement change. In addition, information and knowledge must be shared, everyone involved must be trained, and there must be focused direction and purpose to improve curriculum and instruction.

Furthermore, SBM requires a detailed plan which must include a clear vision, definition of terms, decision-making parameters, standards, monitoring and assessment procedures. Rochester, NY has an SBM plan that can be viewed as a model, and it even has a waiver process in case any part of the plan was found to restrict a school's effort to improve.

One of the most challenging problems involved in planning for SBM is to balance school autonomy and flexibility with certain centralized operations that require consistency, coordination, and legal constraints.

Unfortunately, research studies have concluded: "Such programs rarely decentralized significant portions of the budget, provided substantive personnel authority, were comprehensive or improved student achievement...and that few such efforts engaged teachers in curriculum and instruction change." In addition, the less successful schools were stuck on power and housekeeping issues.

What is most disappointing and surprising is that the research has not found a link between SBM and gains in students' academic achievement, lower dropout rates, increased attendance, and reduced disciplinary problems.

However, the Center for Organization and Restructuring of Schools analyzed data from more than 1,500 elementary, middle and high schools throughout the United States and it concluded: "School restructuring can indeed improve student learning, but there is no magic bullet...for restructuring effort to work, it must be clearly focused on student learning, instruction, collective responsibility and external support."[848]

It could be that SBM will simply prove to be another educational bandwagon that has charged through the schools without any real success. .

However, to put it in blunt terms, site-based management may well become "site-based madness." The bottom line is that SBM, to be successful, must be driven by a passionate quest for improvement in order to achieve quality outcomes for each school and every student. Most schools simply cannot maintain the focus because of changing administrations and environmental, political, and financial realities.

School Councils

Another governance practice found in just a few districts is to have governing councils at each school site where authority is shared with teachers, employees, parents and community members; in other words, collaborative decision making.

New York City established 32 elected community school boards in 1970 as a way to give communities greater control over how schools were managed. It has not been a successful reform effort. "Too many boards are wrapped up in petty squabbles." As a result of repeated corruption and patronage scandals the state Legislature in 1996 divested the boards of nearly all their power. In 2002, the mayor took control of the city school board and he stripped the community boards of their role in appointing district superintendents.[849]

This endeavor to decentralize this behemoth school system was destined to fail because of built-in political patronage, and with this virus comes waste and mismanagement (WaMi) Is it any wonder that the schools it was designed to help the most, those in the poorest neighborhoods, got worse, not better?

Denver found that its 11-year experiment to "democratize" schools through shared decision-making has also proved rather messy. Some of the councils have bogged down in disputes over parliamentary procedures and one school acknowledged it could no longer keep its panel together.

"There is a real problem with tolerance and respect for different views and approaches and styles...and they are picking and choosing which parts of the bylaws to follow."

As a result, the teachers' union and school administration has formed a commission to assess the future of such a shared decision-making structure.[850]

In a deviation from the council or shared decision-making models, another is to invite parent participation on state boards of education. What seemed like a harmless idea turned into a "tug-of-war between the state Parent Teachers Association and Governor Mitt Romney." He did not accept recommendations to the board by the PTA because he felt that they did not represent the interests of all parents. The tugging war is in a state of limbo.

Other

Oregon's Educational Act for the 21st Century has shifted primary funding responsibility from local to state control and, as a result, the legislature has imposed its will over curriculum and instruction. The purpose of this "futuristic" change in school governance is to hold schools accountable for state imposed standards. Of course, with the dollars come the inevitable controls, mandates and loss of local control.

In Massachusetts, a rather novel experiment was tried 14 years ago. The Chelsea school district of 5,800 students is being managed by Boston University even though there is an elected board. However, BU has sole authority in naming the superintendent and has the power to "perform all of the management functions otherwise vested to the school board by state and local law." This governance change was made "after school board members and other politicians were accused of everything from nepotism to organized crime and collected indictments on a regular basis."[851] Again the results have not been very encouraging. Although politics has essentially been removed, test scores in many cases are still below average, and attendance still cannot meet new federal standards.

Magnet schools have been tried and some are very successful; the problem is that they are expensive and cannot be replicated to serve any large number of students.

A movement that is growing rapidly is home schooling and estimates place the number of such children at about 1.5 million. This is a group that has become alienated from the schools and, therefore, is not supportive of them.

International

England has an interesting approach to school governance problems in that schools can "opt-out" of a district's control. Such schools operate much like a chartered school. However, the impact of too many schools "opting-out" is that some districts have had to eliminate the entire central office staff. As a result, the schools receive 15% more dollars so that they can purchase their own support services previously supplied by central office staff.

There is another movement under foot to transform their schools. An example is the opening of Bexley Business Academy, a secondary school. "It is a new school in every way, private funding mixes seamlessly with government support, and people from government and the private sector work side by side." The building, designed by a private company, has a new principal who is free to select only the best teachers who apply. "It is designed to challenge disadvantaged students intellectually and to give them a look at a life that is different in almost every way from the rough neighborhoods in which they live, and it gets results. Despite a dramatic growth in enrollment and an increase in the number of very low-income students, test scores are up dramatically."[852]

Summary

Clearly, there are a variety of efforts being made with the hopes that schools can have more positive outcomes, but thus far nothing has jumped out of the pot of efforts as being effective and, more important, replicable by other states and districts.

However, what cannot be forgotten is that regardless of what the changes may be, money will still be involved; and, as such, the trail of corruption (WaMi and FraSte) will lead to each and everyone. Policymakers simply do not learn that corruption follows money. If this rather simple lesson can be learned, then appropriate measures can be put into place to protect the education treasure chests from being plundered.

Why is this so difficult for policymakers, school boards, school administrators and employees to learn and understand?

CHAPTER TWELVE

The Final Corruption

"The worst enemy of human hope is not brute facts, but men of brains who will not face them." Max Eastman

The previous chapters certainly reveal that corruption comes in many forms and in many disguises; and, although the corrupt acts are discouraging, shameful, and arrogant, there is a final corruption that is found in many schools and with too many policymakers. It is the failure to take timely, honest, and aggressive action when needed that is the most deplorable corruption of all and it is inexcusable. It is such inaction that fertilizes CheDe and allows the cultivation of WaMi and FraSte.

This is not to say that schools, school boards, state departments of education, legislators and the federal government have not taken action to address some of the myriad of problems facing public education. On the contrary, there have been a proliferation of actions; unfortunately, they tend to be deceitful. Deceitful actions are, in fact, responsible for much of the decline in Education America.

The corruption that has been vividly described and documented certainly indicates that personal gain and aggrandizement overshadows and overwhelms the trust that has been placed in the hands of those responsible for the education of all children. In fact, such corruption can literally be described as the "educational rape" of the nation's children. There are numerous examples of deceitful actions.

Deceitful action was taken to create the most outlandish whopper of a lie that "all students can meet high standards." Where is the proof? It defies all logic, all scientific evidence, and all common sense.

Although the politically correct dogma believes that everyone is equal, the fact is that everyone is not equal.

Although the politically correct dogma believes that everyone has equal opportunity, the fact is that everyone does not have equal opportunity.

Although the political correct dogma believes that given the right set of circumstances everyone will make the same effort, the fact is that effort can never be equalized.

Therefore, if anything, the proof is that far too many students are not and cannot meet higher standards, many students do not have equal opportunity, and "effort" can never, ever be equalized, and no amount of money, rhetoric or political and education gibberish can make it happen.

The corruption of inaction is that this lie has created a false illusion of what students can accomplish and that no action is being taken to discount the lie.

Deceitful action was taken to create the web of fabrication concerning standards—creating the image that standards are being raised and adhered too while at the same time using "smoke and mirrors" to lower the standards so that most students can pass them or simply be excused from them. The lie persists because it "feels so good and sounds so good"—self-esteem is more important than honest achievement. What thinking adult can honestly believe that a student who is not succeeding—and students certainly know when they are not succeeding—has a positive self-esteem? Self-esteem comes from "knowing" that you have succeeded honestly.

The corruption of inaction to maintain standards continues to flood the educational landscape. Oh, there will be those who say the standards are too high and must be lowered; however, the fact remains that the industrialized nations with much higher standards consistently best U.S. students.

Deceitful action was taken by policymakers—school boards, state departments of education, U.S. Department of Education—to perpetrate the fraud that small class sizes will improve academic achievement without real changes taking place in instructional practices, curricular improvement, teacher training, and a real focus on academics. The costly debacle of the living laboratory of small class sizes in California is dramatic proof that it is a very costly mistake.

The corruption of inaction to be honest about what small classes can and cannot do, as well as, the impact it has on other educational programs and services and even community needs are never explained. Florida has voted to have small classes and the negative results it will have on education in general and on other non-education needs is just beginning to be realized.

Deceitful action was taken by teacher unions, the media, and many policymakers to create the lie that higher teacher salaries will improve school outcomes. Tell this to the parents and taxpayers of Connecticut, with one of the highest teacher salaries in the country, where more than half of its students cannot achieve proficiency on the state test.

The corruption of inaction to dispel this myth by being honest and forthright that increased salaries are needed to retain teachers even though it does not make them better or more effective will continue to give parents and communities' false hopes.

Deceitful action was taken to create the illusion that lower pupil-teacher ratios are a key indicator required for quality education. Pupil-teacher ratio is, in fact, a meaningless number because it actually disguises what really is happening in schools.

The corruption of inaction by not revealing the important ratios: teacher-pupil load, by grade and by course (the number of students a teacher has during the course of the day and week). These ratios vary greatly among teachers and the teacher unions are absolutely silent on this issue.

Deceitful action was taken to promote the fallacy that more professional development is needed in order to improve student achievement. The reality is that most professional development is haphazard, unconnected, and not monitored for results in the classroom.

The corruption of inaction to take positive steps that professional development be on going each year, well planned, connected with instruction and curriculum, and be monitored for implementation in the classroom is gross corruption of supervision.

Deceitful action was taken to define precisely the meaning of "high quality teachers" found in the No Child Left Behind Act. The reality is that "high quality" is a great rhetorical term that, in the final analysis, will simply mean a certified teacher in the classroom—even that would be some progress.

The corruption of inaction to delineate exactly what is meant by "high quality" beyond mere certification and to effectively monitor school districts will demean the effort of the NCLB Act and further the deterioration of academic achievement.

Deceitful action was taken to censor textbooks and recreating history to satisfy political correctness agendas is creating an abyss that will propel the fabrication of facts because when censorship prevails, it knows no bounds.

The corruption of inaction to stop such practices is a violation of one of the most basic tenets of freedom because it hides the truth; and education, without truth, cannot endure.

Deceitful action was taken to delude parents and taxpayers that more money is the problem facing public education. The fact is that as more money is pumped into the treasure chests, nothing really improves except the amount wasted and stolen.

The corruption of inaction to properly and effectively monitor school dollars from FraSte and WaMi is not only costly and wasteful, but it betrays the covenant of trust taxpayers and parents have a right to expect.

Deceitful action was taken by research universities in that they did nothing to call attention to the problem of corruption in schools. "When we close our eyes to fraud, corruption, and mismanagement in the schools, we forfeit the right to call ourselves school reformers. Even more importantly, when we ignore wrongdoing in the schools, we become co-conspirators to conduct that endanger children."

The corruption of inaction by higher education to conduct research and publicize the problem of corruption makes such institutions professionally impotent and corrupt.

Only when facts are faced honestly and openly can there be any hope for solving problems in a way that will make positive differences. In a sense, Education American has censored the truth in order to cleanse itself of the political pain required for real reform. Of course, those who advocate for schools will say that enough money has not been provided—another deceitful myth, and it is dramatically and forcefully illustrated in a real life laboratory of a school reform effort in one of the largest urban districts where money was no object.

The Kansas City School District (KCSD) Debacle[853]

A fascinating and devastating study made by the Cato Institute (No. 298, March 16. 1998) tells a story that not even Hollywood could conceive. In 1985 a federal judge took partial control over the troubled Kansas City school district on the grounds that it was an unconstitutionally segregated district. He then challenged the district officials to come up with a "cost is no object" education plan and ordered local and state taxpayers to find the money to pay for it.

A plan was developed with a price tag of $250 million twice the school budget of $125 million, and through court ordered tax increases and state segregation dollars the money was provided. It multiplied to a total cost of over $2 billion. Needless to say, it had an impact: Per-pupil expenditure was raised to $11,700—more money per pupil, on a cost of living adjusted basis, than any other of the 280 largest districts in the country; teacher salaries were increased 40% along with all other school employees; and the student-teacher ratio was reduced to 12 to 1, the lowest of any major school district in the country.

Fifteen new schools were built with such amenities as Olympic-sized swimming pools with a underwater viewing room, television and animation studios, a two story library, an arts gallery, a robotics lab, a 25-acre wildlife sanctuary, a zoo, a model United Nations with simultaneous translation capability, and field trips to Mexico and Senegal. In addition to the new schools, 54 more were totally renovated and five magnet schools were built to entice white suburban students to attend KCSD. If the white suburban students were not on a school bus run provided by KCSD, taxi service was provided costing $50,000 a month. The regular bus routes that numbered 100 increased to 850 and it was not uncommon to find 10 children at a single bus stop to be going to 10 different schools.

Other amenities included Russian-born teachers who taught physics, elementary grade students learning French from native speakers recruited from Quebec, Belgium and Cameroon, and performing arts that included ballet, drama, and theater production. Students in the classical Greek athletic program had weight rooms, racquetball courts, and a six lane indoor running track better than those found in many colleges. A former Soviet Olympic fencing coach coached the high school fencing team.

In every Montessori-style elementary school, there was $25,000 worth of beads, blocks, cubes, weights, balls, flags, and other manipulatives.

The district even provided working parents with all-day kindergartens and before-and-after-school programs for older students.

The previous KCSD that could only be described as "Paradise Lost" became "Paradise Found" and then some.

In other words, the school officials were given the challenge that every school district in the country would like to have: provide for every need and want without regard to cost. What the plethora of dollars did not impact was what the desegregation order was all about e.g. to have a 60/40 split of minorities and whites and to increase student achievement to national norms.

"Test scores did not rise; the black-white gap did not diminish; and there was less, not greater, integration." The white students enrolled from suburbia, originally estimated to be 10,000, never went beyond 1,500, and by 1996-97, there were only 387 students. Failure to close old and dilapidated schools and the addition of new schools created spaces for 54,000 students, but the student enrollment never exceeded 37,000. In fact, the high schools were considered financial "white elephants" and were described as "rattlingly empty."

And a little CheDe added an interesting touch to the entire process when the 60/40 split was finally seen as an impossible goal; and instead of trying to attract more suburban students, they allowed more blacks to drop out of school. Can it get anymore deceitful than this?

By 1997 even the federal judge "threw in the towel" at not being able to raise test scores after devoting 20 percent of his time over a dozen years to the case. Of course, the U.S. Supreme Court also overruled him in that he could not raise taxes. In addition, despite repeated requests by him, the district couldn't put together a security plan, a staff development program, or a core curriculum—all desperately needed, but money was instead spent on "wants" rather than needs.

Educators who promised what they could not deliver deceived the judge, and the judge deceived the public into believing that his guiding hand would make a positive difference. The reality was that everyone was deceived.

For example, if the KCSD succeeded in reaching national test norms, it would no longer receive the extra money; and since it built so many costs based on money available, it would probably have to go bankrupt.

With so much money being poured into the education treasure chest, the Robin Hood Hogs were provided with unlimited opportunities, and corruption reared its ugly head openly, unashamedly, and with arrogance that was unimaginable; even worse, there was no punishment to fear.

Hundreds of thousands of dollars worth of equipment and supplies were lost to "rampant theft" every year. Purchase orders overwhelmed the finance office at the rate of 12,000 a month. The rush to build or remodel so many schools found contractors were starting work before educators had fully decided exactly what they needed, and equipment arrived before the schools were ready to receive it. The buildings cost 75% more than similar and neighboring school districts. A display case was purchased for $40,000, but there were no trophies to put in it. Computers were purchased and became obsolete without ever having been in a classroom. The State Attorney said that the district could not account for some 23,000 items including TV sets, CD players, bookcases, office furniture and a baby grand piano.

The central office staff was five times larger than other comparably sized public school districts, yet there was no stable leadership. In 9 years, there were 10 superintendents, with five superintendents still on the payroll because of contract buyouts.

Shockingly, but not surprisingly, 54% of the budget never made it to the classroom. Incredibly, 44 percent of the entire state education budget was going to just 9 percent of the state's students living in Kansas City and St. Louis. As a result, there was a shortfall to other school districts causing them to fire teachers, freeze salaries, defer maintenance, etc.

There were some opportunities to try other reform strategies but they were rejected by KCSD. The Missouri Department of Education wanted to run demonstration schools but because it insisted on hiring its own teachers, it was not implemented. Fifty private schools were willing to take 4,000 students and educate them in return for vouchers for one-third to one-half of what the district was spending; this too was refused because the district feared it would lose jobs, power and influence. To put it into blunt terms, the district was interested in being an employment agency first and foremost, and the children's education be damned.

A guidance counselor really "hit-the-nail-on-the-head by observing: "It's not unconstitutional to give the students a lousy education; it's only unconstitutional to give them a segregated one." What everyone failed to understand was that the real issue was low student achievement, not segregation.

It's hard to understand how a judge who felt he had the power to tax, and the power to act, did not exert his power to demand results. He could have demanded that a process was needed to evaluate the performance of teachers and administrators and that promotions be based on merit. Perhaps he realized that the politics of KCSD made it impossible to fire incompetent teachers and principals. He could have demanded (he only requested) that a core curriculum be put in place and that a staff development program be implemented. These would have been basic steps in helping to turn any school system around, but it would have been more painful—even more painful than raising taxes.

There was one rather astonishing result from this "experiment in financial and human disaster." Black elementary students who went to magnet schools (which had the highest percentages of whites) scored no better on standardized tests than blacks that attended black schools. In other words, the desegregation effort that was built on the belief that blacks would increase their achievement by attending schools with middle-class whites proved false, as it has in other districts that were integrated in the hopes of achieving improved achievement.

This was unfortunate because the examples of schools that were turned-around successfully cited in Chapter Ten are ample proof that minority dominated schools can be improved when there is focus and effort to do so.

Ultimately, this tragedy of opportunity lost with money galore and years of effort resulted in the district being decertified in October 1999 because it failed to meet any of 11 academic performance standards. It did finally receive provisional accreditation when it met 4 of the 11 academic standards, the minimum required for provisional status. This remarkable transformation took place in just two years. However, it's interesting to note that there would have been a state takeover of the district had they not received provisional accreditation.

There is one very basic lesson to be learned from the KCSD tragedy, e.g. the transformation of a failing school or school district must be based on truth and honesty to do the right things, in the right way, for the right reasons, and in the most efficient and effective manner in terms of dollars and human resources.

Those who would still excuse the Kansas City debacle as an exception or anomaly need only look at another very interesting situation where ample money also did not prove to be a solution.

Sausalito, California[854]

The tiny elementary district of 284 students spends $12,300 per student nearly three times the state average. Class size is about 16, in well-maintained buildings surrounded by manicured lawns and plenty of playground equipment. This wealthy, liberal 7,200 population of writers, artists, and professionals is 94 percent white with an average family income of over $100,000.

Yet, "test scores are the lowest in Marin County, a third of the students are in special education classes, classrooms are chaotic, teachers are frustrated, distressed and exhausted, and afraid to turn their backs on their classes."

The problem is that Sausalito shares its district with Marin City, mostly black, that has a 38 percent unemployment rate and where two-thirds live in public housing "known for fostering dependence on welfare, crime, alcoholism, and drug abuse."

The problem that students were disruptive, ill-trained, ill-prepared and lacking the most basic academic and social skills was blamed by the school board on poverty, unemployment, and drugs; but some parents pointed out, and rightly so, that there were schools in nearby areas where students had just as many disadvantages and they were doing just fine.

Sausalito could have tried some effective remedies such as a better curriculum, stronger administrative leadership, encouraging parental involvement, improving communication, firing incompetent teachers, rewarding good teachers, giving parents vouchers and working to help dysfunctional families. Perhaps the most important strategy would have been to replace an obviously inept board because they had the power to institute needed changes. However, these strategies required more effort and in some case far more pain.

Money obviously was not the problem rather having the will to do what's best for children was the problem. It's so much easier to throw-up-your-hands in frustration and use blame without shame.

Summary

Clearly, the problems facing public education cannot be solved and have not been solved by more and more money being shoveled into the treasure chests that become a feeding ground for FraSte and WaMi. Those who preach and advocate for more money to solve the problems facing Education America are perpetrating the CheDe syndrome. Fancy buildings will not solve the problem of low achievement, higher salaries will not solve the problem of low achievement, and smaller classes and lower student-teacher rations, will not solve the problem of low achievement. It has all been tried, repeatedly. Time and time again, it has failed to produce the desired results.

It's interesting to note that the Kansas City debacle and others like it receive practically no attention in the education literature and certainly not in the mass media. The problem is that policymakers, educators, and politicians refuse to believe that these fairytale approaches will not improve school results and student achievement. To aggravate the problem further is their refusal to accept the abundance of research, reports, and information indicating what action is needed for success. Ignoring and not accepting the facts when they do not support their perceptions of reality is really the final school corruption. The final corruption can best be described as the "stupidity by choice" syndrome, and there doesn't seem to be any antidote for it.

When will it change? In the words from an old time radio show, "Only the Shadow knows."

Chapter Thirteen

Conclusion and Remedy

"Begin with the end in mind." Unknown Source

There will always be hogs that will be tempted to feast on the school treasure chests. The only real security for schools is obsessive and even excessive vigilance. However, this can only be achieved if all who are responsible for guarding and using the treasure chests accept their responsibility as a sacred covenant—a legal, moral and ethical contract with those who continually fill the chests in the belief that the resources will be used honestly, wisely and for the benefit of the children. The reality is that the widespread culture of greed and sense of entitlement too often prevail over vigilance and honesty.

Another issue that needs to be understood was expressed eloquently and accurately by L. Thomas Hopkins: "In crises the people in power tend to refine and intensify the status quo system which eventually destroys them. This is the present movement in education."[855]

The problem with America's public education system is that it is operating in the same mode as the Japanese economy. Why such a comparison? The Japanese are most reluctant to do what is needed to get its economy on the move again. It has been stuck in a bureaucratic and traditional business culture for over a decade just as American education has been for decades. Oh, there have been attempts to revive the economy in the same way attempts (reforms) have been made to resurrect education performance from its stance of decay, but none have really succeeded.

The problem with the Japanese economy and the public schools is the same. The hard decisions that must be made are not being made. Both are locked in a box of an antiquated and outmoded model of how business should be conducted. What has not been faced is that the present system of education is outmoded and overloaded and that is why it is not working.

It's extremely important to understand the "overload" concept. What happens in schools time and again is that everything new that they want or must do gets tacked onto everything else they are doing. You can keep some balls in the air, but you can't keep adding more without all of them falling to the floor. In other words, educators never really stop to think about the impact a new or required activity, program, or regulation creates. Something has got to give!

> "Educators are much better at piling things higher and deeper (especially on teachers) and not particularly good at learning to get rid of what doesn't work, what isn't needed or what gets in the way of our main work—teaching students. Put another way, as the old spiritual exclaims, 'Everybody talk'n 'bout heav'n, but ain't nobody go'n!'"856

Jack Welch, former CEO of General Electric and one of the most influential executives of the corporate world, provides the model that may be appropriate to consider. In his book, Jack: Straight From the Gut, he explains what is required: drastic job cuts, closing of unprofitable businesses, and fostering of fresh talent. It may sound simply, but it is extremely difficult and very painful.

This may be what is needed for the corporate world, but how does this model translate to the school environment? Jobs make up the largest part of the payroll so the job roster must be looked at first because that's where most waste will be found and, therefore, where the greatest savings can be made. For example, how personnel are utilized and allocated is never really examined with forensic eyes; basically, current positions are all seen as necessary and more personnel simply get added. That's why budgets are usually offered as "maintenance" budgets where everything must remain or stay the same while more is piled on.

The public school system is embalmed for preservation (status quo) rather than being resurrected and reenergized to face new needs and challenges. Without drastic job cuts that can be made in overstaffed programs, and eliminating ineffective programs, the embalmed system stays frozen in place; therefore, the same results of continued poor performance and results can be expected. The response from Education America is always the same: The painful and slobbering scream that there is not enough money.

At the same time, the needs of the job market have changed. Technology has reshaped and redefined how business is done along with globalization. Yet, it has not changed the business of education in any significant way. New positions are needed and some current positions need to be redefined. Yes, it is happening in a small way with personnel needed for technology, but that's where it stops.

The current problem is that high schools need real reform if they are to prepare youth for the world in which they must compete, but it's not happening. The next major reform effort will, in fact, be high schools. They are the elephant in the education chain.

Can technology reshape and redefine other positions? Does a teacher have to teach the same class in the same way day after day? Technology affords the opportunity to have a combination of large classes and small group instruction. Technology can provide distance-learning classes so that every school does not have to have the same small class such as physics. In fact, this approach to math and science teaching could solve the shortage of teachers in these fields by having a master teacher conduct the distance learning supported by other support staff. Yet, buildings are still being built the same way they were 50 years ago instead of space being redesigned to take advantage of what technology can provide.

Practices must also be examined with forensic eyes and based on factual data and research not with preconceived, emotional and false beliefs. For example, lowering class size has been touted by the professional establishment as the answer to better education, but it is not viewed as less work for those who advocate it. Of course, parents then believe the drumbeat of the philosophy and go along.

The nation only needs to look at the most ambitious and costly effort to lower class size that has taken place in California and the results after six years amount to zero—none. Will this make a difference? Of course, not because the profession and parents are literally embalmed in their belief that lower class size makes a significant difference in student achievement. It is an unprofitable business practice! The fact is that smaller group instruction can take place at times if technology is used to assist in the learning process.

What must also be examined is whether all of the subjects being offered are really needed and whether the way in which they are offered is most effective and efficient.

At the same time, unprofitable activities should be "sold off" and contracted out to entrepreneurs who can manage such activities more efficiently and make a profit. This, of course, is being done with lunch programs, transportation, maintenance, etc. In fact, some systems are beginning to view school buildings as being "contracted out" by having a company build a new school and lease it to the school system.

Another unprofitable business that needs to be examined is school board governance. As they currently exist, boards are unprofitable, and the numerous examples of mismanagement and waste cited in the previous chapters are testimony to this fact. Boards are inept in doing their jobs for the simple reason, as previously stated, that they are not trained and educated for the complex job they are held responsible to do. The vast majority of board members are elected and no skills are required to be placed on the ballot. To believe that they can then become skilled by some form of osmosis is ridiculous and rather insane. However, it is not just a matter of training and education, board members must be vigilant as well. The best example is provided by the Enron debacle. It had a board of directors that certainly had been trained and educated in the corporate world; unfortunately, they didn't take their position seriously by being more vigilant and now the results are a sad history. It's the same in Education America.

Finally, fresh talent is needed if public schools are really to be revitalized (reformed). Some school districts think that they are looking at fresh talent by hiring superintendents who are not certified from the business and political world. Several are now in place in large urban districts. However, what Jack Welch meant was somewhat different because he believes in the need to "foster" fresh talent. This means developing such talent through new training and education programs. The non-traditional superintendents being hired now have not been developed and trained for the job, and the results they have achieved thus far are nothing to brag home about.

To develop such fresh talent requires that schools of education must rethink and redefine what they do and how they do it. It also means that the certification process required by state departments of educations must also be revised so that fresh talent can be attracted and developed. Certainly attracting business executives, entrepreneurs, and line workers would offer a fresh and different pool of candidates, but it can only be accomplished if certification requirements are revisited and revised. Alternative routes to certification offered by many states is an attempt to attract outside talent, but all it does is to abbreviate the regular certification process and, as a result, the candidates are in the same mold.

The issue of the decline of schooling, however, is more than the need to change systems and structures. What is an indispensable need is that the culture of a school must also be changed so that it is in harmony with other changes. The reality is that schooling has declined because a new societal culture emerged that replaced the emphasis on academics and learning with an unrelenting and passionate emphasis on "curing and correcting" all social ills. Curing obesity, and serving dinner meals are simply the latest in the quest to "cure and correct." What is sitting on the horizon waiting to be activated is residential public schools where students will be boarded. Make no mistake about it, it's the next move to take the homeless children off the streets and eventually take away the responsibility of parents who no longer parent. If anyone should doubt this, visit the SEED school in Washington D.C. where the students are boarded.

One of the critical problems is: "America's schools are part of government, subject to public whim and will. By and large, we have the kind of schools that people want. While they acknowledge need for improvement in other people's schools, most Americans are reasonably content with their own."[857]

Parents are also a central part of the problem. Too many are failing to parent, and just as much of a problem is that in their zeal to want the best education for their children, they blindly and obediently fall prey to old clichés that more money and smaller classes are needed to improve school results. All this does is provide "cannon fodder" for Education America to continue in their relentless drumbeat that more of everything is needed, and that's why the schools are failing more often than succeeding. As a result, corruption not only continues but also grows because complacency is preferable to challenge and change.

John Dewey wrote: "Familiarity breeds contempt, but it also breeds something like affection. We get used to the chains we wear."

The current system is, in fact, inexorably chained to perceptions, politics, personalities, paradigms, parental passions, and poor performance. Breaking the chains would be a painful process. However, until it happens, there will be no escape from the present paralysis of change without change, reform that doesn't reform, and rhetoric that sends soothing thoughts to the ears, but accomplishes nothing.

An excellent report and resource that should be read by all policymakers and others interested in maximizing educational resources argues: "Money can and must be made to matter more than in the past if the nation is to reach its ambitious goal of improving achievement for all students."[858] A rather simple but provocative statement!

In essence, the challenge is how to harness the relentless increase in education dollars so that they are spent more productively, efficiently, and effectively, (words that educators growl at) in order to attain the goal of improved school outcomes.

"Public school management is stuck in the mid-20th Century with systems designed decades ago that still predominate."[859]

But in order to make some of the fundamental changes required, an obstacle must be breached: "School boards are reluctant everywhere to face down to unions and to make tough decisions even though there is an abundance of evidence that such decisions produce savings that can be put back to the classroom."[860]

As an example, in Detroit, Michigan, "only 46 percent of public education employees are teachers."[861]

What must also be understood is that the way schools are organized, and financed makes it almost impossible to teach students to high standards. Many changes are needed. One of the important ones is that the school culture must be changed to an academic emphasis. Furthermore, data usage must be a central instrument to analyze and plan needed changes.

One of the leaders in this aspect of change is the New American Schools. Their school design is affordable for most schools and assistance is available in finding needed dollars.

Consider the impact and importance of just one factor. "First the school is not buying a program to be layered on top of what the school already does, or adding on new features. Restructuring involves discarding ineffective practices and building on strong ones to create a more successful school."[862] This approach addresses the problem of most schools in implementing reforms by recognizing and eliminating the overload syndrome

Of course, new leaders or recycled/retrained leaders are needed to manage any such change from the status quo. Recently changes in education doctorate programs have been proposed to make them more effective. However, proposing change does not necessarily mean that it will, in fact, be more effective unless they are the right kind of changes.

State financing structures also need to be reviewed and probably changed to distribute funds more equitably and some states have been discussing this thorny problem. It will also be important to analyze how school districts actually spend the money

South Carolina has become the first state to introduce a new and innovative cost analysis system that fundamentally changes the way education finance is analyzed and reported. The Finance Analysis Model (FAM) was developed by Cooper and Lybrand and replaces a regulatory model with one focused on clear, complete, and useful management information.[863]

The Council of Chief State School Officers (CCSSO) has initiated a project to develop documents that will help state department of educations design, improve or review their state accountability and reporting systems.[864]

A new and novel effort is being considered in Arizona called the "65% solution," and if this initiative is passed, it would require that 65% of the district's operating budget be spent on classroom instruction.[865] It sounds like a very interesting approach.

What must be added to this mix is the information contained in an entire volume published by the Journal of Education Finance on the importance of school based data and analysis of school level spending.[866]

"District-level analysis masked significant variation in the allocation of use of resources at the school level for both equity and adequacy analysis and…it's virtually impossible to accurately link resource use patterns to educational strategies, particularly instructional quality…schools don't intentionally lie about how dollars are actually spent, but they are most negligent in full disclosure (CheDe)."

So it's hard to tell whether these and other such efforts will make a significant difference. However, what must be pondered is the history of many reform efforts that implemented every change considered important to improve school outcomes; yet, the results were dismal.

The question that must be raised is whether there are indeed answers to correcting the public school failures. Of course, there must be better answers, but it seems that the same antidotes are tried again and again and the patient still doesn't seem to get well.

Finally, what must be branded into the educational hides of all policymakers are the words of Tom Peters expressed in his book, <u>In Search of Excellence</u>: "If you always do what you always do, you will always get what you always get." In addition, so far, education is getting the same failed results because it continues to do what they always do in the name of educational reform, and the consequences are always evident with too many failures of schools and failing children.

<u>The stark and shameful reality is that children are held as hostages for getting more and more, but getting less and less in results.</u>

Such corruption betrays the public trust that has been bestowed on the policymakers, educators, and politicians and, consequently, the public and children are betrayed.

<u>A Simple Remedy</u>

There is no way school districts can maintain a focus on monitoring the system to prevent WaMi and FraSte, and that's one reason so much of it has occurred and is occurring. There is a very practical and no-cost remedy that can be applied in every school district that is an absolutely win-win situation for everyone.

There are three groups in every community that have a stake in the schools, and who are relatively independent. The first group is the parent organization (PTA/PTO), the second is the chamber of commerce, and the third is the retiree group. All the groups have local, state and national affiliations, and all are in place so nothing new has to be created.

What needs to be done is for the groups to develop a working relationship to provide assistance to the schools in focusing on corruption particularly in terms of prevention. The business community would probably be quite thrilled to participate because they will know whether their tax dollars are being spent wisely. The parent group would also be ecstatic to do more than have bake sales, and the retiree group would be more than delighted to participate in such a useful and worthwhile endeavor. What must be emphasized is that within these groups are legions of skilled, knowledgeable, and willing people who would gladly volunteer their time and expertise in such a worthwhile endeavor.

After all, for the most part, school boards and town boards are all volunteers so this concept is nothing new.

The size of the school district would determine the number of people who should serve on such a task force that would be called a Forensic Auditing Corps (FAC). There should be a committee of the whole of about 12-18 looking at district wide issues, and school building sub-committees (3-6) looking at building issues. Specialized teams can be created to focus on particular issues or problems.

School boards should realize that the FAC would have absolutely no power, but it would have the authority and responsibility to access needed data and information. It could be instrumental in creating and analyzing the data needed that is vital in helping to determine what the problems are and recommend possible solutions. One of their first tasks could be to develop an asset management system and track down all the assets of the school and monitor the inventory. This data collection would be shocking revelation of FraSte gone mad.

The FAC would report to the school board or subcommittees as needed on a regular basis to keep them abreast of their activities and findings. Some of their findings, if done forensically, will probably not be pleasant to hear about. However, a positive way to deal with this issue is to have them work closely with the administrators to work out proposed solutions or recommendations so that any reports to the board would be very positive. Of course, some of the findings may relate to the board itself in terms of their inept management and monitoring of the school district.

No, it would not be easy, but it can be done, it must be done, and it is owed to the public and the children. Because the structures are in place, it can be done quickly; however, the FAC would need initial and on-going training so that the members would know what to look for, how to look for it, how to develop and analyze data, and how to deal diplomatically with the problems that can be expected to emerge.

It can begin in any number of ways. The local PTA/PTO can contact the chamber of commerce (or vice-versa) to see if there would be interest. Getting support from the town or city leaders would also be helpful. A presentation can then be made to the school board to see if they would support the idea. If so, a written agreement can be developed outlining the responsibilities and procedures to be followed. Having such an agreement would be vital so that there would be no misunderstandings of what can be done or how it can be done.

The process can begin at the state level with both groups developing a strategy for getting support from the state department of education, the legislators, governor, the various education associations, etc. Having the state school board association support such an initiative would help local boards to be more responsive.

The national PTA/PTO and chamber of commerce can get together, develop a national strategy, and perhaps start some pilot programs in different parts of the country to show how the FAC system would work.

Retiree groups in the community, or at the state and national levels, can be asked to join at any stage of developing the FAC idea.

In other words, the FAC can be started by any of the groups, at any level, at any time; even a school board can start the process by encouraging the creation of a FAC. Such action on their part would show courage, leadership, and real responsibility.

The state or national organizations of the groups should develop joint training manuals, videos, etc. It would be an incredible opportunity for the three groups to work together on such a positive "reform effort," and it could be a godsend to every school district.

Of course, every school district would not want to have such "meddlers" in their midst because it would interfere with their feeding freely at the trough of the school treasure chest along with power and control issues. Their decision, whether or not to support a FAC, is an issue of choice.

There will be those who will say another layer of overseers is not needed, and it is simply a matter of the school boards doing a better job. The reality of the current system of governance is that it does not work effectively enough. Boards are too connected and involved with the school system to be objective. Yes, they should be the watchdogs, but as stated previously, too often they are the lapdogs sleeping every so soundly rather than sniffing out the corruption occurring under their watch.

The numerous examples of CheDe, WaMi, and FraSte, certainly demonstrate that boards simply cannot do everything they are required to do in a responsible manner no matter how willing they may be. Lack of education, training, time and politics hamper their efforts to be more effective.

What must not be forgotten is that public education affects every community and taxpayer. In addition, it is a very emotional and extremely important issue. Boards should realize that they can get far more support by having a positive involvement with the community. The FAC could provide such support.

The Beginning

This book has provided the reality of what takes place in Education America in terms of CheDe, WaMi and FraSte, and their destructive impact on the education of children and the public trust. The multitude of references and cases provide a wealth of information in terms of the problems and issues.

A remedy has been proposed; it's simple and has no real cost, but initially it will take a little time and effort to implement. There should be no doubt that it could be viewed as threatening by some. However, the very fact that a FAC is put into place will certainly deter much of the FraSte from happening, and it will put a damper on WaMi as well.

The Appendix provides checklists for what needs to be done, but certainly more can and should be added.

It all makes for a challenging beginning to formalize the sacred covenant that has been entrusted to the school board and its employees. The board has the obligation, responsibility and professional duty to ensure that the public and children will not be betrayed as they have been by so many others who have failed in their duty and obligation.

There is a quote from a New York State Department of Education document that sums up the problem in simple and eloquent words. It should serve as a thoughtful reminder to everyone who feels a real responsibility to the children and the public.

> "The problem is not that the legions of dedicated people are limited or uncaring, nor that they are unwilling to exert themselves to serve our children with intelligent, conscientious, even idealistic people eager to be effective.
>
> The problem is that the system they are in has become obsolete.
>
> For all the changes around us, the American school today is more as it was in 1900 or 1950 than it is different. And what worked in the 1900's will not work in the 2000's.
>
> Tinkering with the status quo is not enough.
>
> We must change the system so that we may achieve the results we need. And, we are running out of time; either we will make the changes that a new century and new era require, or we will sink into mediocrity."[867]

However, good intentions are not good enough, they must be followed by action and resolve. It is sad to report that at this writing "there is a bill in the New York state legislature that could strangle reforms by allowing some schools to evade rigorous state tests…this in spite of the fact that the policy developed in the 1990's is beginning to yield impressive results, especially in inner-city areas."[868]

The resolve is apparently fading, as do all reforms. The lowering of standards is happening in more and more states and local school districts. The lesson from this is that too often there is great rhetoric, but the focus and resolve fade away all too often, and the children and public are betrayed again, and again, and again.

It should not happen, but it does! The lowering of standards also fall under the heading of "corruption," and it is among the reasons why corruption can be found in every single school district.

Education America must either "make the changes or sink into mediocrity." The acceptance of mediocrity is also corruption and among the reasons why corruption will be found in every single school district.

An excellent article makes reference to what is really happening when meaningful reforms and not mere window dressing reforms are tried:

> "The constituencies who benefit from failing districts have proven infinitely more powerful at maintaining these systems than the transformers have been at changing them. Negative trends in achievement, dropouts, suspensions, graduation rates, violence, teacher turnover and ever-rising costs have become quite predictable."[869]

To this can be added that the lack of meaningful accountability is also among the reasons why corruption will be found in every school district. Accountability cannot be achieved solely from within the system and that is the fundamental problem in Education America. In fact, this is the reason why there is growing opposition to the NCLB legislation because it is an outside force on schools trying to garner some level of accountability. The reality is that there must be outside forces to maintain the focus, resolve, and legitimacy, and the Forensic Auditing Corps can certainly help to accomplish this critical task.

Although much in this book has been "doom and gloom," there is hope because there are, in fact, many legions of people eager to be effective. One of the critical roles and responsibilities of school boards and state departments of education should be to harness these forces for the benefit of the children and every community.

Everything else has been tried without success, and Chester Finn sums it up quite dramatically:

> "We've spent billions on reforms of every sort. We've shrunk classes, hired more teachers, installed computers, built new schools, stiffened graduation requirements, added kindergartens, replaced textbooks, devised test, written manifestos, conducted studies, held summits, set standards, created charter schools, experimented with vouchers, out-sourced school management, inserviced teacher, hired nontraditional superintendents, and on and on...Dozens of governors have pledged to turn around their states' education systems...business leaders beyond counting have signed up for commissions, task forces and roundtables, all pledged to fix the schools. The result is that the reforms have not brought about a major tunaround."[870]

As negative as this may be, even though it is truthful, there is an extremely important fact cited by a prominent CEO. It is an issue for all to consider and should never, ever be forgotten:

<u>"Public education was this democracy's greatest achievement...and making public schools work remains the last best hope for that 90 percent still being educated in public schools."</u>[871]

It is obviously a time for a new beginning and for new hope that would be simple, cost free, and easy to implement. There is nothing, absolutely nothing, to lose with the FAC approach, and everything to gain. Failure to forge such a new beginning would be the ultimate betrayal of the children and the public trust.

However, these words should serve as a lighthouse warning, constantly shining the beacon on the reality:

> "Unfortunately, when most people call for solutions, a different way of thinking is usually the last thing they have in mind. What they want instead is something that will not challenge their assumptions, shock their sensibilities, or violate the conventional wisdom."[872]

Texas Governor Rick Perry adds a simple and direct perspective on the basic issue facing Education America:

> "The measure of our success is not whether we provide more money for education, but more education for our money."[873]

In conclusion, it may be well to ponder the words of General Douglas MacArthur who said in his farewell address:

> "Duty, honor, country—those three hallowed words reverently dictate what you want to be, what you can be, what you will be. They are your rallying point to build courage when courage seems to fail, to regain faith when there seems to be little cause for faith, to create hope when hope becomes forlorn."[874]

A rather sobering and thoughtful reminder to all school boards that there is a duty to have honor in their dealings, deliberations, and decisions—not betrayal. It is also a reminder to all school employees that they have a duty to perform their jobs responsibly and ethically. Furthermore, they all have an obligation to the country and their constituents to do what is best for the children, and to dutifully accept the responsibility entrusted to them by the public.

Only by accepting the challenge of a new beginning can trust be resurrected and restored so that the betrayal of the children and the public trust will, hopefully, fade away.

Appendix I
Guiding Principles

- Assume that fraud, theft, and embezzlement are occurring—look for it.
- Assume that mismanagement exists—look for it.
- Assume that there is waste in the system—look for it.
- Assume that financial management controls are inadequate—tighten the process.
- Assume that staff has not been properly trained and educated in budget management—provide on-going training particularly for key personnel
- Assume that there are employees who know where there is fraud, waste, and mismanagement—encourage, reward, and resolutely protect "whistle-blowers."
- Assume that any report or information dealing with financial matters does not provide sufficient details—ask for more details.
- Assume that board policies are not being implemented properly—ask for progress reports.
- Assume that audits do not uncover fraud—insist on forensic auditing.
- Accept the fact that board members lack the skills and knowledge required to effectively monitor the budget—they must be trained.
- Accept the fact that vigilance must be constant—good enough is never good enough.
- Accept the fact that board members must have easy access to detailed information and data that are used to develop financial reports and monitor progress—develop a meaningful reporting system.
- Accept the fact that decisions made by the board will be scrutinized by the staff and the public to see if their financial rhetoric to protect school dollars from fraud, waste and mismanagement is matched against its actions—weigh every discretionary decision carefully for consistency and common-sense.

What must be understood and accepted by every board member is that they do not have to leave the board table in order to analyze and monitor school dollars; it can be done at the board table by examining information and data; the key is to know what information and data is needed and what data is important.

Any board or superintendent who has the courage to develop and implement a proactive program to identify and prevent corruption will hear a recurring phrase: "Why don't you trust us?" There is a positive response to such a reaction: "This has nothing to do with trust, it has to do with responsibility."

APPENDIX II
Prevention

Addressing the problem of corruption does not require rocket science knowledge or skills; in fact, most of what is required is common sense. Developing sound financial practices and policy decisions are not at all costly and perhaps that's the problem, if it doesn't cost a lot of money it can't be worth doing—how wrong a notion to have. However, what is required is to have the "will and desire" to stem the tide of corruption.

There are many practices and policies that need to be in place, but a few basic ones are listed for any school board and school leader to contemplate.

The Four Start Steps

The first step is to prove that there is corruption to some degree (no one really wants to do it, but it's the only way to bring reality to the problem). Once this is done, no one can dispute what needs to be done and that it is a serious matter.

1. Asset Management

List all of the assets that have been purchased in the past 10 years; in all likelihood, there will be no asset management system in place. However, a list can be compiled simply by going through past purchase orders. The next arduous task is to try and locate the assets. Many will be missing—computers, TV's, cameras, tools, projectors, furniture, furnishings, office equipment, etc. Determining what could have happened to the missing assets is the next step—broken, outdated, traded-in, worn-out, etc. These possibilities may explain some of the "missing," but the honest conclusion will be that most have been stolen.

2. Forensic Auditing Corps (FAC)

The information obtained from the Asset Management process should be enough to demonstrate that the management system is not what it should be or ought to be. A school board truly interested in developing an effective monitoring system to prevent and identify FraSte and WaMi must establish the Forensic Auditing Corps indicated previously. The FAC, of course, would need open access to all financial records (which are public), and unfettered access to records or activities dealing with or involving money.

However, the FAC would have no power so the board does not lose any control. It would report to the entire board on a monthly or quarterly basis that would include its activities, any abuses found, as well as, commendations, and recommendations for prevention activities, regulations and/or policies.

3. School Statistical Data Base (SchStat)

Information is an absolutely key component to identify and prevent FraSte and WaMi. There are companies that provide software for this purpose, but it can be done in-house and, there is no reason why that it can't be among the first activities for the FAC.

Data needs to be compiled on finances, students, staff, programs and services that would be useful in doing benchmark studies with other similar districts, and that can be reviewed regularly for "red flags." As just one example, a useful data source would be teacher absences and when they occur (day of the week, the month and the year).

4. Education and Training

Everyone responsible for handling financial transactions or monitoring and supervising dollars in any way needs to be provided with education and training so that they will know how to supervise and monitor effectively—how to analyze budgetary information, where to look for possible fraud, what reports are needed, etc. Education and training sessions must be updated and conducted regularly during the year.

The Critical Checklist

1. The duties of key personnel are segregated so that no one person is handling an entire financial process (some systems combine the function of the school finance officer and the town finance officer—this is a prescription for financial disaster).

2. Anyone responsible for financial transactions is supervised and their activities monitored regularly. Surprise audits are conducted during the year.

3. Regular monthly and detailed financial statements are provided to the board and superintendent. The detailed financial statements clearly delineate all transfers of funds, all encumbered funds, and projections for the year.

4. Financial information is verified independently on at least a quarterly basis. An effective way to do this is to have the financial officer report month-

ly directly to the school board, the town finance committee, selectman or mayor, and the superintendent all at the same time. For this procedure to be effective, the finance officer must have a contract that only the school board can fire and not renew the contract.

5. All employees involved in any way with financial transactions or financial oversight are required to take their vacation time and someone else is assigned to take over their duties. Much embezzlement is uncovered when a "substitute" takes over.

6. A credit check is made on everyone hired that will be involved with any financial transactions or oversight; and credit checks are made at least every three years.

7. There is a hot line or other confidential means for employees or others to report possible FraSte and WaMi. The hot line must be external to the system. It can be made to a police department designee, town finance committee members, town selectman or mayor, or a volunteer Forensic Auditing Corp.

8. There is double verification of all cash transactions for budget items, student activity funds, and any fundraisers.

9. The yearly budget preparation document should show what each department requested signed by the department head, supervisor, director, administrator, etc. and whether any request was changed with an explanation. The budget figures are compared with the current budget and the prior year budget.

10. There is an asset management system in place and updated whenever purchases of equipment, furniture and furnishings are made.

11. A yearly inventory is taken of all assets—equipment, supplies, furniture, furnishings and any cash accounts.

12. No credit cards are issued.

13. No school cars are provided, but car expenses or allowances with guidelines are provided.

14. There is a double-verification process (more than one person involved) in reviewing expense reimbursement requests.

15. There is a clearly defined policy on how budget transfers are made and who needs to approve them. All transfers are reviewed by a board finance subcommittee on a monthly basis.

16. A credit check is made on all companies that are not known or established companies (to verify that they are real and not a "false" invoice), and copies are provided to the finance sub-committee.

17. There is a stringent bidding policy, as well as, a very strong procedure for waiving bids.

18. All fund raising activities are formally requested in writing and approved by the administrator or supervisor in charge, the superintendent and the board finance sub-committee.

19. All student activity fund accounts are <u>double verified</u> monthly by the school supervisor and central office finance department.

20. All grant opportunities are provided to the board as they occur, and the board finance sub-committee approves any formal applications.

21. All grants received are monitored by the finance office and progress of each grant is reported to the board finance sub-committee on a monthly basis. Monitoring involves reviewing what expenditures are involved, how the grant money is actually spent, and whether any grant money is returned.

22. All consulting contracts are approved by the superintendent and the finance sub-committee.

23. There is a policy outlining "reimbursable expenses" and caps placed on specific expenditures such as food and lodging.

24. The employee benefit list is checked yearly and whenever employees leave during the school year to verify that benefits are provided according to the status of the employee.

25. The board receives a monthly budget report that includes prior year expenditures, current line item expenditures, line item encumbrances, and projections by line item for the remainder of the year.

26. Programs and services are given intensive forensic reviews every three years to determine staffing requirements or changes, program effectiveness, and future needs. Such a review must be conducted with outside-the-school-system personnel included on any evaluation committee.

27. A yearly report is provided on teacher-student loads—actual number of students each teacher has per period per day per week.

28. Purchases of maintenance supplies are reviewed and monitored by the finance officer and superintendent.

29. Petty cash funds are reviewed monthly by the immediate supervisor, the finance office and the superintendent, and each reviewer affirms in writing that they have examined the account balances.

30. All contracts for maintenance work, remodeling and construction must be monitored with the utmost diligence because it is the area where most of the WaMi and FraSte occur. The FAC can be very instrumental in helping to monitor such projects (many retirees will be construction workers of all kinds and would know what to look for).

Endnotes

1 Barbara Ann Kipfer, Ph.D., 21st Century Thesaurus (dictionary form), Bantam-Doubleday Dell Publishing, NY, 1992
2 Ron Isaac, "Spellbound," EducationNews.org, 6/16/2005
3 Seema Mehta, "O.C. principal's memo stirs teachers, district," Los Angeles Times, 6/15/2005
4 Rosalind Russell, "Top-paid school staffer earns $375,000," Chicago Sun-Times, 5/29/2005
5 Beth Reinhard, "Contract buyout of New Orleans chief spurs lawsuit," Education Week, 2/25/1998
6 Dana Hull, "San Jose school secretary sought in $483,000 theft," Contra Costa Times, 6/8/2005
7 "Superintendents on the Take?" Texas Journal, 6/14/2005
8 "Financial laxity leads to corruption in schools," Birmingham News, 11/4/2000
9 Richard Fossey, "Corrupt, mismanaged and unsafe schools: Where is the research?" Education Week, 10/25/1995
10 The Deliberate Dumbing Down of American, Conscience Press, Ravenna, Ohio, 1999
Note: This book is an absolutely fascinating history (fully documented) of the dumbing down of American education.
11 Virginia Birt Baker, "Public Schools, Home Schools, and Private Schools—A History Lesson and a Warning," Education News, 4/8/2001
12 Marsha Richards, "School superintendents want funding for Mission Impossible," Evergreen Freedom Foundation, Olympia, WA 3/30/2005
13 Ibid
14 John Archibald and Charles Dean, "Shelby administrator paved easy way out for teacher missteps," Birmingham News, 12/3/2000
15 Armando Roggio, "ISRI seminar looks at fraud and embezzlement," American Metal Market Magazine, 7/20/1998
16 John Archibald and Charles Dean, "Lax rules, oversight let millions disappear," Birmingham News, 12/3/2000
17 Ibid
18 Mark Walsh, "High court ruling makes districts liable for 'false claims'," Education Week, 3/19/2003
19 David W. Kilpatrick, "Education's funding follies," EducationNews.org, 11/2002 (also PA townhall.com)

20 Ibid
21 Joetta L. Sack, "Tangled in politics statistics position remains in limbo," Education Week, 2/6/2002
22 Details in chapter eight
23 "Federal executives afforded $32 million in bonuses last year," Fox News, 1/23/2002
24 Chuck Finnie and Julian Guthrie, "Schools: stop using bond fund for payrolls," San Francisco Chronicle 12/5/2001
25 Beth Barrett, "Million owed in records dispute," Los Angeles Daily News, 12/5/2001
26 Edward Wyatt, "Panel assails board control of building," New York Times, 7/27/2001
27 Charles Savage, "Travel bonuses don't add up," Miami Herald, 11/2/2001
28 Alan Richard, "Hands in the till," Education Week, 1/31/2001
29 Robert F. Kennedy Jr, "Deadly immunity," Salon.com, 6/16/2005
30 Lydia G. Segal, <u>Battling School Corruption in Americas Public Schools</u>, Harvard University Press, 2005
31 Craig Coogan, "The ethical choice," American School board Journal, 5/2004
32 "Embezzlement," Diocese of Providence, RI, 5/21/1998
33 <u>How to Protect Yourself and Your Business from Fraud: America's #1 Crime</u>, Broadway Books, Random House, NY, 2001
34 David Kilpatrick, "We Don't Get 'Nuff Money Blues," U.S. Freedom Foundation, 3/14/2003
35 "The 2002 Report Card: The Ethics of American youth," The Josephson Institute of Ethics, Los Angeles, CA
36 Catherine A. Carroll, "Cheating is pervasive problem in education, forum participants say," Education Week, 2/25/2004
37 <u>Winners Never Cheat</u>, Wharton School Publishing, 2005
38 "K-12 Testing," Fair Test, Cambridge, MA
39 Alfie Kohn, "Fighting the Tests," Phi Delta Kappan, January 2001
40 Jay P. Greene, "Testing High "Stakes Tests: Can We Believe the Results of Accountability Tests?" #33, 2/2003
41 "Paige scolds states," News in Brief, Education Week, 10/30/2002
42 "A Status Report: Title III No Child Left Behind," Council of Great Schools, Washington, D.C. Fall 2004
43 Tom Loveless, Brown Center Report, Brookings Institute, 9/2002
44 Ibid, 2004
45 American Legislative Exchange Council, Washington, D.C., 10/2002
46 John Marks, Center for Policy Studies, London, England, 1/21/2002
47 "Organization for Economic Cooperation and Development, Paris, France

48 Lisa Snell, "How schools cheat," Reason Foundation, 6/2005
49 Matthew Robinson, "Wave of cheating teachers hits southern California coast," Claremont Institute, Claremont, California, 1/31/2000
50 Matthew Robinson, Op.cit
51 James Traub, No Child Left Behind; Does it work?" New York Times, 11/10/2002
52 Source unknow
53 John Leo, Town.hall.com, "Ethics are made easy when anything goes," 7/15/2002
54 The Doyle Report, #51, 11/2/2002
55 USA Today, 8/30/2000
56 Associated Press, "52 Teachers accused in competency test scandal," New Haven Register, 8/18/2000
57 Diane Ravitch, "The language police," New York Times, 6/5/2002
58 Ibid
59 Zogby Poll, Op.cit, Chapter Two
60 USA Today, 10/17/2002
61 Diane J. Schemo, "U.S. reports makes no all on for profit schools," New York Times, 10/30/2002
62 "Evaluation of the National Youth Anti-Drug Media Campaign," Westate, Rockville, MD, 12/22/2003
63 Laurence D. Cohen, "Head Start tough nut to crack," Hartford Courant, 4/24/2005
64 Bridget Schulte and Valerie Strauss, "School rethinking Head Start," Washington Post, 12/4/2002
65 "School system troubles," Birmingham News, 12/3/2000
66 Pat Flannery, "Lawmakers broke school funds law," Arizona Republic, 6/19/2002
67 "Deceit and Betrayal," Arizona Republic, 11/15/2002
68 Monica Mendoza, "Deer Valley official kept $1.6 million deficit secret," Arizona Republic, 11/8/2002
69 Michelle Malkin, "Deleting 'F' from the report card grades," Washington Times, 6/21/2002
70 Michael Fletcher, "Failing schools find hole in law," Washington Post, 8/29/2002
71 Erik Robelen, "Audit faults districts on unsafe schools data," Education Week, 4/6/2005
72 Sars Neufield, "Schools test scores helped by cheating," The Mercury News, 6/14/2002
73 Howard Blume and Dennis Dockstader, "Degrees of Deceit," Los Angeles Weekly, 7/19/2002
74 BayArea.com, 11/12002
75 Francis Mejia, "Cheating teachers," CNNfyi.com, 5/5/2000

76 David Huff, "As stakes rise definition of cheating blurs," Education Week, 6/21/2000
77 Helen O'Neil and Denise Lavoie, "Erasergate principal out over tests," AP, South Coast Today, 4/6/1997
78 Michele Malkin, "Deleting F from the report card grades," Washington Post, 6/21/2002
79 Ed Martel, "Dear Educators, Parents and All Concerned with Education," EducationNews.org, 6/15/2002
80 Justin Blum, "Grading disparities verified in D.C.," Washington Post, 8/27/2002
81 Dave Weber, "Schools aren't toeing the line in retention," Orlando Sentinel, 6/26/2002
82 Editorial, "New school-grade label compounds the politics," Pam Beach Post, 6/17/2005
83 Laura Diamond, "Board OK's out-of-field teachers," Times-Union, 11/6/2002
84 Elizabeth Duffrin, "The cheating analysis," Catalyst News Magazine, Chicago, Ill, 9/1/2001
85 Rosalind Russell, "Cheating probe widens to 16 teachers and principals," Chicago Sun Times, 11/20/2002
86 Catalyst News Magazine, Chicago, Ill, 9/1/2001
87 "School heads face suspension for test tampering," Beloit Daily News, 6/27/21000
88 Elizabeth Duffrin, "The cheating analysis," Catalyst News Magazine, Chicago, Ill, 9/1/2001
89 Jodi Wilgoren, "School cheating scandal tests a town's values," New York Times, 2/14/2002
90 Diane Carroll, "Teacher quits in dispute with school board over student plagiarism," Kansas City Star, 1/29/2002
91 Monica Roberts, "Dispute heads to court," Herald-Leader, 11/15/2002
92 Randy Reynolds and Chuck Reynolds, "Large percentage of all statewide cheating," KEZP, 7/23/2001
93 John Naughton, "In Maryland, fudging on scores," Washington Post, 7/16/2000
94 Erika Niedowski, "City students promoted despite not meeting goals," Baltimore Sun, 6/15/2002
95 Sun Staff, "City schools exceed budge," The Baltimore Sun, 11/9/2002
96 Kathy Slobogin, "Cheating sandals test schools," CNNfyi.com, 6/23/2001
97 Anand Vaishnav, "MCAS rule faces challenge," Boston Globe, 10/30/2002
98 Julie Ross, "MEAP charges raise chief's wrath," Detroit Free Press, 6/14/2001
99 Judy Putnam, "Group wants to cut list of failing schools," MichiganLive, 8/31/1002
100 "Officials misuse waivers to inflate test scores," The Education Reporter, 3/1997

101 "Credibility gap grows wider," District Roundup, School Reform News, 11/1998
102 "NYC schools get an A for duplicity," Time Daily, 12/8/1999
103 Karl Reid, "NYC union report blasts cheating probe," Education Week, 1/10/2001
104 Alison Gendar, "Critical teacher stats vanish," New York Daily News, 11/9/2002
105 Gabrielle Burman, "The Whistleblower," New York Resident, 11/15/2002
106 "Ah, Love, Let Us Be True, or at least be accurate," New York Times, 1/30/2003
107 "Grade tampering" The News and Observer, 9/29/2000
108 Reginald Fields, "Akron schools break promise," The Beacon Journal, 11/1/2002
109 "Cheating teachers race for the best scores fueling adult deceptions," Jefferson City News Tribune, 6/9/2000
110 Auditor General Report, 407-02, 11/20/2002
111 Jeff Archer, "RI halts exams," Education Week, 3/17/1999
112 Janet Elliott, "TAKS passing score my be lowered," Houston-Chronicle, 11/1/2002
113 Robert Johnston, "Texas presses districts in alleged test tampering cases," Education Week, 3/7/1999
114 Editorial, "State dropout figures distort real picture," San Antonio Express News, 8/24/2002
115 "Cheating teachers race for the best scores," Jefferson City News Tribune, 6/9/2000
116 Bess Keller, "Cheating scandal ends in no-contest plea," Education Week, 1/16/2002
117 Barbara Whitaker, "Prosecutors says indictment of Austin Schools will help deter test tampering," New York Times, 4/8/1999
118 Robert Johnston, op.cit, 3/7/1999
119 Eric Hansen, "TASS scheme investigation," Houston Chronicle, 6/19/2002
120 Peabody Zanto, "Assistant principal is moved," Houston-Chronicle, 4/3/2003
121 Ronnie Lynn, "School may lower passing scores," Salt Lake City Triune, 12/5/2002
122 Liz Seymour, "Student newspaper expose school's misbehavior," Washington Post, 4/5/2001
123 "Cheating teachers race for the best scores," Jefferson City News Tribune, 6/9/2000
124 Mike Baker, "What makes teachers cheat?" BBC News, 6/15/2002
125 School Administrator, 11/2002
126 David W. Kirkpatrick, "Why are public schools so expensive?" School Reform News, 10/30/2002
127 Based on the author's personal experience as a superintendent
128 Ibid

129 Ibid
130 Ibid
131 Ibid
132 The American Legislative Exchange Council (ALEC), Washington D.C., April 14, 2000
133 "Time to rethink how we pay for education," Other Opinion, Hartford Courant, 6/10/2005
134 Allison Sherry, "DPS literacy efforts stymied: Millions spent, but few gains reflected," Denver Post, 6/10/2005
135 Peter Brimelow, <u>The Worm in the Apple: How Teacher Unions are Destroying American Education,</u> Harper Collins Publisher, 2/1/2003
136 "Money Goes to Aides," Arizona Republic
137 "General Accounting Office Report #02-393
138 Lisa Fine, "Medicaid Money Goes Untapped By Many Schools," Education Week
139 "Medicaid Scam," School Reformers
140 "Reasons for Closings," Education Week
141 Richard Rothstein, "Lessons for School Ills: The Sugar Pill," The New York Times,
142 Michelle Davis, "Hill hearings focus on Head Start finances," Education Week
143 "Head Start a Tough Nut To Crack," Hartford Courant
144 John Archibald and Charles Dean, "Lax rules, oversight let millions disappear," Birmingham News
145 "Alabama School system Ripe for Theft," Alabama Tax Watch
146 Ibid
147 John Archibald, Op.cit.
148 Jen Sansbury, "Brown blamed for lost millions in Birmingham," Atlanta Journal-Constitution
149 Charles Dean and John Archibald, "Financial laxity leads to corruption in schools," Birmingham News
150 John Archibald and Charles Dean, "Shelby County's model system tracks everything," Birmingham News
151 "Arizona ASP plan mired in controversy," eSchool News Online
152 Pat Kossan, "Charter schools crackdown," Arizona Republic
153 Pat Flannery, "Stop raiding school fund, judge warns," Arizona Republic
154 Pat Kossan and Maggie Galehouse, "Arizona flat broke for school repairs," Arizona Republic
155 "Arizona district seeks to recoup insurance," Education Week
156 Beth Falco and Sally Anchors, "Suspended superintendent draws salary," Arizona Republic

157 Sally Anchors, "Interim chief of Wilson district ousted," Arizona Republic
158 Bess Keller, "Arkansas schools won't have to pay for $50 million accounting gaffe," Education Week,
159 Lisa Snell, "LAUSD should let builders build new schools," Reason Public Policy Institute, Los Angeles, CA
160 Robert Holland, School Reform News, Heartland Institute, Chicago, Ill (1/2001)
161 Beth Fouhy, "Public school failures raise questions," San Francisco Chronicle
162 Lisa Snell, "Scandals prevalent in public schools," School Reform News, Heartland Institute, Chicago, Ill
163 Beth Fouhy, Public school failures raise questions of political leadership," AP, San Francisco Chronicle, 4/4/2005
164 Nanette Asimov, "2 charter operators claim same school," San Francisco Chronicle
165 Bob Egelko, "California to repay millions in federal grants," San Francisco Chronicle
166 Ramon Coronado, "Jury stings education chief and state," Sacramento Bee
167 "The pain and injustice of Alum Rock Schools," Mercury News
168 Walter Yost, "$2.3 million budget gap stuns schools," Sacramento Bee
169 Catherine Gewertz, "California superintendent leaves school district in disarray," Education Week
170 State Education Roundup, School Reform News, Heartland Institute, Chicago, Ill
171 "LA school district sets bad precedent," USA Today
172 Office of the Inspector General
173 "Funding cuts hamstring audits," Los Angeles Daily News
174 Beth Barrett, "District $600 million short," The Los Angeles Daily News
175 Solomon Moore, "Board says it was misled," Los Angeles Times
176 Sonia Giordano, "LAUSD watchdog role eyed," Los Angeles Daily News
177 Miquel Bustillo, "Panel OK's bill on school watchdog," Los Angeles Times
178 Duke Helfand, "District Ends Legal Battle," Los Angeles Times
179 Sonia Giordano, "LAUSD board backs hire even before measure OK'D," USA Today
180 Troy Anderson, "LAUSD accused of misspending," Los Angeles Daily News
181 "Jury says schools misused lottery funds," Los Angeles Daily News,
182 "Audit finds that state was deceptive," Los Angeles Daily News,
183 Laura Randall, "School days in the Hotel California," New York Times,
184 Sonia Giordano, "Conflict of interest found" Los Angeles Daily News
185 "Accountable public schools squander funds," School Reform News, Heartland Institute, Chicago, Ill
186 Soloman Moore, "Quake fault under Belmont school is studied," LA Times,

[187] Tom Harrigan, "Los Angeles DA finds no evidence," Associated Press
[188] Cara Mia DiMass and Erika Hayasaki, "LA Board votes to finish troubled Belmont Project," Los Angeles Times
[189] Lisa Snell, "LAUSD Should Let Builders Build New Schools," Reason Public Policy Institute, 11/10/2002
[190] ibid
[191] "Contract terminated," Los Angeles Daily News
[192] Helen Gao, "Education board gives ultimatum," Los Angeles Daily News,
[193] Beth Barrett, "Consultants cost district twice as much as staff employees," Los Angeles Daily News
[194] Catherine Gewertz, "California audit cites litany of troubles in Oakland schools," Education Week
[195] Lisa Snell, "Corruption in Public Schools Costs Taxpayers," School Reform News, Heartland Institute
[196] Nanette Asimov, "Study puts Oakland dropout rate at 52%," San Francisco Chronicle
[197] May Meredith and Seth Rosenfeld, "Bankrupt Dreams: How idealistic education's grand plan turned into a fiscal nightmare," San Francisco Chronicle
[198] Kate Folmar, "San Jose school chief resigns after 7 months of turmoil," San Jose Mercury News
[199] Kate Folmar, "Report details district failings," San Jose Mercury News,
[200] Sara Neufeld, "District fined," San Jose Mercury News
[201] Sara Neufeld, "Judge questions district integrity," San Jose Mercury News
[202] Peter Schmidt, "Grand Jury Blames Richmond Bankruptcy on Board," San Jose Mercury News
[203] Lori Posas Santos, "Commentary," Hispanic Vista
[204] Chuck Finnie and Julian Guthrie, "Schools: stop using fond fund for payrolls," San Francisco Chronicle
[205] Chuck Finnie and Julian Guthrie, "Signs of Trouble," San Francisco Chronicle
[206] Lisa Snell, "Scandals prevalent in public schools," School Reform News, Heartland Institute
[207] Nancy Mitchell, "Difficulties plague school board," Rocky Mountain News
[208] Nancy Mitchell, "State seeks safeguards for school borrowing," Rocky Mountain News
[209] Jeff Archer, "Budget errors leave schools feeling pinch," Education Week
[210] Marcos McQueen, "St. Vrain bailout accord near," Denver Post
[211] Nancy Mitchell, "State seeks safeguards for school borrowing," Rocky Mountain News
[212] Chris Frates, "St Vrain was warned in '01," Denver Post
[213] Richard Weizel, "Amity voters head to polls," Hartford Courant

214 Brian McCready, "Amity board told early of crisis," New Haven Register
215 Brian McCready, "Amity budget rejected 7th time," New Haven Register
216 Brian McCready "Budget fails for the 11th time," New Haven Register
217 Michele Jacklin, "A raw deal for taxpayers," Hartford Courant
218 "Hartford's Bloated Payroll," Editorial, Hartford Courant
219 Richard Fossey, "Corrupt, Mismanaged and Unsafe Schools," Education Week
220 "Mere change or real reform," Washington Times
221 Ibid
222 Ibid
223 Ibid
224 Justin Blum, "Lawyers capitalize on DC school gaps," Washington Post
225 "Board probes charger problems," The Washington Times
226 Vaishali Honawar, "Charter schools overstate counts," Washington Times
227 A Post staff writer, "Audit faults DC special-education finances," Washington Post
228 "More bad news," House Editorial, Washington Times
229 Jim Saunders, "School Board pay gets spotlight," The Florida Times-Union
230 "Highlights of how state money is spent," Herald-Tribune
231 Office of Program Policy Analysis and Government Accountability Report #99-07
232 Ibid
233 Robert King, "School review turns up $3 million," St Petersburg Times
234 Bill Hirschman, "School chief orders audit, "Sun-Sentinel
235 Steve Harrison, "Tenacious inspector a puzzle for supervisors in school system," Miami Herald
236 Laura Diamond, "Audit questions school spending," Florida-Times Union
237 "Audits involving three Broward schools find misspending and theft," Miami Herald
238 Ibid
239 "Tenacious inspector, Op.cit.
240 Robert King, "School district's inventory shrinks," St. Petersburg Times
241 "Hillsborough school deficiencies," Editorial, St Petersburg Times,
242 "Student's lose, others gain...millions spent on questionable projects," Miami.com
243 "Wealthy Miami school board member pleads guilty to mail fraud," AP, Naples Daily News
244 Charles Savage, "Report: School District Bloated," The Miami Herald
245 Ibid
246 Ibid
247 Ronnie Greene and Jason Grotto, "As schools confront tough challenges, millions spent," Miami Herald
248 Jason Grotto and Ronnie Greene, "Firm was paid to run school," Miami Herald

[249] Ronnie Greene and Joseph Tafani, "Lobbyist hold major role in school district," Miami Herald
[250] Ronnie Greene and Jason Grotto, "Florida's costliest school gets pricier," Miami Herald
[251] Charles Savage, "Private maintenance work pits school board vs. unions," Miami Herald
[252] Charles Savage, "Schools shun 'freebie': pay big for TV tower," Miami Herald
[253] Charles Savage, "State audit shreds Dade schools," Miami Herald
[254] Lisa Snell, "Corruption in public schools cost taxpayers," Heartland Institute
[255] Steve Harrison, "School building refund demanded," Miami Herald
[256] Daniel Grech, "Miami-Dade schools OK position of IG," Miami Herald
[257] "Crumbling schools," Miami Herald
[258] "At Beach High, when it rains it pours," Miami Herald,
[259] Carl Hiaasen, "Putting students in harms way," Miami Herald
[260] "Tossing McKay Dollars," Editorial, St. Petersburg Times
[261] Collins Connor and Kent Fischer, "One director, two schools mismanaged," St. Petersburg Times
[262] "Enemies from within," editorial, Palm Beach Post
[263] James Salzer, "Budget overrun sparks state education staffers' firing," The Atlanta-Journal Constitution,
[264] Lucy Soto and Paul Donsky, "Shrenko deals voided," Atlanta Journal-Constitution,
[265] Laura Brown, "Dept of Education remakes 'Silence of the Lambs,'" The Hawaii Reporter
[266] "Private Education Trust Reaches Settlement with Hawaii Over Alleged Mismanagement," News in Brief, Education Week
[267] "Expensive travel," Idaho Statesman
[268] Kerry White, "Audit questions oversight," Education Week
[269] Ann Bradley, "Agent fills new Chicago post to probe waste and fraud," Education Week
[270] Ann Bradley, "Inspector's report blasts lack of accountability," Education Week
[271] Joanne Richardson, "Dozens targeted in corruption probe," Education Week
[272] Rosalind Rossi, "Schools get millions; results unclear," Chicago Sun-Times
[273] Michael Martinez and Stephanie Banchero, "3 teachers who hit OT jackpot probed," Chicago Tribune
[274] Stephanie Banchero, "Power struggle, lack of cash stalls progress," Chicago Tribune,
[275] George Clowes, "Accountable public schools squander funds," School Reform News

276 Joseph Sjostrom and Diane Rado, "District learns fiscal lessons hard way," Chicago Tribune
277 "A review of the school technology program," Office of the State Auditor
278 Kathy Bolten, "Schools misspent, audit says," Des Moines Register
279 Kathy Bolten, ""School district has $9.1 million in errors," Des Moines Register
280 Carrie Watters, "Schools lose reading aid," Des Moines Register
281 "Tough Times, Tough Choices," AP, NJ.com
282 "Charges filed," Education Week
283 Beth Reinhart, "Contract buyout of New Orleans chief spurs lawsuit," Education Week,
284 Brian Thevenot, " N.O. schools insurance pact blasted," The Times Picayune
285 Jeff Archer, "Budget errors leave schools feeling pinch," Education Week
286 "PG school board gets off easy at audit hearing," Washington Times
287 Nancy Trejos, "Metts pins deficit on per diem teachers," Washington Post,
288 "Overstaffing, Accounting blamed for school deficit," Washington Post,
289 Matthew Mosk and Nelson Hernandez, "Lawmakers alarmed by growing costs of school construction," Washington Post,
290 Jonathan Rockoff, "PTA president asked to resign," Baltimore Sun
291 State Education Roundup, School Reform News
292 David Kilpatrick, "Why are public schools so expensive," School Reform News
293 Ed Hayward, "Group's study finds education reform wastes $," Boston Herald
294 Maria Sacchetti, "State plans school construction probe," Boston Globe
295 News in Brief, A National Roundup, Education Week
296 Anand Vaishnav, "Accounting issues mire a district in red ink," Boston Daily Globe
297 Patrick Healy, "Consultants told Governor Romney of Waste in Public Colleges," Boston Globe
298 "Michigan administrative expenses top $1.4 billion," Michigan Education Report
299 Peter Schmidt, "Thefts in Detroit spur inventory control effort," Education Week
300 George Clowes, "Accountable public schools squander funds," Education Week,
301 "Stopping Theft Before it Happens," Education Week
302 "Cut waste in school budgets, not class instruction." Detroit News
303 Jodi Cohen, "Detroit schools' PR: $1.5 million," The Detroit News,
304 School House Beat, American School and University magazine
305 Jodi S. Cohen, "School audits show ripoffs, broken rules," Detroit News
306 Michigan Education Report
307 Bill Johnson, "Detroit kids share classes with roaches," Detroit News
308 "State is foolish to turn down $500 million," Detroit News

309 Chastity Pratt, "Schools' auditor says cash misspent," Detroit Free Press
310 John Welsh, "Outsider 'balances' district's books" Pioneer Press
311 Jake Wagman, "Audits detail problems in school finance," Post-Dispatch
312 "Tough Times-Tough Choices," AP, NJ.com
313 Ed Vogel, "Educator's letter irritates lawmakers," Las Vegas Review-Journal
314 "Has money improved education in Claremont?" AP, Boston Globe
315 Jason Schreiber, "Raymond school official defends $19 K Hawaii trip saying its federal money," The Union Leader
316 Robert Moran, "State report cites massive waste in schools program," Philadelphia Inquirer
317 Millicent Lawton, "NJ auditors cite district's waste, nepotism," Education Week
318 Melanie Burney, "The district will have to make some sacrifice," The Philadelphia Inquirer
319 Office of the State Auditor
320 "NY career school scandal," Education Week
321 Mike Cervantes, "State gives low grades to middle schools," Buffalo News
322 News in Brief, School Reform News
323 James Hertling, "City agency cites mismanagement," Education Week
324 "Trade school official pleads guilty," Education Week,
325 William Snider, "Panel is set to probe NYC corruption scandal," Education Week,
326 Caroline Hendrie, "Five arrested, fraud alleged," Education Week
327 "Stancik's greatest hits," Education Week
328 "Credibility gap grows wider in NYC schools," School Reform News
329 Ibid
330 Governor's Press Release
331 Edward Wyatt, "Panel assails board control of building," New York Times
332 Carl Campanile, "School building work is $ky-high," New York Post
333 Kenneth Lovett, "Ed. Board Too Perk-Y," New York Post
334 Alison Gendar, "Ed Board Perks Under Fire," New York Daily News
335 Joe Williams, "Educrats' 40G trip," New York Daily News
336 Carl Campanile, "Writing off $2.7M," New York Post
337 Carl Campanile, "Teachers do lunch for big $," New York Post
338 Carl Campanile, "Boar of Education summer school cafeteria program a waste," New York Post
339 "The case of the missing teachers," Editorial, New York Daily News
340 Jacques Steinberg, "Report says city is paying too much to build schools," New York Times
341 Carl Campanile, "Shocker of booted students," New York Post
342 Joe Williams, "Report slams bilingual education," New York Daily News
343 Frankie Edozien, "Classroom taken for 529G ride," New York Post

344 Abby Goodnaugh, "Trainer says he almost quit twice," New York Times
345 Phil Mintz, "Audit rips textbook procedures," Newsday
346 George Clowes, "Accountable public schools squander funds," School Reform News
347 Herbert Cohen, "Contractor accused of fraud," Port Washington News
348 Celeste Hadrick, "Audit rips phone scam," Newsday
349 "School board ousted," New York Times
350 State Auditor Performance Audit Summary #151
351 Cara Froedge, "Notebooks detail case," Statesville Record & Landmark
352 "Audit critical of charter school oversight," The Plain Dealer
353 Auditor of the State Report
354 "Grand retreat" The Plain Dealer
355 Andrew Welsh-Huggins, "Charter school owes Ohio," The Cincinnati Enquirer
356 Patrick O'Donnell, "Spending adds up at school retreats," The Plain Dealer
357 Jeff Archer, "Budget errors leave schools feeling pinch," Education Week
358 Melissa Jones, "More school workers collect 2 paychecks," Oregon.Live.com
359 Susan Snyder, "Tutor dollars are going to waste," Philadelphia Inquirer
360 Geoff Mulvihill, "Court ordered work eluding Abbott schools," Philadelphia Inquirer
361 Auditor General Report #407-02
362 Auditor General Report #036-01
363 Auditor General Report #036-01
364 Auditor General Report #036-01
365 AG Report 382-01
366 Susan Snyder, "City school to hire IG," The Philadelphia Inquirer
367 George A. Clowes, "Accountable public schools squander funds," School Reform News
368 Chris Brennan, "School reformers OK $3.1 M in payouts." The Philadelphia Inquirer
369 AG Report 453-00
370 AG Summary Report
371 AG Report 726
372 AG Summary Report
373 AG Report 582
374 AG Report 354
375 AG Report 395
376 AG Report 398
377 "Chester Upland ordered to pay charter fully, on time," The Philadelphia Inquirer
378 Aimee Edmondson, "Schools' backer cuts off funding," GoMemphis.com

[379] Review 2001
[380] Review 9/1995
[381] Review 8/2000
[382] Review 8/2001
[383] Review 2001
[384] Review 7/2001
[385] Review 6/2000
[386] Review 4/2002
[387] Ibid
[388] "School fund management probe goes to grand jury," Houston Chronicle
[389] Tawnell Hobbs, "Audit shows activity fund problems," Dallas News
[390] "Schools may have overpaid millions," Star-Telegram
[391] Melanie Markley, "Charter school chief gets $235,000 payout," Houston Chronicle
[392] Salatheia Bryant, "Charter school chief hiring of kin," Houston Chronicle
[393] Salatheia Bryant, "One used building, prime location, Call HISD," Houston Chronicle
[394] State Auditors Office Report
[395] Joshua Benton, "Master urged for district," Dallas Morning News
[396] "Schools' supply-side economics," Editorial, Washington Post
[397] "Overspending probe requested," Education Week
[398] "Jessica Portner, "Five members of Va. School Board resign," Education Week
[399] Gregory Roberts, "Ethics inquiry focuses on former state schools official," Seattle Post-Intelligencer
[400] Diane Brooks, "Superintendent paid $320,000 to resign," Seattle Times
[401] Martin Ringhofer, "Mismanagement wrong priorities," Seattle Post-Intelligencer
[402] Keith Ervin, "Audit again shows problems at Seattle schools," Seattle Times
[403] Linda Shaw and Vinh Tan "$33 million in blunders," Seattle Times
[404] Keith Ervin, "Seattle school district's financial woes grow," Seattle Times
[405] Keith Ervin, "Seattle schools name auditor," Seattle Times
[406] Linda Shaw and Christine Williamsen, "How Seattle schools botched their budget," Seattle Times
[407] Amy Hetzner and others, "30 working without licenses in schools," Milwaukee Journal Sentinel
[408] BBC News
[409] "Betrayals in Public Education," LewRockwell.com, 3/30/2005
[410] "Teacher whistle blowers harassed," New York Post
[411] Carl Campanile, "Teachers union wants Klein to join 'waste watchers,'" New York Post

412 Austin, Texas
413 Joseph T. Well, "Why employees commit fraud," Association of Certified Fraud Examiners, Austin, Texas, 2/2001
414 Peter Schmidt, "Bid rigging among schools suppliers," Education Week
415 Kathleen Manzo, "Book distributor charged with overcharging schools," Education Week
416 Thomas Toch, "Thousands of educators bought false diplomas," Education Week
417 Mark Pitsch, "Three school milk suppliers indicated on price fixing," Education Week
418 Peter Schmidt, "Bid rigging among school suppliers," Education Week
419 Ibid
420 Peter West, "Computer theft is hidden cost of tech boom," Education Week
421 Ellen Sorokin, "Complaint accuses NEA of misusing funds," The Washington Times
422 Julie Blair, "Missing $400,000 spells bankruptcy for staff trainers," Education Week
423 Philip Brasher, "Ineligible kids get free lunch," Chicago Sun-Times
424 Lisa Snell, "Scandals prevalent in public schools," Heartland Institute, Chicago, Ill.
425 "Financial laxity leads to corruption in schools," Birmingham News
426 "School system troubles," Birmingham News
427 Ibid
428 "Alabama school corruption: The case histories," Birmingham News
429 Ibid
430 State Education Roundup: Focus on Public School Corruption, School Reform News, Heartland Institute
431 "City schools "air-conditioners found in houses," Birmingham News
432 Ibid
433 "Alabama school corruption: The case histories," Op.cit.
434 John Archibald and Charles Dean, "Lax rules, oversight let millions disappear," Birmingham News
435 "School systems troubles." Birmingham News
436 Peter West, "Arizona probes alleged misuse of thousands in school funds," Education Week
437 Auditor General Report
438 Monica Mendoza, "Parent asks district to probe car use," The Arizona Republic
439 Monica Mendoza, "Departing Hill will get $158,245" The Arizona Republic
440 Mel Melendez, "PTO hurt by scandal," Arizona Republic

441 Pat Kossan, "Mesa charter school owner facing charges of theft, fraud," Arizona Republic
442 Auditor General Report
443 News in Brief, Education Week
444 Betty Reid and Daniel Gonzales, ""Husband apologizes to PTO for wife's woes," Arizona Republic
445 Auditor General Investigative Report
446 Auditor General's Office Investigative Report
447 Peter West, "Arizona's chief in the eye of the storm," Education Week
448 Karla Reid, "Arkansas boards group wins restitution in kickback case," Education Week
449 Catherine Gerwertz, "Teacher test proctor, 9 others indicted in cheating probe," Education Week
450 "Alum Rock school accountant going to prison," Mercury News
451 Sean Webby, "Warrant details case against school," Mercury News
452 Erika Hayasaki and Cara Mia DeMassa, "School district's IG resigns his post," Los Angeles Times
453 Peggy Caldwell, "Teachers charged with obtaining phony credits," Education Week
454 Doug Smith, "$300,000 in quake money is unaccounted for," Los Angeles Times
455 "A fishy deal," The Daily News
456 Beth Barrett, "Millions owed in records dispute," The Los Angeles Daily News
457 "Bookkeeper accused of embezzling," The Los Angeles Daily News
458 "No contest pleaded in phone scam," The Los Angeles Daily News
459 Gretchen Hoffman, "Claims filed against LAUSD," Los Angeles Times
460 David Reyes and Mark Platte, "School embezzler dies in prison," Orange County Register,
461 Nancy Mathis, "State oversight likely as district is engulfed in theft and patronage scandal," Education Week
462 People News, Education Week
463 Sara Neufield, "State launches financial probe of district," Mercury News
464 Peter West, "Computer theft is hidden cost of school technology," Education Week
465 Sherry Parmet, "School employee placed on leave in possible scam," Union-Tribune
466 Corey Murray, "Police investigate alleged computer theft," e-School News
467 Jason Van Derbeken and Nanette Assimov, "S.F. schools scam alleged," San Francisco Chronicle
468 "Ex-SFUSD official arrested in energy scam," San Francisco Chronicle

469 David Kravits, "Indictments issued on e-rate fraud," AP Atlantic Journal Constitution
470 "Former employee charged with embezzlement," News Release, District Attorney Office, Los Angeles
471 Kristi Belcamino, "Fraud eyed in school funds case," Contra Costa Times
472 Moline Hazle, "School leader faces 9 charges," Record Searchlight
473 Christine Kovakes, "Ex-chief must pay," Sacramento Bee
474 Kara Shire, "Ex-West County teacher sues school district, union," Sacramento Bee
475 Lisa Fine, "California superintendent charged with felonies," Education Week
476 May Meredith, "West Fresno school board probed," San Francisco Chronicle
477 "Aurora facing theft charges," Rocky Mountain News
478 John C. Ensslin, "Cops find bizarre layout," Rocky Mountain News
479 Maureen Harrington, "Audit cuts no factor in theft," Denver Post
480 Marilyn Robinson and Keiran Nicholson, "Custodian arrested in theft," Denver Post
481 Joey Bunch, "School district by the books," Denver Post
482 Ann Schrader, "Ex school employee avoids jail," Rocky Mountain News
483 "Bill Cummings, "Double dip by school employee probed," Connecticut Post
484 "Former school official jailed." Hartford Courant
485 Amy Zitka, "Embezzling case postponed," Middletown Press
486 Peter Schmidt, "Bid rigging among school suppliers," Education Week
487 "Custodian steals lunch $," Associated Press
488 "Suit alleges trustees misspent scholarship funds," The Hartford Courant
489 Lee Foster, "Ex clerk for schools sentenced," The Hartford Courant
490 Michael York, "Money was taken from elderly woman," Washington Post
491 "School employee resigns," Washington Post
492 District News Roundup, Education Week
493 Valerie Strauss, "D.C. meal tab doesn't add up," Washington Post
494 Karla Reid, "Former union president is at center of probe," Washington Post
495 Justin Blum and Valerie Strauss, "Charges filed in union scandal," Washington Post
496 Neely Tucker, "Teacher union driver pleads guilty," Washington Post
497 Jim McElhatton, "A big schools budget but few watchdogs," Washington Times, 4/25/2005
498 Office of Auditor of Accounts
499 Ibid
500 "Florida principal pleads guilty to stealing," CNN News
501 Steve Harrison, "Principal stole cash," Miami Herald
502 "Coaches charged with grand theft," Miami-Herald
503 "Manager get free catering," Miami Herald

504 Daniel Grech, "Dade schools' blood deal criticized," Miami Herald
505 "Former high school bookkeeper sentenced for embezzlement," Daytona-Beach News Journal
506 "Georgia woman accused in PTSA theft," Savannah NOW
507 Leteef Mungin, "Teacher arrested in theft of Ritalin," The Atlanta Journal-Constitution
508 Teresa Stepzinski, "Ex-Ware school recorder arrested," Florida Times-Union
509 Jan Skutch, "Billy Knight indicted," Savannah NOW
510 Jennifer Hiller, "Aide charged, more promised in Felix probe," Honolulu Advertiser
511 "Unnecessary spending," Idaho Statesman
512 Cities News Roundup, Education Week
513 "CU account probed in school embezzlement," Credit Union Journal Daily
514 "Heroine wearing a wire nabs bribing bus contractors," Education Week
515 Joanne Richardson, "Dozens targeted in Chicago corruption probe," Education Week
516 Peter West, "Computer theft is hidden cost of tech boom," Education Week
517 Michelle Roberts, "Feds to probe Clemente spending," Chicago Sun-Times
518 John Gehring, "Parents implicated in probe of financial aid fraud," Education Week
519 Rosalind Rossi and Nancy Moffett, "Did ex-principal embezzle?" Chicago Sun Times
520 Diane Rado, "Auditors target teacher academy," Chicago Tribune
521 Art Golab, "7 years for looting poorest schools," Chicago Sun Times
522 "Athletic chief admits charges," Education Week
523 Carolyn Starks, "School nurse pleads guilty," Chicago Tribune
524 Julie Sowers, "3 yr plan seeks to erase red ink," The DesMoines Register
525 Jonathan Weisman, "Vote fraud charges cap dispute over school site," Education Week
526 George Clowes, "How well are our public schools run?" School Reform News
527 "School fraud to cost former Topeka man $22.6 million," AP, Kansas News
528 Jessica Sandham, "Audit accuses Ky Ed Dept of fiscal subterfuge," Education Week
529 Joseph Gerth, "Kimbrough admits embezzlement," Courier-Journal
530 Megan Woolhouse, "Embezzlement case rocks school system," Courier-Journal
531 "Dead school board bookkeeper charged," Lexington Herald-Leader
532 Megan Woolhouse, Op.cit.
533 Beth Reinhard, "Contract buyout of New Orleans chief spurs lawsuit," Education Week
534 Lisa Snell, "State probes Louisiana district on overtime," Education Week

535 "Investigation turns up $669,000 in stolen property," Times Picayune
536 Brian Thevenot, "Orleans school insurance probe," Times Picayune
537 Brian Thevenot, "Consultant's repair work deals spark investigation," Times Picayune
538 Lisa Snell, "Corruption in public schools costs taxpayers," Education Week
539 "New Orleans probe yields more charges," News in Brief: A National Roundup, Education Week
540 Jennifer McMenamin and Sheridan Lyons, "Settlement seen in theft of PTA funds," Baltimore Sun
541 Lisa Leff, "School official gets 5 years," Washington Post
542 Julie Blair, "MTA official charged with larceny," Education Week
543 Kevin Rothstein, "Audit: School boss spent kid's cash," Boston Herald
544 "School superintendent placed on paid administrative leave," AP, MassLive.com
545 Melinda Leader, "Ex-principal admits theft," Standard Times
546 Dave Wedge, "School employees eyed for mishandling of taxpayer funds," Boston Herald
547 George Clowes, "How well are our public schools run?" School Reform News
548 Dennis Niemiec and others, "Schools fight new battle of the books," Detroit Free Press
549 Karla Scoon Reid, "Detroit audits reveal fraud," Education Week
550 District News Roundup, Education Week
551 "Principal charged in school fraud case," The Detroit News
552 "Ex-bookkeeper charged," Detroit Free Press
553 Peggy Sarnecki, "Schools make the taxpayer's pay for price of corruption," Detroit Free Press
554 Jodi Cohen, "Audit rips principal," The Detroit News
555 Ibid
556 Jodi Cohen, "Detroit schools to hire auditor," Detroit News
557 Jodi Cohen, Detroit schools chief questions leaders' bills," Detroit News
558 Jodi Cohen, ""School audits show rip-offs," Detroit News,
559 Gene Shabath, "Former school aide admits guilt," Detroit News
560 Gene Shabath, "School scandal isn't over," Detroit News
561 "Businessman admits falsifying invoices," Detroit Free Press
562 Kim North and David Ashenfelter, "2 accused of exchanging favors," Detroit Free Press
563 Ryan List, "Pleads guilty to embezzlement, forgery," The Daily News
564 Dennis Niemiec, "District fears new embezzlement of PTO funds," Detroit Free Press
565 "Three charged in embezzlement," AP, The Detroit News
566 Cecil Angel, "School officials are suspended," Detroit Free Press

[567] Dennis Niemiec, "Officials were told of shady spending," Detroit Free Press
[568] Office of the State Auditor
[569] News in Brief: A National Roundup, Education Week
[570] Peter Schmidt, "Bid rigging among school suppliers" Education Week
[571] "School employee charged with embezzling," Hannibal Courier-Post
[572] Peter Schmidt, "Bid rigging among school suppliers" Education Week
[573] "N.J. report says schools are ripe for labor scam," Philadelphia Inquirer
[574] Lisa Snell, "A lesson from NJ special education contracting," Reason Public Policy Institute, Los Angeles, CA
[575] Catherine Gerwetz, "Former NJ mayor accused of bilking" Education Week
[576] Caroline Hendrie, "Murder leads to probe" Education Week
[577] Michele Davis, "Superintendent charged with soliciting bribe," Education Week
[578] "IRS raids school offices," School Reform News
[579] Office of the State Auditor
[580] "District investigating possible embezzlement," Amarillo Globe-News
[581] Christine Proctor, "Woman pleads guilty," Tahoe Daily Tribune
[582] Mike Henderson, "Employee held on embezzlement charge," Reno-Gazette Journal
[583] Anjeanette Damon, "Ex-administrator accused of using school funds," Reno-Gazette Journal
[584] Joanne Richardson, "Custodian abuses," Education Week
[585] "Official pleads guilty" Education Week
[586] Richard Fossey, "Corrupt, mismanaged and unsafe schools," Education Week
[587] Peter Schmidt, "18 held in probe of fraud" Education Week
[588] "Stancik's greatest hits," Education Week
[589] Richard Fossey, Op.cit
[590] Carl Campanile, "School big…" New York Post
[591] Barbara Stewart, "Teacher accused of selling first aid certifications," New York Times
[592] "NY food company and its top executives plead guilty" U.S. Department of Justice press release
[593] "Five executives and three food companies plead guilty" U.S. Department of Justice press release
[594] Carl Campanile and Ryan Sabey, ""School window scandal," New York Post
[595] Carl Campanile, "Levy aide caught" New York Post
[596] Carl Campanile and Daniel Schiff, "Readin, "Ritin and Rip-off," New York Post
[597] Jessie Graham, "School Scammers," New York Post
[598] Andrew Smith, "Ex-school treasurer guilty," Newsday
[599] "Stancik's greatest hits," Education Week
[600] Patricia Hurtado, "Guilty plea in embezzlement," News Day

[601] "Principal removed," News Day
[602] Carl Campanile and Daniel Schiff, "Readin, 'Ritin and Rip-Offs," New York Post
[603] Mary Pasciak, "School chief relieved of duties," Buffalo News
[604] Lisa Snell, "Corruption in public schools costs taxpayers," The Heartland Institute
[605] "Auditors Sued," National Roundup, Education Week
[606] Frank Eltman, "Four plead not guilty in million-dollar school scandal," AP, Newsday, 6/8/2005
[607] "Grade tampering" The News and Observer
[608] Jennifer Moxley, "School worker accused of embezzlement," Salisbury Post
[609] Jennifer Moxley, "School secretary embezzled $27,000," Salisbury Post
[610] "Audit shows overcharges by charter" The Plain Dealer
[611] George Clowes, "Accountable public schools squander funds," School Reform News
[612] Sheila McLaughlin, "Ex-school official sentenced in theft," Cincinnati Enquirer
[613] Steve Trevler, "School chief deals to avoid time," Beacon Journal
[614] News in Brief: A National Roundup, Education Week
[615] April Copeland, "Employee accused of misusing school district credit cards," The Plain Dealer
[616] District News Roundup, Education Week
[617] "Ex-school official indicted" Cherokee Press
[618] Diane Barker-Harold, "Charges filed in school embezzlement case," Cherokee Press
[619] Office of the State Auditor and Inspector Report
[620] Ibid
[621] Ibid
[622] "Playground equipment $ embezzled," Oregon OnLine
[623] Mark Walsh, "Districts victimized by alleged financial scheme," Education Week
[624] Peter Schmidt, "Bid rigging among school suppliers," Education Week
[625] "Academy accused" Wired News,
[626] District News Roundup, Education Week
[627] George Clowes, Op.cit.
[628] "School chief charged with theft," Washington, Pa. Observer-Reporter
[629] "Former principal promises to reimburse school system," AP, Star-Ledger
[630] "Cianci corruption trial turns to school building, lease deal," Boston Herald
[631] "Man files counterclaim in embezzlement case," Charleston.net
[632] Scott Deacle, 'School district seeks legal action" Wake Weekly
[633] Don Jacobs, "Ex PTA treasurer charged," News-Sentinel
[634] "Officials worried theft may hurt PTA," News-Sentinel

635 Peter Schmidt, "bid rigging among school suppliers," Education Week
636 "Three charter schools at center of fraud investigation," AP, DFW.com
637 Salatheia Bryant, "Charter school chief hiring of kin," Houston Chronicle
638 George Clowes, Op.cit
639 Jennifer Packer, "Carroll ISD credit card use investigated," Dallas Morning News
640 Graham Underwood, "Former employee gets 15 years," Lubbock Avalanche Journal
641 Lamar S. Jason, "Former employee faces embezzlement trial," Opengovtcoppell.com
642 Bess Keller, "Employees suspended," Education Week
643 "School maintenance workers indicted," Houston Chronicle
644 Bess Keller, "Former Dallas superintendent sentenced to 15 months," Education Week
645 "Activity fund theft" Dallas News
646 "School district contractor found guilty," Corpus Christi Caller Times
647 "Former school employee sentenced," The Dallas Morning News
648 "Ex-school manager sentenced for embezzlement," El Paso Times
649 Lisa Snell, "Corruption in public schools costs taxpayers," The Heartland Institute, Chicago, Ill
650 State Auditors Office Report
651 "FBI descends on W-H," The Dallas Morning News
652 Joshua Benton, "Master urged for Wilmer-Hutchins schools," The Dallas Morning News
653 Joshua Benton, ""Questions, answers on Wilmer-Hutchins," The Dallas Morning News
654 State News Roundup, Education Week
655 "Three dairies sued," Education Week
656 Cohen D'Vera. "Former Fairfax treasurer fined for embezzling $8,000," Washington Post
657 "Finance officer charged," Metro Section, Washington Post
658 "PTA teacher charged with embezzlement," Washington Post
659 "School official arrested," Washington Post
660 Michael Shear, "Fairfax school funds missing," Washington Post
661 Joanne Kelly, "Treasurer charged with embezzlement," The Fairfax Journal
662 "Education assistant arrested," Washington Post
663 "Administrative Assistant charged," Washington Post,
664 Daniel Tevlock, "Former PTO treasurer indicted in embezzlement," The Winchester Star
665 Daniel Tevlock, "City woman is charged in embezzlement," Winchester Star
666 Maria Golad, "PTO president charged with embezzlement," Washington Post
667 Chester Katzman, "Police say shop teacher sold car," Washington Post
668 Avis Thomas-Lester, "Parent group's former leader arrested," Washington Post

669 Josh White, "PTO treasurer charged with theft," Washington Post
670 "Former Miss Virginia indicted," Washington Post
671 Ann O'Hanlon, "Teacher faces drug, fraud charges," Washington Post
672 "Roanoke educator, spouse charged in church embezzlement scheme," MSNBC News
673 Josh White, "Hylton employee charged with embezzling," Washington Post
674 Michele Malkin, "$430,000 question: Who is minding the store?" Seattle Times
675 Keith Ervin, "Seattle schools official quits during ethics probe," Seattle Times
676 Brad Pierce, "Former school secretary charged with embezzlement," The Journal
677 "District secretary accused of theft," Wisconsin State Journal
678 "Woman gets seven months for school thefts," Milwaukee Journal Sentinel
679 "Woman gets 30 days for embezzlement," Milwaukee Journal Sentinel,
680 Ed Trevelen, "Former Dells school worker charged with embezzlement," Wisconsin State Journal
681 Rachana Rathi, "300,000 kids qualify for free tutoring," Los Angeles Times, 6/17/2005
682 News staff, " NCLB resistance mounts," eSchool News, June 2005
683 Capitalism Magazine, 7/28/2001
684 Eileen White, "$160 million improperly spent," Education Week, 12/14/1981
685 Education Week, 12/21/1984
686 "Task force finds E.D. could cut $2.83 billion," Education Week, 1/25/1984
687 "E.D. management invites waste, fraud," Education Week 2/10/1988
688 Mark Pitsch, "Audit finds $665 million in unused funds idle at E.D.," Education Week, 9/4/1991
689 Meg Sommerfeld, "Significant problems remain in student-aid programs," Education Week, 8/3/1994
690 Julie Miller, "Past impropriety could imperil grant eligibility," Education Week, 6/15/1998
691 Joetta Sack, "Hoekstra accuses Education Department of mismanaging funds," Education Week, 12/15/1999
692 ERIC document, ED #443182, 2000
693 Associated Press, 9/19/2000
694 "Concerns raised over education theft," AP, New York Times, 9/19/2000
695 Erik W. Robelen, "GAO prepares for Education Department audit,"Education Week, 9/27/2000
696 State Education Roundup: Focus on School Corruption, School Reform News, 11/2000
697 Erik Robelen, "Riley grilled on travel, department fraud allegations," Education Week 11/1/2000

[698] "Education agency riddled with fraud," Free Republic.com, Fresno, CA, 4/3/2001

[699] Associated Press, 4/3/2001

[700] Glenda Cooper, "Education Dept. credit cards seized in anti-fraud effort," Washington Post, 7/18/2001

[701] "Report of investigation in response to whistleblower's allegations of gross mismanagement at the U.S. Department of Education," U.S. Office of Special Counsel, Press Release, 1/31/2001

[702] ERIC document, #ED 453593, 2001

[703] Greg Toppo, "Paige says team to tackle education department finances," AP, Washington Post, 4/21/2001

[704] Patty Reinert, "Paige's team works to recover department's wasted millions," Houston Chronicle, 7/17/2001

[705] "Facilitator of $1 million DOE fund and theft scheme pleads guilty," DOE Inspector General Press Release, 1/17/2002

[706] U.S. General Accounting Office, "Financial mismanagement problems," TownHall.com, 6/27/2002

[707] Anne Lewis, "State takeovers of filing urban schools: ECS Conference Highlights," 1997

[708] Wayne Barrett, "Déjà vu all over again," Village Voice, 6/12/2002

[709] Clarence Chambers, "State Takeovers," School Board News, 7/11/2000

[710] "State Takeovers and Reconstitutions, Updated January 2002," Policy Brief, Education Commission of the States, Denver, CO

[711] Pat Kossan, "State decides to takeover 11 failing schools," Arizona Republic, 3/28/2005

[712] Anne Ryman," Napolitano denies school district's request," Arizona Republic, 6/26/2002

[713] Anne Ryman, "Scrutiny is ended at school district," Arizona Republic, 8/10/2002

[714] David Hoff, "Takeovers threatened: 25 Arkansas districts address deficiencies," Education Week, 10/2/96

[715] "State Takeovers" Op.cit

[716] Karen Degmueller, "Academic deficiencies force takeover," Education Week, 9/16/1992

[717] Karla Reid, "California returns Compton District," Education Week, 9/19/2001

[718] Caroline Hendrie, "Down on Top-Down," State Journal, Education Week, 9/5/2001

[719] Nancy Mathis, "State oversight likely as Oakland district is engulfed in theft and patronage scandal," Education Week, 9/13/1989

[720] Education Week, 9/13/1989

721 "County appoints financial expert to handle Oakland schools budget," AP, SFGate.com, 10/16/2002
722 "State Takeovers," Op.cit
723 Brian Melley, "State takeover proposed," AP, San Francisco Chronicle, 11/5/2002
724 "State Takeovers," Op.cit.
725 Robert Frahm, "Across nation mixed results," Hartford Courant, 6/3/2002
726 "Takeovers in other states," Detroit Free Press, 2/23/1999
727 Steve Harrison, "Failing schools takeover targets," Miami Herald, 3/31/2005
728 "State Takeovers," Op.cit
729 Ann Bradley, "Daley names team to takeover at Chicago schools," Education Week, 7/12/1995
730 George Clowes, "Business group gives Chicago schools an 'F,'" Heartland Institute, 10/1/2003
731 "State Takeovers," Op.cit.
732 Lonnie Harp, "State moves to oust East. St. Louis school board," Education Week, 4/10/96
733 Sean Hamill, "State panel set to run schools," Chicago Tribune, 8/23/2002
734 "Board in Iowa seizes control of tiny district," Education Week, 11/28/1990
735 "State Takeovers," Op.cit.
736 Reagan Walker, "2 Ky districts deemed deficient, face state takeover," Education Week, 1/18/1989
737 Ibid
738 Lonnie Harp, "Audit spurs board to eye takeover of Ky district," Education Week, 5/25/1994
739 "State Takeovers," Op.cit.
740 Aesha Rasheed, "All school board alternatives rejected," Times-Picayune, 10/30/2002
741 "New Orleans superintendent resigns," AP, Los Angeles Times, 44/12/2005
742 Amy Argetsinger, "State plans school takeovers," Washington Post, 1/5/2000
743 Howard Libit, "School board powers curbed," Baltimore Sun, 2/5/2002
744 Peter Greer, "BU and Chelsea: First lessons," Education Week, 5/16/1990
745 Robert Johnston, "Lawrence reaches deal with state," Education Week, 2/4/1998
746 "Swift signs bill taking over finances of school district," AP, The Boston Globe, 10/11/2002
747 Mario Ortiz, "Ready to run schools," Detroit Free Press, 2/13/1999
748 Chastity Pratt, "State expert takes over," Detroit Free Press, 8/9/2002
749 Christopher Singer, "State to run Highland Park," The Detroit News, 6/14/2002
750 Joanna Richardson, "For profit to run district," Education Week, 11/10/1993

751 Meg Summerfeld, "Mississippi poised to take over cash short district," Education Week, 11/17/1996
752 "State Takeovers," Op.cit.
753 Ibid
754 Missouri Department o f Education, News Release, 4/17/2002
755 Paul Ciotti, "Policy analysis #298," CATO Institute, 3/16/1998
756 Catherine Gewertz, "Eyes private manager to run schools," Education Week, 5/28/2003
757 David Lieb, "School district loses accreditation," St. Louis Dispatch, 6/23/2002
758 Melanie Burney, "Camden schools face more reins," The Philadelphia Inquirer, 6/14/2002
759 Dwight Ott, "No takeover planned for Camden," The Philadelphia Inquirer, 8/29/2002
760 Lisa Jennings, "Bd in New Jersey completes takeover," Education Week, 10/11/1989
761 Mark Walsh, "State takeover of Jersey City schools seen yielding significant improvements," Education Week, 2/17/1993
762 Karla Reid, "Newark sues state, district over losses," Education Week, 2/14/2001
763 Richard Jones, "Education chief urges restoring local control," New York Times, 6/20/2002
764 Robert Holland and Don Soifer, "State control of schools has failed to help Paterson, NJ children," Lexington Institute, Arlington, VA, March 2005
765 "State Takeovers," Op.cit.
766 Press Release, Office of the Governor, 6/12/2002
767 William Raspberry, "Fixing what ails the schools," Washington Post, 4/25/2005
768 "Legislature approves a school takeover," AP, New York Times, 4/9/2002
769 Elissa Gootman, "Changes beginning to appear," New York Times, 10/2/2002
770 Anne Lewis, "State takeovers of failing urban schools: ECS conference highlights," Education Commission of the States, Denver, CO, 1997
771 "State Takeovers," Op.cit.
772 Robert Johnston, "Pa targets districts for takeover," Education Week, 5/17/2000
773 Jacques Steinberg, "In largest school takeover, state will run Philadelphia's schools," New York Times, 12/22/2001
774 "Teachers inside story shows why state took control," The Morning Call, 6/7/2002
775 Robert Johnston, "State chooses 3 companies to run Pa district schools," Education Week, 3/28/2001
776 Morando Rhim, ""Restructuring schools in Chester-Upland, Pa: An analysis," Education Commission of the States, Denver, CO, 3/2005

777 Dale Mezzacoppa and Connie Langland, "Principal just the tip of woes," Philadelphia Inquirer, 4/12/2005
778 "State Takeovers," Op.cit.
779 Karen Diegmueller, "Troubled RI district becomes first to request state takeover," Education Week, 4/3/1991
780 "State Takeovers," Op.cit.
781 Aimee Edmonson, "Tennessee placing 63 troubled schools on probation," Memphis Mid-South News, 8/23/2002
782 "State Takeovers," Op.cit.
783 Joshua Benton, "Court order overturned," Education Week, 4/2/2005
784 "3 states move to intervene in failing school districts," Education Week, 8/3/1988
785 "Kevin Bushweller, "Under the shadow of the state," American School Board Journal, 8/1998
786 Lisa Fine, "Troubled W.Va. district invites takeover," Education Week, 11/21/2001
787 Richard Brennan and Tess Kalinowski, "Board awaits cuts in cash," The Toronto Star, 8/28/2002
788 Anne Lewis, Op.cit.
789 Richard Seder, "Balancing Accountability and Local Control: State Intervention for Financial and Academic Stability," Policy Study #268, Reason Public Policy Institute, Undated
790 Brian Carpenter, "Takeover as a reform strategy," Heartland Institute, Chicago, Ill, 2/1/2005
791 Kevin Bushweller, Op.cit.
792 Caroline Hendrie, Education Week, 6/12/1996
793 Michael W. Kirst, "Mayoral Influence, New Regimes, and Public School Governance," Consortium for Policy Research in Education, Univ. of Penn, May 2002
794 Kenneth Wong, and Francis Shen, "Does school district takeover work?" Department of Leadership and Organization, Peabody College, Nashville, TN, 9/2001
795 Reason Public Policy Institute, Op.cit.
796 Tracy Morrlehem, "School takeover is no guarantee," Detroit Free Press, 2/23/1999
797 Larry Hardy, "Building block of reform: Is 'reconstitution' the answer for struggling schools?" American School Board Journal, 2/1999
798 "Turning around low-performing schools," U.S. Office of Education, May 1998
799 "Can reconstitution fix failing schools," NEA Today Online, 1/1999
800 Ibid

[801] Jessica Portner, "Six suburban schools in Md. To be reconstituted," Education Week, 6/11/1997
[802] Larry Hardy, Op.cit.
[803] Joanne Daemmrich, ""Russo to guide failing schools," Baltimore Sun, 2/1/2001
[804] Caroline Hendrie, "In S.F. reconstitutions, Rojas softens the blow," Education Week, 6/25/1997
[805] Larry Hardy, Op.cit.
[806] Ibid
[807] "Turning around low performing schools," Op.cit.
[808] David Bacon, "Reconstitution—The Clint Eastwood solution for low-performing schools," The Workplace, 10/22/1997
[809] Mark Sanchez, "School reconstitution a total failure," San Francisco Chronicle, Op-Ed. 1/12/2005 (Note: He is a commissioner on the Board of Education).
[810] David Bacon, "The Resistance: San Francisco teachers reject reconstitution," Substance Newspaper, Chicago, Ill, 2/2005
[811] NEA, Op.cit.
[812] "Turning around low performing schools," Op.cit.
[813] Beth Reinhard and Caroline Hendrie, "At two Cleveland schools, overhauls mark a dramatic response to 'desperate times,'" Education Week, 9/24/1997
[814] "Denver backs reconstituting schools," Education Week, 2/16/1997
[815] Maria Sacchetti, "An uphill battle for better schools despite increase stability, only modest improvements," Boston Globe, 5/22/2005
[816] Barbara Miner, "Reconstitution trend cools," Rethinking Schools, Milwaukee, WI, Vol. 13, #1, Fall 1998
[817] "Turning around low performing schools," Op.cit.
[818] Ibid
[819] Ibid
[820] Ibid
[821] Dave Weber, "Some schools granted reprieve," Orlando Sentinel, 6/10/2005
[822] John Murphy and Denise P. Doyle, "Redesigning the Operating Environments in School Districts," Governance Notes, Education Commission of the States, Denver, CO, 6/2001
[823] "Governing America's Schools: Changing the Rules," National Commission on Governing American Schools, ECS, Doc #1172, 11/1999
[824] "Can schools be managed," Schools and Education, Center for the Study of Alternative Futures (CSAF), Website (csaf.org) 3/23/1996
[825] Katie Farber, "Report: Dishonest education reporting by states is 'widespread'," Human Events, 6/2/2005
[826] "A League Table of Educational Disadvantage in Rich Nations," Report Card, Issue #4, 11/2002

827 "The Condition o f Education, 2000," National Center for Educational Statistics, Washington, D.C.
828 Jane Elizabeth, "School boards' worth in doubt," Post-Gazette, Pittsburgh, PA, 11/30/2003
829 "Everett board boosts pay of schools chief, despite indictment," AP, boston.com, 6/17/2005
830 Jay Matthews, "An end to school boards?" Washington Post, 2/16/2001
831 Michael Kirst, Michael Usdan, Jacqueline Danzberger, "Governing Public Schools: New Times, New Requirements," Institute for Educational Leadership, Inc., 1992
832 Ibid
833 Ibid
834 "Leadership Matters: Transforming Urban School Boards," National School Boards Foundation, Alexandria, VA, 6/1/1999
835 Frederick M. Hess, "School Boards at the Dawn of the 21st Century," National School Boards Association, Alexandria, VA, 2002
836 Jane Elizabeth, Op.cit.
837 "Governing America's Schools," Op.cit.
838 "Thinking Differently: Recommendations for 21st Century School Board/Superintendent Leadership, Governance and Team Work," NESDC, 1999
839 "Leadership for Student Learning: Recognizing the State's Role in Public Education," A Report of the Task Force on State Leadership, Institute for Educational Leadership, Washington, D.C. May 2001
840 Ibid
841 Alison Gendar, op. cit.
842 "Governing Americas Schools," Op.cit.
843 "School Principal Survey Reveals Fear of Liability Limits Educational Opportunities for America's Children," American Tort Reform Association, Washington, D.C. 9/8/1999
844 Jay Mathews, "Playing politics in urban city schools," Washington Post, 9/10/2002
845 "Pennsylvania school privatization effort collapses" AP, CNN.com, 6/1/2005
846 Pat Kossan, "Charter schools failing on reform goals," Arizona Republic, 6/12/2005
847 Alan J. Borsuk and Sara Carr, "Lessons from the voucher schools," Journal-Sentinel, 6/11/2005
848 Fred M. Newmann and Gary G. Wehlage "Successful School Restructuring," Wisconsin Center for Education Research, Madison, WI, 10/30/1995
849 Alison Gendar, "Ax school boards," New York Daily News, 2/17/2002
850 "Shared decision-making messy," Denver Post, 8/28/2002

851 Jane Elizabeth, "School board in Massachusetts hands over controls to university," Post-Gazette, Philadelphia, PA, 12/1/2003
852 Paul T. Hill, "Lessons from Blair's School Reforms," Hoover Institution, #131, June & July 2005
853 Paul Ciotti, "Money and School Performance: Lesson from the Kansas City Desegregation Experiment," Cato Institute, Policy Analysis #298, 3/16/1998
854 Ibid
855 David W. Kirkpatrick, "Education Reform, The Task, School Choice, The Goal," Center for Education Reform, 6/1996
856 Gary S. Mathews, "Learning to Abandon what doesn't work," School Administrator, AASA, 11/2002
857 Ronald Perry, "Do Reformers Survive?" Education Week, 9/1992,
858 Helen Ladd and Janet Hansen, "Making money matter, financing America's schools," Committee on Education Reform, National Research Council, National Academy Press, Washington, DC, 1999
859 Editorial, "School can cut budgets without harming kids," The Detroit News, 2/5/2002
860 Editorial, "School boards: Make tough budget calls to aid kids," The Detroit News, 8/4/2002
861 Ibid
862 Allan Ogden, "How to Rethink School budgets to Support School Transformation," New American Schools, Arlington, Va. (undated)
863 "Tracking/Accounting for Education Spending," Policy Update, National Association of State Boards of Education, Alexandria, VA, 1/1997
864 Brian Gong, "Accountability Systems and Reporting," Council of Chief State School Officers, Washington D.C., 1/2002
865 George Will, "Schools 65 Percent Solution," Hartford Courant, 4/11/2005
866 Allan Odden and others, "Defining school level expenditures structures that reflect educational strategies," Winter 2003
867 <u>A New Compact for Learning,</u> New York State Department of Education, 1991
868 "Education standards under assault," New York Times, 6/17/2005
869 Martin Haberman, "What can be done with dysfunctional urban school districts?" EducationNews.org, 6/14/2005
870 "Education: Reform fatigue," Jacksonville.com, 1/15/2003
871 Hodding Carter III, "Democracy's Bedrock: Public Education—an American idea and ideal," Miami Herald, 10/23/2002
872 William Ophuls, <u>Requiem for Modern Politics</u>, Westview Press, Boulder, CO, 1997
873 "Texas Governor calls for financial accountability, takeovers of failing schools," School Reform News, 7/2005
874 Editorial, "MacArthur: Duty, honor, country," Washington Times, 5/27/2002

978-0-595-36557-9
0-595-36557-4

Made in the USA
San Bernardino, CA
27 February 2014